FIELD GUIDE
to the
SPIRIT WORLD

"The depth and quality of research exemplified by Susan B. Martinez, Ph.D., in her previous books are evident again in *Field Guide to the Spirit World*. The spirit world is all around us all the time, and this very helpful book provides a key to the spiritual world and a guide to working with it for the treatment of mental disorders caused by 'overshadowing.' As Whitley Strieber says in his foreword, 'Step out of the prison of materialism in order to see such experiences in ways that might deepen our understanding of ourselves and the amazing universe'—as Strieber demonstrates when he talks about the loss of his wife, Anne, and how that opened his spiritual vision."

ROBERT R. HIERONIMUS, PH.D., COAUTHOR OF *THE SECRET LIFE OF LADY LIBERTY: GODDESS IN THE NEW WORLD* AND COHOST OF *21ST CENTURY RADIO*

"From all accounts, the world beyond the veil is a labyrinth chock-full of entities both good and ill. With her new book *Field Guide to the Spirit World: The Science of Angel Power, Discarnate Entities, and Demonic Possession*, Susan B. Martinez has contributed an important work that helps to demystify the other side. It warrants an important place on your Fortean bookshelf and, more importantly, in your hands as you read and learn."

JIM HAROLD, HOST OF THE *PARANORMAL PODCAST*

FIELD GUIDE

to the

SPIRIT WORLD

The Science of Angel Power,
Discarnate Entities, and Demonic Possession

SUSAN B. MARTINEZ, Ph.D.

Bear & Company
Rochester, Vermont

Bear & Company
One Park Street
Rochester, Vermont 05767
www.BearandCompanyBooks.com

Text stock is SFI certified

Bear & Company is a division of Inner Traditions International

Cataloging-in-Publication Data for this title is available from the Library of Congress

ISBN 978-1-59143-332-3 (print)
ISBN 978-1-59143-333-0 (ebook)

Printed and bound in the United States by Lake Book Manufacturing, Inc.
The text stock is SFI certified. The Sustainable Forestry Initiative® program
promotes sustainable forest management.

10 9 8 7 6 5 4 3 2

Text design and layout by Debbie Glogover
This book was typeset in Garamond Premier Pro with Appareo, Smoking,
Gill Sans MT Pro, Bernhard Modern Std, Old Claude LP Std, and Papyrus used
as display fonts

To send correspondence to the author of this book, mail a first-class letter to the
author c/o Inner Traditions • Bear & Company, One Park Street, Rochester, VT
05767, and we will forward the communication, or contact the author directly at
poosh8@gmail.com.

To Joan Greer aka Gypsy,
beautiful and beloved daughter of Jehovih

CONTENTS

FOREWORD

By Whitley Strieber

The near-death experiencer, the UFO abductee, the out-of-body traveler, the medium, the psychic—who are these people and are their unusual perceptions of the world around them somehow linked?

In this powerful book, Susan Martinez sets out to explore the soul from the standpoint of a new scientific vision that discards the materialist assumptions that have so far limited the willingness of professionals in the field to address unusual phenomena without those assumptions.

As an out-of-body traveler and UFO witness who was married to a woman who had a life-changing near-death experience, I am well acquainted with the strange unwillingness—or is it inability—of scientists to approach these phenomena in a way that might actually advance knowledge.

I must say that I think that spirit itself is on Susan's side. Let me tell you why.

In April of 2016, I was attending a conference at the Institute of Noetic Sciences in Petaluma, California, when I had an extremely unusual experience. Every night of my life, I meditate at eleven and again at three. This is trying, of course, but I have compelling reasons to do it involving contact with my deceased wife, but we will get to that shortly.

On that night, I was exhausted from a long day of travel and participation in the conference. Nevertheless, I woke myself up at three and did the meditation. Then I fell back into bed. An hour later, a terrific shock went down my spine. I sat up in bed, startled wide awake. I said to myself—and to whomever I meditate with—"I've already meditated, don't wake me up again." But I sat and meditated for another ten minutes anyway, then fell into the bed.

An instant later, I found myself in the corridor of the small dormitory in which I was housed. I was astonished. How had this happened? My door was closed. Was I now locked out until morning?

Then I realized that I was once again out of my body. I'd been in this state a number of times before, and previously on occasion had enabled people to see me. I thought to myself that I should try to make myself seen at this conference of scientists and professors. I was here to upset the paradigm, after all. And as I cannot leave my body on my own (I've tried for years), somebody had done this to me, and my guess was that it was to challenge the very paradigm that Susan so brilliantly upsets in the following pages.

I went through the wall into the conference leader's room, but he was absolutely asleep. I have no idea how a bodyless person might awaken somebody who is asleep, so I then went from room to room until I found a conferee who had his eyes open. I went beside his bed and looked down at him. He reacted with surprise that I was in his room. I thought, "Am I out of my body or not?" He didn't seem to think so. We spoke together for a few minutes. I was able to see his life hopes and fears almost as if they were somehow written on his face, carved into his expression, as it were.

Then I abruptly shot upward, completely out of control, until I was so high that I could see the curvature of the Earth and the line of dawn far to the east. I was shocked to my core. Compared to this, my previous OBEs had been child's play. I then shot downward and eastward, finding myself on what appeared to be a college campus. The sun was either rising or setting. I could not tell which. But it had been about 4:15 a.m. in Petaluma; therefore I assumed that I was in the eastern United States and it must be 7:15 a.m.

I moved about on the campus, trying unsuccessfully to show myself to a young man I saw walking along a sidewalk. Then I went into a building, which proved to be a dormitory. I went down a hall and into a room, but found the occupant sound asleep.

I'd never been so far from my body in this state, so I decided that I wanted to go back. I went outside and tried to think how I would do that. As I did, I rose into the air, once again going to a great height, then sped down and back into my body.

Exhausted, excited, and a little frightened, frankly, I thought I would get up and greet the dawn. I did not feel at all sleepy. But the next thing I knew, my travel alarm was ringing and it was seven thirty.

Not expecting much, I went to breakfast where, to my surprise, everybody was talking about the fact that one of conferees had waked up and found me in his room. He had talked to me for a short time, whereupon I had gone out through the ceiling!

I was naturally called upon to explain myself, so I told the full story of the experience. Two of the other conferees recognized the campus. It was theirs.

A year later, they invited me to join them there, and I had the remarkable experience of actually entering a building that I had seen previously only in the out-of-body state, going down a hall and standing at the door of the dorm room I had entered.

At the present time, science dismisses all of this as impossible. Supernatural poppycock. OBEs can be induced in the lab, after all. (They can, but nothing even close to this has ever been reported.) As to the man who saw me, he must have been dreaming. Chalk that one up to coincidence. And the campus? Maybe I'd been there before, or maybe the two professors simply wanted to believe and innocently confabulated their belief that I was describing my campus.

I would submit that Susan makes an important argument in *Field Guide to the Spirit World* that these phenomena are not in some way "supernatural" and therefore outside of the realm of scientific inquiry, but rather that they are part of the natural world and our experience of it that we do not yet understand.

On August 11, 2015, my beloved wife of forty-five years, Anne Strieber, died. As I lay beside her body, enveloped in grief, all of my belief in afterlife left me. I was devastated. Her terrible stillness screamed out to me: You're alone. She's gone. You're *alone!*

From the depth of my love and grief, I asked her, "Do you still exist? Can you let me know?"

An hour and a half later, a friend who did not yet know of her death called. She said, "Whitley, I just had the feeling that Anne wanted me to call. Is she all right?" I said to her, "Belle, Anne died at 7:15."

Thus began the most powerful and mind-changing life experience I think I can imagine. Anne had begun what soon became a methodical process of contacting friends that left me with little doubt that the soul continues on after death, and that individual consciousness survives. A week later, I was sitting on a bench in the mountains above Palm Springs, California, consumed with grief and once again asking Anne if she was there. Literally at that moment, my cell phone rang and there was a friend from Nashville, Clare Henry, who proceeded to say that she'd just gotten a message from Anne that she should call me. (She knew Anne was dead, of course.)

Those were two of many such incidents. I eventually recalled that the two of us had made a plan back in the 1990s that the first one to die would try to make contact if possible. But given that we are both such skeptics, we would first try to contact friends and tell them to contact the one still living.

The moment that I realized that Anne was carrying out our plan was unforgettably powerful. Tears came to my eyes. The gratitude and joy were just indescribable.

They led to an intimate, ongoing relationship between us that has transcended death completely, and led to the book that we wrote together, *The Afterlife Revolution.*

Field Guide to the Spirit World performs an essential function in that, with its careful scholarship and cogent insights into what is being missed by the materialistic paradigm that now dominates science, it offers the reader a chance to reground herself in such a way that stories like the ones I have told here are no longer mysterious, distant, and seemingly impossible, but rather that they represent what I think we should call "ordinary experience of the extraordinary."

We need to step out of the prison of materialism in order to see such experiences in ways that might deepen our understanding of ourselves and the amazing universe whose consciousness we are privileged to share, and if there ever was a key to the door of that prison worth possessing, it is Susan Martinez's *Field Guide to the Spirit World*.

WHITLEY STRIEBER is author of *Communion, Warday, Superstorm, Super Natural,* and most recently *The Afterlife Revolution.* His books *The Wolfen, The Hunger, Communion,* and *Superstorm* (as *The Day After Tomorrow*) have all been made into movies. His book *Alien Hunter* was made into the SyFy series *Hunters.* His website is Unknowncountry.com, and his podcast, Dreamland, which explores the edge of reality, has been online continuously since 2000.

THE FINAL BOUND

The Truth is not hidden from us
We are hiding from it.

REB YERACHMIEL BEN YISRAEL

We look at it and we do not see it;
Its name is The Invisible.
We listen to it and do not hear it;
Its name is The Inaudible.
We touch it and do not find it;
Its name is The Subtle.

LAO-TZU, *TAO TE CHING*

Spiritual! Psychic! Supernatural! Ghosts! Angels! Novelists are toying with it, movies are exploiting it, government is using it (ESPionage), and talking heads are making self-conscious jokes about it. But are we ready for the real thing? Hardly. That which we call psi is still in the tawdry category of horror as far as retailers are concerned; while the mainstream skeptic claims, falsely, "Any evidence of ghosts . . . just doesn't hold up. The spiritual movement in the U.S. was built on scams" (Angel 2015, 75).

But what about the "tunnel"? Dividing this world from the next, the tunnel—aka the void, the vacuum, the valley, the vortex—has recently become the main metaphor of the near-death experience (NDE).

1

Among those who "die" but revive, descriptions of the transition include "moving very rapidly through a long dark tunnel"; "I found myself in a tunnel . . . of concentric circles"; "I was in a sort of whirling state"; "I felt as if I were moving in a vacuum . . . in a cylinder"; "I was moving through . . . this long dark place"; "I went through this dark, black vacuum at superspeed"; "I entered . . . a narrow and very, very dark passageway"; "I was moving through a deep, very dark valley"; and the like (Moody, 1975, front page, 30–34).

In Dr. Melvin Morse's 1990 study of NDEs in children, I found more than twenty-five testimonials that specifically describe a tunnel, the place, as Dr. Morse terms it, "where the material and the spiritual worlds meet" (1991, 126). But entering the tunnel—or "touching the darkness"—is by no means limited to the NDEr. This in-between place, this limbo, has been depicted in almost every variety of ASC (altered states of consciousness). We find the tunnel described everywhere: in the literature of MPD (multiple personality disorder), of autism, of astral projection and mediumship, of hypnosis and dream, of demonic possession, and even in cases of criminal psychopathy! In criminology, we have the psychopath (sociopath). In demonic possession, the subject is a victim. In psychiatry, it is the client. In psi, it is the medium or sensitive. In the occult, it is the EEr (Extraordinary Experiencer). In MPD, it is the patient and her "alters." In poltergeistery, the experiencer is the "focal agent."

Although these appear to be disparate areas, once we delve into spirit influence we find a common link, an underlying Factor X. But because specialists are so insulated from other fields of knowledge in today's world, it is rare that we glimpse the remarkable *similarities* that exist between multiples, somnambules, narcissists, obsessives, autistic children, psychics, as well as cases of possession, schizophrenia, sociopathy, hysteria, and poltergeistery. The common denominator is ASC—dissociation from ordinary reality. In this book, we delve into that separate reality, that nonphysical existence in which the disembodied being might find himself.

When Kenneth Ring found striking links between people with

NDEs and UFO encounters, he called these folks EErs, or Extraordinary Experiencers. Not surprisingly, abductees tend to be psychic. These EErs get high scores in ESP tests; they have paranormal experiences, are prone to trance, and there are quite a few MPDs among them. EErs "tend to have dissociative personalities." They are "sensitives" who have not developed their gift. Most have been psychically vulnerable since childhood and are "natural recipients" for extraordinary phenomena "of all sorts" (Ring 1992, 142, 129).

Consider the mounting literature on—and more frequent occurrence of—the baffling phenomenon of MPD and OCD (obsessive-compulsive disorder). Closely related to these are numerous cases, worldwide, of spirit possession. A touch away is the matter of (psychic) mediumship, and at a stone's throw we have the mysterious "voices" and foreboding whispers that prompt antisocial behavior—even crimes of the most ghastly, yet inexplicable, kind. We will visit them all.

I have long been writing to prove that the spirit world is not an invented thing, but a reality with which we have fallen out of touch. There is a biblical prophecy in Acts 2:17–8 (by Joel) according to which the use of psychic powers will one day be widespread among people and commonly accepted: "I will pour out my Spirit upon all flesh . . ." Psychic powers are coming back around the mountain, "the use of ESP also aiding the moral rebirth of mankind" (Ryzl 2007, 101).

With secondary selves we have not only a chronic form of ASC, but also a virtual state of siege. MPD seizures, as Dr. Charcot once observed, can be mistaken for epilepsy. In one MPD case (Kit Castle), Dr. Beidler noted the mediumistic Kit's history of "epilepsy" and its curious connection to the poltergeist activity surrounding her. It is especially in the switching process (switch and twitch)—from one persona (alter) to the other—that the multiple is "seized," sometimes flailing and writhing. In the case of Billy Milligan, "his lips twitched . . . he was quivering" (Keyes 1981, 54). Epileptoid symptoms are not uncommon in MPD: When another multiple, Beth, switched to her alter Anna, "her eyes rolled up to the ceiling" (Mayer 1989, 20).

No Earthly Power

Let me take hyperpraxia as a single example of a baffling experience with a paranormal underpinning (hyperpraxia denotes feats of extraordinary, unearthly strength). In one instance, having been assured by the hypnotist that it was as light as a feather, a man of low muscular development took a 20-pound weight, which ordinarily he could barely lift, and twirled it around his little finger (Inglis 1992, 193). The well-known "mental traveler" (OBEr, out-of-body experiencer) Vincent Turvey explains his long-distance clairvoyance as "appearing to see through a tunnel." His biographer comments, "Here we have a perfect description of etheric flight. When Mr. Turvey's double was capable of physical exertion—he once lifted a bed with two people on it, though incapable, when in the body, of lifting a small child—he was of course drawing on some psychic force" (Battersby 1979, 93).

Hyperpraxia is one of the cardinal signs, according to the *Rituale Romanum*, of entity possession. Though Dr. Peck's patient Beccah was "dramatically underweight . . . gaunt like a concentration camp victim," she exhibited superhuman strength during her exorcism (Peck 2005, 134, 151). Thrashing and contorting, the victim of possession is often impossible to restrain; even the slight thirteen-year-old boy (*The Exorcist* real-life child) threw off a team of full-grown men. Possession working at full strength in a human being can be overwhelmingly forceful: During the exorcism of the woman called Therese, Fathers Pier-Paolo and Giustino (in Italy) could not restrain her. "She seemed to have a hundred times her normal strength" (Christiani 1961, 139). In a similar French case, the woman was "so violently possessed, that her strength was above five women's," not unlike a Chinese case where the woman's "strength was almost superhuman" (Ebon 1974, 92, 140).

As for the Haitian *loa:* Wade Davis, in his brilliant analysis of *The Serpent and the Rainbow,* sat as an observer during the Haitian rite of spirit possession; the woman was "mounted by the divine horseman;

she had become the spirit. . . . Never in the course of my travels in the Amazon had I witnessed a phenomenon as raw or powerful as the spectacle of vodoun possession that followed. The initiate, a diminutive woman, tore about the peristyle, lifting large men off the ground to swing them about like children" (Davis 1985, 45). This supernatural strength Davis calls "the mystical agility."

Multiples, too, have performed prodigious feats of strength, like Billy Milligan who smashed the toilet bowl with his fist. Jennifer, another multiple (who describes her own dissociated state "as if I were in some dark tunnel") broke a tennis racket in half during one of her rages. "I can't believe I broke it . . . like it wasn't me . . . like somebody else had taken over" (Schoenewolf 1991, 26–28).

The epileptic may also be imbued with this paranormal power: "The strength he exerts during the attack seems to exceed his natural endowment" (Lhermitte 1963, 28). Overshadowed by malignant spirits, the psychopath may be a candidate for both epilepsy and hyperpraxia—Richard Ramirez, the LA Night Stalker, had been epileptoid in childhood, and as a man, "when he was in killing mode, his strength increased, and he carried her [the victim] like she was a weightless rag doll" (Carlo 1996, 142). John Wayne Gacy, serial killer, had also been a sickly boy with spells of fainting, rolling back eyes, swooning. The doctors found nothing, but during a hospitalization at age seventeen, he was diagnosed as having an epileptic fit. "According to the doctor," Gacy told FBI super-agent Robert Ressler (1992, 86), "when I had an epileptic seizure, I had eight hundred times my own strength." (The seizures, we suggest, have something to do with Gacy's belief that his crimes "had been committed by someone other than himself") (Ressler 1992, 247).

But also the medium and adept, like John Ballou Newbrough, who lifted a ton "without apparent effort" (Fodor 1966, 263)—just as his contemporaries, the Fox sisters and the Koons boy (all in the 1850s) exhibited remarkable feats of strength. Then, in 1884, it was Georgia's Lulu Hurst who captured American audiences with her inexplicable prowess.

LULU HURST

(THE GEORGIA WONDER)

Writes her Autobiography and for the first time

EXPLAINS AND DEMONSTRATES

The Great Secret

OF HER MARVELOUS POWER.

Fig. I.1. *"The Electric Maid": On stage, three men would pile on a chair, and Lulu would move it into the air with her hands. A group of men would grasp a cane, brace themselves, and Little Lulu would grab the cane and drag the men back and forth across the stage, flinging them all into the footlights (Miles 2000, 251).*

Most interestingly, "rolling eyes . . . twitches or marked changes in facial expression," observes Dr. MacNutt, also happen to be signs of spirit possession (Head 2004, 58), though also evident in the trance convulsions of the trained medium. It is understandable that the overwhelming loss of control in trance-mediumship can occasion involuntary spasms. Mrs. Piper, falling into trance, would be subject to slight convulsive movements, something like an "epileptoid fit." So we ask: Isn't there some overriding factor at play in these freakish displays of multiples, the possessed, the schizophrenic, the psychic, the hysteric? Tourette's syndrome, we might add, also resembles possession: tics, sudden jerks, gutteral sounds, shouting, obscenities—and these, in turn, dovetail with the displays of some autists, whose symptoms range from clairvoyance to MPD and OCD. Dr. Arthur Guirdham (1982, 52–53) has said, "What used to be called St. Vitus Dance or chorea is now known as obsessional tics. In these, the child suffers from uncontrollable twitchings. . . . [These] children were prone suddenly to burst out in obscene language* with no relevance to the immediately preceding topics of conversation. . . . Whether or no this particular manifestation should be called obsessive or due to possession, the basic fact remains that *the two conditions are allied to each other*" (emphasis added). People with Tourette's, moreover, are likelier to have ADHD, impulsivity, OCD, learning disabilities, and sleep disorders. Most of this is presumably due to their "difficulties with impulse control." *Impulse?* I don't think so. But yes, it *is* a matter of self-control.

Sometimes an earthbound spirit steps in and takes control *[emphasis added] and then there is obsession or possession.*
CARL WICKLAND *THIRTY YEARS AMONG THE DEAD*

---

*Why does *coprolalia* (sudden fits of filthy or abusive language; see appendix A) occur in spirit possession, criminal pathology, OCD, and MPD? Guirdham's patient Annette "passed in a second from her natural . . . charm to a state in which she strung together the most vile collection of four letter words the doctor had ever heard" (1982, 52).

What shall we make of the serial killer, like J. W. Gacy, who feels that someone *else* is controlling his actions? Eric Chapman, for another, believed that people were "controlling him with their thoughts" or that the CIA was plotting to control his brain (Markman and Bosco 1989, 304–8). Along the same lines: Why do certain paranoid schizophrenics imagine they are being manipulated by space aliens, Martians, et cetera? Some patients "complain that they have lost control of their minds, and that thoughts are put into their heads by outside influences. . . . Now these are exactly the symptoms one would expect if the theory of spirit obsession were true" (Archer 1967, 101). Usually the victim has no clue of the personality behind the invasion of his own mind and so constructs some fancy to account for it; Dr. Rapoport, an OCD specialist, has encountered kids and teens with "ET, alien, outer space creature scenarios. . . . Debby was one of a dozen kids who had their own science fiction story to explain the planted thoughts." Laura, OCD since age seven, had watched a movie about Martians controlling people on Earth; this, she thought, might explain the foreign thoughts "inside her head." Rapoport's patient Sam was another: "I would imagine myself being the controlled pawn of observers from outer space. How else could one explain the . . . compulsions that I knew were so senseless?" (Rapoport 1989, 113, 139, 54).

Megacontrol in early life has been found at the base of many pathological disruptions of psyche—including dual personality, Capgras syndrome, hysteria, schizophrenia, compulsive crime, somnambulism, extreme depression, OCD, and other spontaneous automatisms like hyperpraxia and coprolalia. Seek and you will find a highly domineering parent (or guardian). Somehow, self-will has been removed from the child, most likely at the hands of an overpowering parent or even a church. The kid who feels powerless is the easiest (for spirit) to control. In many cases, parental megacontrol was exercised amid a total absence of encouragement and affection, which are the water and sunshine of the healthy growing child. Strictness often comes with lack of affection: Rita, mediumistic, tried to please her father, but only invoked his wrath—he had her beaten for an imagined impudence. "Such parent-child relationships are found quite uniformly among the families of all of the Spiritualist mediums interviewed. All have referred to their upbringing as strict and described their parents as undemonstrative with each other and with their children" (Crapanzano and Garrison 1977, 55).

Billy Milligan's stepfather not only abused him horrifically, but was also "an extremely rigid, tyrannical individual with little feeling for others." "Daddy Chal" was also hypercritical, watching the boy constantly; Billy "sat on the couch the way he'd been told to, feet flat on the floor, hands on his knees" (Keyes 1981, 176).

Dr. Mayer recalls, "I once had a [MPD] patient who would often hear a voice berating and cursing him . . . he was convinced he was possessed by a dybbuk, a Jewish demon which . . . would yell at him." Susan, another multiple treated by Mayer, had been dominated by her church-deacon father who "tried hard to control her." Lauren's mother "was always picking on her." Toby's mother was domineering and sadistic—scalding her with boiling water (Mayer 1989, 165, 126, 145, 251).

The mother of Sybil, a famous multiple, always had her "by the arm." Hers was a family of zealots; the radio, laughter, and other pleasures, were "the work of the devil"; home life was filled with religious strictures, fundamentalist prohibitions, "evangelical rantings and puritanical rigidities" (Schreiber 1973, 256).

In the case of Audrey, OCD, the twenty-eight-year-old was the product of strict parochial school upbringing. Excessively preoccupied with prayer and confession, she was certain that Satan himself was implanting sinful thoughts in her mind. As a rule, possessed people "know that 'something is wrong,' as if another force were gripping them; they're out of control, something is living underneath their skin" (Burnham 1990, 138).

There is something chillingly similar between the personality of the sociopath (APD, antisocial personality disorder) and that of the bodacious alters of the MPD. It is almost as if the sociopath is himself ruled by a dominant alter who is rebellious and obnoxious. We know this: Extreme selfishness underlies both the sociopath and the unmanageable alters of the multiple; the same unbridled self-interest is the final criterion of the lowest-grade spirits. "In the study of criminal psychology, one is forced to the conclusion that the most dangerous of all types of mind is that of the inordinately selfish man" (Costello 1994, 31). The lowest mortal grade in the Oahspe system is the most self-serving, thus easy prey to drujas, the lowest of the low in the spirit world.

Another reasonable question: Why does memory loss occur so consistently in possession, in ASCs, MPD, criminals, and self-cutting—as well as among trance mediums, who usually do not know what happened until told afterward? Then there is the amnesia of those possessed by the spirit in Haitian vodoun (Davis 1985, 216). Too, Kenneth Ring (1992, 65), who compares shamanic rites and ordeals to UFO contactees, especially notes the return phase, which is marked by "feelings of confusion, disorientation, time loss and memory impairment." The multiple, too, sometimes "hears the statements of others that she slapped someone, or screwed with some person she doesn't even know, and on and on" (Cohen et al. 1991, 41). This makes it easier to consider that "many persons who suffer from amnesia are in reality MPs" (Schreiber 1973, 449). The super-multiple Truddi Chase (1987, 63, 88) did not remember her childhood at all and was even unaware "of things discussed moments before." Mayer's multiple Susan had no memory before the age of twelve.

I have yet to meet the psychologist who can explain why MPD and OCD have so much in common. Eve, the famous multiple, gave a Rorschach that showed marked OCD traits (Thigpen and Cleckley 1957, 109). There is often so much overlap that doctors don't know *what* to diagnose. In the case of Ginny, for example, a suicidal patient treated with ECT, doctors diagnosed schizophrenia, depression, and bipolar, in turn. Such promiscuous diagnoses are more common than we realize.

Can we, moreover, really differentiate between possession and MPD? After all, the "evil spirit will make every attempt . . . to appear to be one and the same person . . . with its victim," as one exorcist put it (Martin 1976, 18). Said another, "While some clinicians deeply suspect my cases of purported possession are actually cases of MPD, I have come to suspect . . . that their purported cases of MPD might actually be cases of possession" (Peck 2005, 102). The classic case of Mary Roff was a terrific blend of possession and MPD (secondary personality). One can hardly distinguish between them.

> *I was fed up. After listening to four or five doctors come up with four or five different explanations, all of which were dead wrong . . . I realized that the doctors were groping around in the dark, in this infant science called psychiatry.*
>
> DANNY, QUOTED IN NAIFEH,
> *A STRANGER IN THE FAMILY*

We know that victims of both poltergeists and demonic possession often loathe religious objects, venting their fury at formal rites. In fact, one theorist put poltergeistery as a type of possession. So why not put together under possession: MPD, OCD, schizophrenia, et cetera?

Because . . . Because . . . The Big Picture does not suit today's narrow specialists, particularly if the underlying principle has a supernatural ring. But the man on the street? Surveys tell us that there is a good deal of general interest in the paranormal, and that 40 percent of Americans believe there is such a thing as haunted houses, while 65 percent accept some form of survival after physical death. Nevertheless, the *official* word remains with the scoffers. For quite a number of reasons, psi phenomena continue to fly under the radar, kept in the proverbial closet. Detractors have been whitewashing the spirit world for hundreds of years, because it fits neither the religious nor scientific model.

Editors [may] secretly believe, but openly denounce.

HENRY STEELE OLCOTT,

PEOPLE FROM THE OTHER WORLD

Many individuals, too, have kept secret or unspoken their own paranormal experiences. Why the big secret? Is it because we fear ridicule—or that no one will understand?

Psychic attacks are far commoner than is generally realized. . . . There is very much more in the mind than accounted for by the accepted psychological theories.

DION FORTUNE,

PSYCHIC SELF-DEFENCE

Nandor Fodor, the greatest twentieth-century compiler of psychic evidence, published many accounts of the psychic "taint," including the prudent decision of one psychic head of state (Canada) to avoid "becoming too actively identified with Psychical Research work"; another account cites the superintendent of schools of New York who "was forced to resign because he publicly stated his belief in spirits" (Fodor 1964, 4, 17).*

The reason for secrecy or denial could be something as pragmatic as the precautions taken in selling or renting out a (haunted) house: the Surratt boardinghouse, for example, where the Lincoln assassination was plotted. The place had a reputation for being haunted, which throughout its long history hurt its resale price. Or take a certain group home, another Victorian building that was featured on Halloween broadcasts and "certified" haunted by a paranormal organization that investigated the complaints of owners. The landlord, dismissing all gossip of hauntings, said, Hey, it's just a nice old house.

---

*Fodor's contemporary, Dr. Carl Jung, kept secret his lifelong spiritual experiences. See my book *Delusions in Science and Spirituality*, chapter 6.

I'm sure there's no ghost there. I put in new wiring, plumbing, and walls, and I haven't seen a single ghost.

But even if he *had* seen one, chances are the skeptics would have explained it away, perhaps as a hallucination. Or imagination. Or rats in the wall. While it is perfectly reasonable to look for a commonplace explanation (like "a trick of the moonlight"), not every apparition or weirdness can be eliminated in this way. And when the evidence for some unseen power is overwhelming, the doubter's line of defense falls to mere semantics—explaining away the phenomena with obtuse verbiage. Trotted out are awkward, ambiguous phrases like

an exteriorized nerve force
dramatization of a telepathic impulse
hyperexcitability
unconscious auto-suggestion or cerebration
primal instinct
some unknown magnetic principle
bundle of projected impressions

Although most of these word groups do not come with a good explanation or clarification, a bit of effort has gone into the concept of "thoughtforms." In which case, it is argued that a house, for example, could hold the thoughts or energy of its former occupants, which then manifest as a haunting. Frankly, whenever I hear theorists resort to thoughtforms or "an energy," I am nonplussed. Energy per se has no intelligence, no personality, no purpose; whereas the entity behind apparitions often does. The term *energy**—in place of *entity*—is simply an evasion, a way to beat around the bush.

---

*As Eugene Maurey (1988, 62), a great twentieth-century exorcist and spiritologist, observes, "Since a spirit entity normally has no physical energy, he can on occasion absorb the excess energy from a small child . . . [or from] the manipulations by a chiropractor." Spirits, he points out, may also accumulate energy by gathering it up from a scene of lively human activity. Any such energy can be "drawn upon to produce poltergeist activity."

"Energy" and Poltergeists

Even so-called experts in the paranormal often resort to the clueless "energy" explanation, which is no explanation at all. In one poltergeist case, Rosemary E. Guiley (2000, 331) makes bold to declare, "Discarnate beings were eliminated as a possible cause, for none had manifested . . . or communicated . . . Virginia [the young focal agent] had never complained about being possessed or harassed by unseen agents. . . . The most likely cause was Virginia herself. Her rapid pubescence may have generated *the energy* [emphasis added] to create poltergeist forces." Inanely, Guiley even suggests, "the entire episode may have been in part an attention-getting device."

I would like to contrast Guiley's vacuous analysis with the knowing words of Ena Twigg, England's foremost medium of the mid-twentieth century. When asked what she thought of the poltergeist phenomena, Twigg replied, "These are people [spirit people] who have a strong reason for coming back to the world. Perhaps they passed on obsessed with some unsatisfied urge." No stranger to poltergeistery, Twigg, in one alarming case, was called to a family home where fires were breaking out all over—chairs, rugs, beds, curtains just catching fire spontaneously. "I had never seen anything like it in my life. . . . It was really terrifying."

As Ena sat with the family in the living room, she suddenly heard a voice:

"I'm Jimmy."

"Who are you?" she asked.

"I'm her brother. I died as the result of a fire when I was three years old."

Then she asked him, "Why are you terrorizing these people like this . . . ?"

"It's my only means of making them wake up to the fact that what is happening in the family is too dreadful for words."

She asked him what was going on in the family that disturbed him so, and he told the whole story. It involved a wicked quarrel and estrangement among family members. The spirit was determined to continue his stunts until peace was meaningfully restored among the family. Twigg then asked him to promise to leave if peace were in fact made between them.

"I promise you that if they make peace . . . there will be no more disturbance."

And there were no more fires (Twigg and Brod 1973, 62, 110).

In 1964 at a Detroit automobile factory, a motor fitter suddenly lurched out of the path of a giant body press, which had been accidentally activated. Afterward he said he had actually been *thrust* out of the way by a tall black man with a scar. Well, some of the older workers recognized the description. Twenty years earlier, during the war, a black man with a scarred cheek had been accidentally decapitated while working in the same area of the shop. Amazed by his own miraculous escape, the 1964 motor fitter asserted that the black guy was real enough to him; he had enormous strength and easily pushed him out of harm's way. "I never believed in spooks before, but if this was a spook, I take my hat off to him."

When the story became public, the ghost (entity) interpretation was replaced by the following redaction: One of the fitter's older co-workers, seeing him in danger, but too far away to pull him to safety, suddenly had a powerful subconscious image of the dead man, the black guy, which he telepathically transmitted to the endangered man. Hmm. I do wonder why this far-fetched loose-jointed scenario is more acceptable than the ghost itself, the entity. I have to laugh at the irony of it all, remembering Colonel Olcott's pique at those who "seem to take it as a personal affront if credited with an immortal soul" (Olcott 1972, 77)!

I am reminded of a passage in another nineteenth-century work called *Spiritalis* that states, "To those who believe nothing . . . we [spirit assemblies] have tried many ways to make them understand. In cases of *sudden death* [emphasis added] . . . we have induced the [deceased] spirit to return to the place and take upon himself the elements necessary for your mortal vision to behold. But you believed not the spirit!" (Newbrough 1874). Here I would direct your attention to the words *sudden death*. It is one of the most relevant circumstances touched on in the chapters to come. But for the moment, let me recommend to the reader an extraordinary book, *The Ghost of Flight 401* by John G. Fuller. A compelling account of modern "ghostery," the book provides a striking parallel with the above story of the Detroit motor fitter: both the deceased pilot (of the crashed Flight 401) and the deceased auto worker (in wartime Detroit) made their return for one reason only—to guard and protect those who followed after them.

> *Angels and ministers of grace . . . defend us.*
> WILLIAM SHAKESPEARE, *HAMLET*

Conversant as we may be with human psychology, the proverbial iceberg lies hidden in a sea of theories, the simple truths of psyche undertowed by a tidal wave of "experts" who know nothing of the unseen dimension of life. The facts, nonetheless, are staring us in the face. Yet we hesitate to connect the dots, for the picture extends from the familiar visible to the unfamiliar invisible world, and we quail on the brink of the unknown, lingering at the threshold of enlightenment.

For 150 years and more, the official science of man has made every effort to explain away the signs and symptoms of the invisible world. Even members of ghost clubs, past and present, have been spiritual agnostics, given to explanations acceptable to materialism. I shouldn't be, but I am always jolted by their conservative conclusions. Take Peter Underwood, for example, longtime president of the London Ghost Club. He states, "The experience of seeing the ghost of a person after they are dead . . . originates from the person of the seer. [It] could be classed as wishful thinking . . . I hesitate to accept that ghosts are evidence of an afterlife" (Underwood 1986, 219).

And with the afterlife thus censored or rebuked by our intelligentsia, we are told that it is, instead, our own "inner life" that holds the answers. I write this book to challenge that assumption. I write this book to speak openly about those dwelling in the next world, those gone before. I write this book to explore the multitudinous ways in which the spirit world touches on our own and to illuminate the ways of the everlasting soul.

> *Until man recognizes that he is an immortal spirit and possesses all the equipment of a spirit—an intelligence that the great majority never even suspect in themselves, a divinity, a genius of the angelic. . . . Until he develops this to the utmost, he will remain as he now is—the most advanced among the higher animals, combative, acquisitive, the slave of himself, the sport of circumstance and of evil forces.*
>
> LEWIS SPENCE,
> *WILL EUROPE FOLLOW ATLANTIS?*

The New Age, with its frankly narcissistic focus on self, is the first to portray these mysteries as "inner," sending us off to ply the so-called subconscious mind, the inner life, for stuff that in reality *impinges* on the soul—from without. This misdirection must be the reason our thinking, our theories, have dead-ended.

> *The world is sick with theories.*
>
> W. B. YEATS

The overworked Inner Mind (whatever that is) has thus stood in for the actual doings of spirits, as in poltergeistery, which is mawkishly blamed on "the mind's inability to cope with strain"—entirely missing the otherworldly element. Likewise has the ghost world often been reduced to hallucinations.* And in the same way are victims of spirit obsession supposedly imagining the interference of unseen personalities:

---

*Hallucination? If we are hallucinating, so are our pets! In one case of a frightening haunting, "four Pomeranian dogs in the house were reduced to abject terror, showing that there was no hallucination upon the part of the human observers" (Doyle 1930, 58).

"What they're really hearing is only their own inner voice, imagined" (Morrison 2004, 134).

Before modern psychology took the stage, people did indeed view insanity as a kind of infestation by external, malevolent forces. Today we smugly call this a medieval point of view. The serial killer who sees "monsters" (evil entities) is blithely told it is "just a product of his wild imagination" (Carlo 1996, 202). The multiple personality, like the famous Sybil or Eve, is also told that her alters (other "selves") come from *within*.

All this smooth talk, whether deceptive or merely naive, amounts to failure on the part of those who have been entrusted with the Science of Mind. Let us, from now on, call it Psi-ence! The times are changing and progress is in store. We are now in the "as if" stage. Let me explain: My colleague and friend, England's Stephen Blake (2014, 197), mathematician and author, makes the astute observation that "modern psychiatry has begun to adjust [to] . . . the widespread effects of discarnate spirit influence. . . . Without acknowledging that discarnate spirits really exist, psychiatrists now can treat their patients *as if* [sic] they did, whilst leaving the intellectual apparatus of their discipline intact." This was indeed the tactic chosen by Dr. Adam Crabtree, who wrote, "Since it is not necessary to come to a final conclusion about . . . possession in order to deal therapeutically with it . . . the *as if* attitude . . . will be assumed. [Thus will] the possessing entity be described as a separate person." Indeed, his patient Maria had "shuddered *as if* [emphasis added] something had possession of me." Anna (also possessed) became incapable of entering a church "*as though* [emphasis added] prevented by some invisible force." Referring to Maria's and Anna's stories, Dr. Crabtree owns, "I discovered that when the possession experience was treated *as if* it were exactly what it appeared to be—invasion and control of the client by another human spirit—the condition could almost always be cleared up" (Crabtree 1985, 41, 95).

But to avoid that final moment of truth, the final bound, most analysts—and patients—turn to the As If simile, thus keeping entity intrusion a hypothetical, unreal supposition. The As If model crops up in response to every form of ASC (altered states of consciousness):

- In mediumship: Describing her entrance into trance, England's psychic-medium Winifred Tennant recalled, "It seemed *as if* somebody else was me, as if a stranger was occupying my body, as if another's mind was in me" (Cummins 1965, 105, 107).

- In OBEs: "I was floating in the air a few feet above the bed . . . moving slowly towards the ceiling . . . *as if* in the grip of some powerful cryptic directing force" (Battersby 1979, 68).

- In the prophet's experience: "This strange thing has come suddenly into his life and imposed itself upon him. . . . In this state, [it is] *as if* . . . a strange power speaks by his mouth . . . as if he were only the spectator of what the strange force says and does" (Oesterreich 1935, 76).

- In bipolar disorder: "It was *as though* there were demons inside me making me do all these crazy things" (Duke and Hochman 1992, 10).

- In MPD: "These personalities [MPD alters] could be demonstrated to be physically, chemically, and psychologically different, almost *as if* [emphasis added] they indeed were different people encased in the same body" (Mayer 1989, 28). Noting the startling changes in the multiple's voice, looks, and movements, another observer comments, "It was *as if* [emphasis added] the therapists were encountering entirely separate people" (Spencer 1989, 195).

- In possession: "It is *as if* [emphasis added] you are no longer looking at the same person," commented one writer on the facial changes that occur in demonic possession (Head 2004; comment by Francis MacNutt). It was "as if someone else were giving the orders," another victim of possession complained (Goodman 1981, 21).

- In criminal pathology: "Most of the time he seemed utterly absent, *as if* [emphasis added] his self had long since left his body behind" (Kirwin 1997, 42–43). One behavioral analyst said the same about Ted Bundy: "It was *as if* [emphasis added] an outside force had taken root . . . come to inhabit [his] psyche" (Depue 2005, 156).

- In OCD: One patient reports that "she felt *as if* [emphasis added] she had lost control of her thoughts completely" (Levenkron 1991, 52). Dr. Rapoport, who has given us so many interesting cases of obsessive-compulsive disorder, discusses Sal's problem (a compulsion to pick up trash!): "It appeared *as if* [emphasis added] it were some outside agent that suddenly provoked the illness" (Rapoport 1989, 8).

If we hark back to the day when it was more customary to speak and think in terms of "some outside agent," we find that certain telling figures of speech linger on in our language. Think of the literal meaning of such phrases as

> What possessed me to . . . ?
> Something got into me
> She's beside herself
> He's out of his mind
> What came over me?

That earlier Era of Belief was upended by the so-called Enlightenment, with its thoroughgoing faith in objective science, one could almost say, by the God of Science. And it has fulfilled its purpose—which was, broadly speaking, to clear away all that was uncritical, ignorant, or unsound in older, provincial thinking. In this it has succeeded—marvelously. But now we face a new era, a new synthesis. The science stronghold, with its arch-rationalism and unstinting materialism, is now faced with this challenge: What to make of the *unseen* forces?

Most traditional societies recognized that force; the Zulus, for one, call the physical body *inyama* and the shadow body *isithunzi,* and the vehicle of a person's spirit is called *umoya.* As Ralph Waldo Emerson once put it, "All I have seen teaches me to trust the Creator for all I have not seen." The move toward spiritology was, in Emily Bronte's words, "the final bound."

Supposed objectivity or rationality is not enough to complete the picture of the human being. Empiricism is not enough. Materialism is not enough. Intellect alone is not enough. Science is not enough. If the recent explosion of NDE (near-death experience) studies means anything, it has brought us closer to an understanding of what lies beyond. In this book we treat the human being in both her forms: the corporean (physical) and the essean (spiritual).

> The spirit I made was separate from the corporeal [physical] life ... O man of the earth, if only your spirit and your corpor stood even in wisdom and power all the days of your life! But you are so delighted in the earth that you have left your spirit unfed. And it stands within you like a spear of grass covered with a stone.
>
> OAHSPE, BOOK OF JEHOVIH 6:10
> AND BOOK OF JUDGMENT 13:11–12

In making the "final bound," we will get past the taskmaster's demand for physical proof of nonphysical things! "I don't need scientific proof," Sir Arthur Conan Doyle wrote in a letter to the *New York Evening Mail* on December 29, 1921. "Nobody does. This is one of the fine things about Spiritualism. Each person can prove it for himself ... and the better you live here, the further you'll go there, progressing finally to the perfect state."

Proof, in the purely scientific, even petty, sense, may turn out to be less relevant than logic, good judgment, reason—or even love. It is as the prophet Ka'yu (also known as Confucius) said so long ago: "To try to find the Creator with love, instead of with a dissecting knife; this leadeth man on the highest road. To trust in Him, wherein we strive to do our best; this is good philosophy" (Oahspe, God's Book of Eskra 36:44).

What I perceive is that the secular model, despite its many successes, has ultimately left us high and dry, its impartiality a sham, its materialism a limitation, its godlessness a stone on the soul. This book I write does not pretend to be an unbiased account of human behavior taking all views into consideration. Rather it is a testimony of the unseen world, the layer of reality that has been brushed aside by the conceit of man. The invisible and unmeasurable world is nonetheless demonstrable in a thousand ways. To ascertain—to show you—the immortal existence of the human spirit is my goal.

Will man ever know he has been raised up?
Will he be believing?
Or will he, too, need to go to some new world
and raise up its first fruits
and toil his hundreds of years
with naked mortals?

OAHSPE, BOOK OF SETHANTES 10:6

Belief is at an impasse. Most people I talk to are undecided, unsure, about ultimate questions like life and death, here and hereafter. Fence-sitting has become a way of life. Yet this is not the safe path we think it is. Uncertainty (and its companion, doublethink) is a breeding ground for hard lessons—and blowback. The desire for truth in these distracted and cynical times is considered idealistic, even quixotic. But I know this: the business of problem solving, *real* problem solving, is not for unripe minds nor is it the business of the politically correct or of any worldly agenda whatsoever. Frank and forthright problem solving inevitably plunges us into murky waters, secret places, even forbidden ground. Bedrock. Nitty-gritty. The plunge, though sober and demanding, will bring us that much closer to the safe, secure, and honest world we all crave.

1
SPIRIT AT LARGE

"The Unbelievable" by Edwin Markham
Impossible, you say, that man survives
The grave—that there are other lives?
More strange, O friend, that we should ever rise
Out of the dark to walk below these skies.
Once having risen into life and light,
We need not wonder at our deathless flight

. . . . .

We can believe the all-imagining Power
That breathed the Cosmos forth as a golden flower
Had potence in his breath
To plan us new surprises beyond death—
New spaces and new goals
For the adventure of ascending souls.
Be brave, O heart, be brave:
It is not strange that man survives the grave:
'Twould be a stranger thing were he destroyed
Than that he ever vaulted from the void.

As you, dear reader, may well know, the Great Age of Spiritualism hit the ground running in America in the year 1848.* In very little time,

---

*That year, 1848, is memorialized in the cosmic bible Oahspe as Year One of the new bright era called Kosmon.

distinguished personalities, including Abraham Lincoln, were taking active interest in mediumistic circles. Sweeping the country like brush-fire, the movement, nonetheless, drew as many detractors as proponents. John Dods, for one, thought he could explain the apparent manifestation of spirits in a purely materialist way. His book, *The Philosophy of Electrical Psychology,* met with great success, especially in the scientific community.

In 1851, Daniel Webster, Sam Houston, and Henry Clay personally invited Mr. Dods to the capital to lecture on his ideas. Spirits, Dods explained in his talk, were not a reality; what we mistook for spirits were merely the body's electrical emanations, produced for the most part by the operations of the brain. A few years later, though, Dods was disturbed by an unnerving experience, an apparition. Four spirits appeared before him, four relatives who were living in Norfolk, Virginia. They told him they had just passed into the spirit world, dead of yellow fever. When Dods later confirmed the fact, his unbelief was shaken. Over the next six months John Dods struggled with his unsettling experience, trying to convince himself that the vision had been some sort of psychological quirk. By early 1856 he gave up the fight and joined the ranks of the spiritualists, publicly embracing the immortality of the soul.

The question is sometimes asked: Why were there so many manifestations and full-form apparitions in the mid-nineteenth century compared to today? One explanation, drawing on the Oahspe bible, lies in the matter of cyclic dawns or *dan'has.* These are times of light, ushering in a new era, which then lasts for some three thousand years. *Kosmon* is the name of the present era, which began in 1848. The light of heaven is revealed at the start of each new dawn:

Jehovih gave this sign to man on earth; which is to say: In the beginning of the light of dan'ha, the spirits of the newly dead shall have power to take upon themselves the semblance of corporeal [physical] bodies, and appear and talk face to face with mortals. Every three thousand years Jehovih gave this sign on earth.

OAHSPE, BOOK OF JEHOVIH 7:4

Like Dods, his contemporary Dr. John Ballou Newbrough (1828–1891) would go the way from skeptic to believer, but again not without a fight. For many years, approximately from 1848 to 1874, Newbrough—though mediumistic and clairvoyant himself—would not commit to any of the going theories. I think he had truly turned a corner in 1874, the year in which he published a small booklet entitled *Spiritalis*. The tract was in a *Q* and *A* format in which he posed questions to his spirit teachers. At one point (Question #19) he inquired about electricity (a la Dods) and magnetism: the favored theory then currently held was that paranormal phenomena devolved on a living magnetism or electricity belonging to the body of the medium; the magnetizer's art was thought to depend on withdrawing that "electricity from the system."

However the jolting answer to Newbrough's Question #19 was that "dead magnetism cannot impart intelligence" and electricity is inanimate—"it grows not." Moreover Newbrough was told that "the power that springs from the living body is spirit"; only spirit could "receive and impart knowledge." (Newbrough, seven years later, became the amanuensis of the Oahspe bible; my biography of Newbrough is called *The Hidden Prophet*.)

I think it follows that energy, like electricity, is an inadequate solution to such manifestations as show intelligence (as discussed in the introduction). Yet, 150 years have done nothing to settle the debate. Even today's parapsychologists—who should know better—tell us that "flying objects in a poltergeist situation, some of them huge and following elaborate patterns—are being thrown about by 'psychic energy' emanating from the 'unconscious.' . . . Most incredible," add Hunt and McMahon (1988, 116), "is the continued insistence of these skeptics that such amazing physical phenomena are caused by the subconscious release of a mental force innate within themselves." Hauntings, it is still stubbornly argued, are not caused by any intelligence, but by *energy* that psychic-sensitives merely "interpret" as personalities. No, ghosts are not ghosts, but "some kind of psychic *energy* [emphasis added] that has been imprinted on the atmosphere and can be picked up by certain people"

(Underwood 1986, 219). Just how this splendid magic is wrought is never explained. Nor are we given the slightest clue how "an impersonal bundle of violent psychic *energy* [emphasis added]" could be "the fallout from an emotional explosion which may have occurred centuries ago" (Spraggett 1967, 164). If this were any other field of study, these theorists would be drummed out for wild speculation and gross incompetence.

Ghostly entities, in fact, exhibit not only intelligence but also cunning—as well as precise timing, showing up, as they so often do, on the anniversary of some pivotal event. How could we possibly call this an "impersonal" energy? I'll tell you how: twaddle that it is, it is nonetheless the materialist's last redoubt against the actual reality of ghosts.

True, it is a separate reality. Ghost and earthbound entities (EB for short) are inhabitants of neither heaven nor earth. Neither here nor there, they wander in darkness.

A great multitude of angels of darkness [are] gathered together upon the face of the earth, and many of them will not hence into the higher heavens. . . . Billions of spirits of the dead do not know the plan of the resurrection to higher heavens, but wander about on the earth, not even knowing the organizations of the kingdoms in [the] lowest of heavens. Many of these angels believe the heavens to be like an unorganized wilderness, void of government, instruction and discipline. And by virtue of their presence with mortals, though invisible to them, do inspire mortals with the same darkness.

OAHSPE, GOD'S BOOK OF ESKRA 1:4–7

You will find their bailiwick described as limbo, the Outer Darkness, or Hades. As England's Dr. Arthur Guirdham (1982, 209) once put it, "the discarnate entities which cause psychiatric disease . . . circulate in what we call Hades, a no-man's land between this world and the next. . . . These are psyches so contaminated by materialism . . . that they remain in close proximity to it."

Guirdham's countrywoman, Dion Fortune (1981, 63) has seen enough of the dark side to know that "the entity causing the trouble may be a soul that is itself in distress . . . and is too ignorant of post-mortem conditions to know the harm it is doing by clinging so desperately to the living." Her wording ("clinging so desperately") is echoed in the words of Eugene Maurey (1988, 48), one of America's most adept exorcists: "I often think of an invading spirit entity as a drowning person, desperately clinging to another for help. . . . When living on earth he was never given directions or an indication what he would find after dying. He may think that possessing a living person is his sole option. He knows of no other place to go."

As a drowning man clingeth to a log, so cling the drujas [Hades spirits] to mortals.

OAHSPE, BOOK OF LIKA 22:11

A grasping, parasitic entity that latched on to a young man was described in the same terms: quite by chance, an experienced medium (Frank Decker) happened to meet that young man, and later avowed that he had perceived a spirit "with him that was hanging around him so closely that he is almost overshadowing the young man's personality. . . . He [the entity] is very unenlightened. He does not know he is dead. He seems to be *clinging* [emphasis added] to the young man . . . not really knowing what is going on" (S. Smith 1970b, 152).

Cases vary: one entity spotted by Dr. Adam Crabtree (1985, 198) was afraid of starvation without someone to feed upon. *Feed?* Oahspe alludes to this: "Millions of them lived with mortals as familiars, depending for their own existence upon the spiritual part of the food mortals drank and ate" (Oahspe, Book of Fragapatti 37:3). Or as Dr. Edith Fiore (1987, 77) has observed, the victim of sudden death may just "latch on to" the nearest person "to stay alive"—or simply because they feel lonely, confused, or scared.

How long can such an attachment endure? "Maybe a few years or it may be hundreds of years," according to Oahspe (Book of Judgment 23:23) and also to British spirit-worker Wilma Davidson (2006, 104) who says that "the length of time a spirit can wander the between-worlds ranges from a few days to several hundred years." The English cases are some of the richest: near Exeter, in 2007, a spirit named Jacob was wreaking havoc in one particular household; through the medium, he divulged that he had been hanged nearby for horse stealing in 1837. In spooky old England, too, near the Channel, a very old house was found to be haunted by a stubborn spirit who ultimately revealed himself as "John Aird. I was murdered in this house 465 years, 9 months, and three days ago, and buried in the garden" (Hurwood 1971, 12). Aird further communicated that he had hidden a quantity of gold in the cellar and wanted it to be found and turned over to his descendants.

It is not that unusual for money matters to hold a spirit back, as in the case of one Jean Clement-X* who recalled with great remorse a crime he had committed during his life, asking that the money that remained be returned to its owner (Fodor 1966, 387). Or take a more recent, American, case: A man dies. His wife cannot find his life insurance policy. The husband comes in a dream, revealing that the papers are in a strongbox in the attic. And that is just where she finds them. Sometimes it is only the deceased who can reveal a hiding place. After the death of Dante, it was realized that the thirteenth canto of his "Paradiso" was missing. Soon, the dead poet appeared to his son Pietro Alighieri, and told him to remove a certain panel near the window of the room in which the poem was written. And there the missing canto was found, mildewed but legible (Olcott 1972, 99–100).

Patterns of haunting are almost identical in all countries and cultures.
HANS NAEGELI-OSJORD, *POSSESSION AND EXORCISM*

Concerning ghost return, there are countless anecdotes pointing to some grievance (of the departed) that keeps him or her lingering on the earth plane. Often we hear of some excarnate house owner disgruntled

---

*Appending an "X" onto someone's name is the standard way that spiritualists refer to a deceased person who returns (usually in a communication), announcing his or her identity as an ex-mortal.

with the new owners and manifesting as a disruptive ghost or even a poltergeist. Others are obsessed with a place—such as the entity who possessed a very young girl because her family built their home on her erstwhile (eighty years ago!) property. Vengeful, the entity had tried to attack the parents, but their aura was too strong, so . . . the child became the victim—and she was made into a very shy, cripplingly fearful child. As a matter of fact, the possessor, as discovered in hypnosis, had been a hanged murderess—she passed on the upset of her traumatic finish to the child.

The troublesome spirit in some traditional societies, on the other hand, is frequently thought to be vexed by his improper burial. In every part of the world, though, return for vengeance's sake has been reported for those who died as victims of murder, persecution, torture, deception, injustice, and the like, retaliating by causing accidents, quarrels, attacks, sickness, or even just a good fright, among the living.

The well-known author Isabel Allende (1993, 224–25) relates the chilling story of General Prats's ghost. This goes back to the 1970s; Prats, Chile's leading general, had refused to participate in the (CIA-inspired) coup ousting the social-democrat president Salvadore Allende (who, incidentally, was assassinated on *September 11*, 1973; it was a Tuesday). The leading families then fled to Argentina but, as Isabel recounts, "on September 29, 1974, a bomb exploded in Prats's automobile . . . after dining with my parents. The force of the explosion . . . dismembered the general, and his wife died in the blazing inferno." Isabel goes on to relate what happened next. "A few days later in Santiago, in the residence of the commander-in-chief where Prats and his family had lived . . . Pinochet's wife saw General Prats in broad daylight, sitting at the dining room table. . . . After her first shock, she [thought] that the vision was a result of bad conscience . . . but in the following weeks, the ghost of the betrayed friend returned many times: it appeared, standing, in the salons, it walked loudly down the stairway, it peered through doorways, until its obstinate presence became intolerable . . . Pinochet had the walls of his bewitched house reinforced and the windows covered with armorplate; he doubled his armed guard, installed machine guns around the perimeter, and blocked off the street so no one could approach. I don't know how General Prats managed to filter through such fortifications."

Back to North America: Dr. Fiore (1987, 92) found an entity hiding in her client Barbara, which had entered her at hospital when Barbara was operated on. The intruder, Dorothy X, had herself died of cancer, after which, Barbara married Dorothy X's widower. This infuriated Dorothy X who was now determined to make her rival sick—she was obsessing her to overeat! Dorothy X's excessive attachment to her husband kept her earthbound and determined to "create turmoil between the two"; she was "delighted that their marriage was indeed crumbling."

Although a grievance or an obsession with money may keep a spirit earthbound, such scenarios are not entirely typical. Rather, the Outer Darkness is filled with stupefied souls, some bewildered by a violent or sudden death. "The dead-who-are-not-at-rest . . . are not so much evil as confused" (Betty 2012, 27). "Confusion," says Fiore (1987, 32), "was common among people who experienced a sudden, unexpected death. Some stayed where they died for hours, months—in some cases even years." The multiple Billy Milligan called it "the Dying Place," where souls remain suspended between heaven and earth. He explained: "I see bad things happening to people. They fall in front of cars, they fall down cliffs, they're drowning" (Keyes 1981, 178, 419).

Vastly underrated, if not largely ignored, is the causal link between sudden death and the *persistent* phantom. Today, more than 150 years since the end of the Civil War, casualties of that bloody conflict still linger, in spectral form, above the place of their demise. "A mass of orbs of all sizes" was recently caught on film at a church where Civil War wounded and dying were treated. At the Antietam National Battlefield and Cemetery, which honors the *23,000* men who lost their lives on that fateful day (September 17, 1862) untraceable shouts and screams can still be heard. Paranormal researchers have been drawn to that haunted battlefield, where phenomena are most evident around Burnside's Bridge. Here, spectral "blue balls of light," like soap bubbles, are occasionally seen floating in the air—sometimes unseen by the naked eye but picked up by camera. Ghost hunters know: the place to look for perfectly round, transparent balls are murder sites, scenes of violent death, places of suicide. Theories? Maybe it is the deceased "attempting to put itself back together" (Ramsland 2001, 205, 296).

Still Battling

Dying in the heat of passion, fear, and anger, [they] become wild and bound on battlefields, or perhaps stroll away into deserted houses and castles, and are lost, bewildered and unapproachable. Of these, there are hundreds of millions; and they are in all countries and among all peoples in the world. . . . Those slain on earthly battlefields are born into spirit in chaos, not knowing they are dead (as to the earth), and so they linger on the battlefields, still battling imaginary foes.

OAHSPE, BOOK OF JUDGMENT 32:9–10

AND BOOK OF THOR 1:15

A ghostly reenactment of the classic Battle of Edge Hill was seen by thousands of witnesses among the Northamptonshire peasantry, clergy, and two officials of the king—only two months after its actual occurrence (Ebon 1971, 48). The clairvoyant who visits the scene of battle may encounter "swirling groups of combatants who had left the body, locked together in an intense emotional stress, fancying they were still engaged in slaughter," fighting in their astral bodies (Clarke 2004, 184). In a third-century Greek case, reported by Flavius Philostratus, a sixteen-year-old boy who was possessed "no longer even has his own voice," as the distressed mother explained. "He utters deep and grave sounds like a grown man. The eyes . . . are not his eyes." At last, the demon revealed himself through the boy's mouth and declared to the mother "that he is the spirit of a man killed in war" (Oesterreich 1935, 10).

In the Pacific Islands, *mauli* are the ghosts and evil spirits that inhabit old ceremonial ruins like the *marae* where human beings were once sacrificed, offered up to the gods or the sun or Venus. Islanders avoid these places like the plague. In the Society Islands, it was supposed that when people died violently their spirits did not move on in the normal way, but that they remained at the place of death. Hence were they dreaded, under the belief that such places, especially the marae and former battlefields, were haunted (Henry 1928, 200).

Neither were Samoans who had died a violent death, especially in battle, able to start on the journey to the next world. Fear was felt by the survivors, lest such spirits should haunt their former abode. Trouble might also arise from a relative who had drowned, remaining a "wanderer in limbo, lacking entrance to the country of the dead" (Williamson 1933, vol. 1, ch. 13).

> *Phantoms, countless, men and women, after death, wandering . . .*
>
> WALT WHITMAN

In the Marquesan Islands, too, anyone who died by enemy action or in some other untimely way, inhabited the place of death and was "particularly annoying, as they inflicted such ills on their [earthly] victims as boils, skin diseases and temporary insanity" (Suggs 1962, 42). Investigators in all parts of the world have concluded that ghosts and poltergeists owe their existence to earthbound spirits (EBs) whose lives were cut short by accident, illness, murder, or suicide.

As we go on, we will find the suddenly or violently dead to comprise the bulk of our perturbed and disturbed EBs. They are the spirits behind so-called past lives. They are the alters (otherwise known as the secondary personalities) of multiples (MPD). Too, they are, as Conan Doyle suggested, the entities who "visit" spirit circles.

> *Many reports that have come through mediums [are] accounts from those who had died suddenly.*
>
> JOHN G. FULLER,
> *THE GHOST OF 29 MEGACYCLES*

In one of Horatio Eddy's "dark circles" (Olcott 1972, 205–6, see below), two discarnates made their appearance. One was a "sailor-spirit" drowned in the wreck of the steamship *President;* the other was a maiden who died of a fever while captive among the Indians of Maine (circa 1770). They were traumatic, untimely deaths. Yet, we cannot overlook the fact that even those who have made a smoother transition may be oblivious to their passing. "It does not enter their minds that they are spirits, and they are loath to recognize the fact" (Wickland 1974, 43). Similarly, spirit mentors have explained "that death is so simple and natural a process that many people do not . . . realize the change and may be attracted by the . . . auras of the living . . . causing mischief and misery. . . . In fact, knowledge is an armor" (Archer 1967, 101).

And there were born from the earth millions and millions of spirits who could not believe they were dead, but maintained they were confined in dark dungeons [coffins?] howling and cursing day and night . . . [Others] were in chaos, still lingering in the places where they were cut off from the earth.

OAHSPE, BOOK OF FRAGAPATTI 2:11 AND 35:5

As a busy medium, England's Ena Twigg had often to deal with "those entities who have lost their physical bodies but continue to haunt this life. . . . These poor unfortunates do not know they are dead." In one instance, Twigg was taken to a haunted theater where a man had died right in his seat. Yet his spirit remained. "He did not know he was dead. He'd frightened the life out of the whole staff. So my job then was to explain to him that the show was finished and he'd just as well get on with his new life" (Twigg and Brod 1973, 107–9).

"I'm not dead, you know! I'm not!" a spirit voice came through hypnosis (Fiore 1987, 32). Believing only in matter, the physical life, one thinks that Earth is the only place for growth and experience: "I was not aware of this side," one excarnate communicated. "I didn't know the potential over here. . . . So when I got here, it was like . . . not knowing where I was at. Like having a bad dream" (Fuller 1986, 134). The confusion is vast: "There were one billion eight hundred thousand spirits wandering about, mostly on the earth. . . . And many of them had forgotten *who they were* [emphasis added] and had no memory of once having lived mortal lives" (Oahspe, Book of Fragapatti 37:3, referring to a time some seven thousand years ago). Yet not much has changed. A man named Per was one of Cam West's various alters (MPD). Cam's wife asked Per, "Who are you?" Per replied (through Cam) "I . . . don't . . . know exactly. . . . It's strange being out here . . . I don't know where I came from" (West 1999, 91). In another multiple case, several lost souls hovered around the woman, "yet were unaware of her and of each other" (Chase 1987, 94). We learn, moreover, that spirits sometimes merge unintentionally (accidentally) with a host and are unable to extricate themselves.

As such, Soldier-X was "trapped in a limbo between worlds." Encountered at a Rescue Circle, he was identified as a Revolutionary War soldier who had been tortured by the British in that very room where the circle was held. "The soldier's ordeal had unhinged his mind and he did not realize that he was dead." He spoke through the medium, in a broken, incoherent voice, "pouring out a pitiful story of horror and confusion. . . . Finally the ghost accepted that he was 'dead' and agreed to leave the place" (Spraggett 1967, 164). Another spirit, speaking through Mrs. Wickland admitted, "I couldn't get out" (of the host's aura) (Wickland 1974, 57). One wag, commenting on this "stuckness," quipped that "the devils themselves would gladly leave, but they cannot" (Christiani 1961, 6). This is true. Many spirits are unable to "go away from the mortals to whom they are bound, and on whom they live" (Oahspe, Book of Fragapatti, 35:7).

But ghosts and poltergeists seem to have a life of their own, to somehow drift into almost physical existence. Exactly how this is done has excited the curiosity of many investigators. Is it, wondered Epes Sargent (1876, 36), "with the aid of some occult alchemy unexplainable to material senses?" Perhaps, he thought, spirits have "the power to extract elements from their surroundings, wherewith they are enabled to present themselves in an exact resemblance to their earth body, together with its clothing* and peculiarities."

Before Henry Steele Olcott jump-started the Theosophy movement with Mme. Helena Blavatsky,† he had earned a fine reputation as a government investigator. Then, after eye-witnessing the materializations at the Eddy household in Vermont, he asked how those spirit-forms, which he saw with his own eyes, could be explained. "We can conceive of the body being made by a supreme effort of the spirits from the invisible atoms of the atmosphere."

On one occasion, "ten spirits appeared to us, among them a lady . . . who had only died the Friday previous. [Her] relative . . . sat beside me and was dreadfully agitated at the thought that one whom she had seen buried *only a few days before* [emphasis added] should so soon have 'burst the cerements of the grave.' Poor woman!" (Olcott 1972, 309, 326–27).

I have given power to spirits of *the newly dead* [emphasis added] to clothe themselves from the atmosphere with corporeal semblances of flesh and blood. . . . When thou hast quit the corporeal body, behold, thy spirit will be free. . . . Thou shalt fashion from the surroundings thine own form, hands and arms and feet and legs, perfectly.

OAHSPE, BOOK OF APOLLO 10:12 AND BOOK OF BEN 4:10–11

Occultists might call this phenomenon the condensation of etheric energy; it is described in the Book of Thor (4:12) as a process in which "ethereans gather up the atomic elements . . . propelling them forth . . . aggregating [them] from a mite." But spirits of a lower order can only gather up whatever energy is available, like "parasites that feed off the electrical system." This is what psychic investigator Paul Eno (2006, 57–58) discovered after looking into several poltergeist cases. In one

---

*As Oahspe has it, spirits learn how to *sargis* (or make manifest) clothing and how to create light and darkness in the College of Creation, according to the fiftieth Divan law.
†Blavatsky also traveled up to the Eddy's where the spirits spoke to her in Russian.

Figs. 1.1 and 1.2. Eddy homestead and circle room

home disturbed by shadow figures, bed shaking, foul smells, and other anomalies, Eno asked the mother, "What has your electric bill been like lately?" She replied, "Funny you should bring that up. Since this crap started, the bill's been sky high . . . and for no reason."

sargis

Fig. 1.3. Sign of sargis

An ancient word for a materializing angel is *sargis*. Sargis, in fact, is either an apparition (materialized angel) or a corporean (mortal medium) in whose presence angels can take on the semblance of mortal forms and be seen. The sargis uses vortexya* for manifestations: "When a prophet hath attained to discharge vortexya so as to make raps at will, he is also subject to the presence of people from the unseen worlds. And these people, spirits, or angels, use this vortexya for a foundation for sargis" (Oahspe, Book of Cosmogony and Prophecy 11:12). A spirit does not take its bulk with it, but fashions a body from its surroundings when it arrives at its destination. It may be only a partial materialization, depending on the skill and advancement of the angel. Just so, the "people from the other world" at the Eddy's explained that such "synthesis" is not easy; the art of materialization (or sargis) is difficult and some of the spirits can only make hands, unable to synthesize a complete form.

Occultists have also accounted for materializations by positing "a chemist in the spirit world [who] withdraws certain ingredients . . . from the medium and those present" (Findlay 1931). Others describe the process in terms of unseen "ducts leading from our bodies" and carrying a vital substance "drawn from the spine and nerve centres principally" (Fodor 1966, 208). Yet others claim that plain old "excess

---

Vortexya is the atmospheric discharge originating in the Earth's vortex, i.e., in its magnetic field.

energy" can be absorbed from people or even animals to make a spirit-form. "As an indication of how this [extra] energy may be accumulated," Rev. Maurey (1988, 62) describes a large and lively dance party he attended, a reunion actually, that was so invigorating he could not fall asleep that night. "Spirits," said he, "accumulate psychic energy in very much the same way as I did at the reunion. When they are in the presence of such energy, they can draw upon it to produce poltergeist activities or for a more useful purpose."

Even the charged energy of a drug high can activate a nearby spirit. Gore Vidal recalled a vivid image of his lost love Jimmie that came back to him "while I was smoking ganja in Katmandu . . . Jimmie materialized beside me on the bed. He was completely present." When Gore touched him, Jimmie opened his eyes and smiled. "He was, for an instant, real . . . but only for an instant" (Vidal 1996, 35).

2
FLIGHT OF THE SOUL

W hen psychologists chalk up enigmatic and inexplicable behavior—like ESP or MPD—to the mechanisms of the unconscious or subconscious mind, they're not saying much. A dead end, it is virtually the same as saying, We just don't know. Serving as the proverbial rug under which countless mysteries may be swept, the so-called unconscious represents not so much the hidden place of the soul as the ignorance of analysts, the same specialists to whom we turn for an understanding of the mind. The same specialists who maintain the cold war between materialism and spiritualism.

Long overdue for the wrecking ball, Freud's overrated Unconscious explains nothing. It's not really because the experts are stumped; no, it's because they are wary—even fearful—of the alternative, which is of course *altered states of consciousness* (ASCs). Open that door and out comes a host of hobgoblins from the unseen world, all the creatures of mind that materialist science would rather ignore or blame on anomaly, hallucination, irrationalism, overactive imagination, or any other throwaway sound bite. Yet the door has already been opened; fifty years ago, the category of ASC joined the jargon—if only parenthetically—yet covering a raft of deviant or dissociative mental states, many of which, significantly, belong on the paranormal spectrum. ASCs, then, would include a great range of conditions, such as

- Dreaming, daydreaming, fantasizing
- Trance, meditative, or ecstatic states
- NDEs and OBEs and other Elsewhereness
- Blackouts and fugue, staring spells, drowsy states
- Brown study or reverie, "lost in thought"
- Hypnogogic states
- Drugged and drunken states
- Shocked or overstimulated states*

That said, I hasten to add that the most distinctive thing about ASCs—the pith of it, really—is the abeyance of self, abeyance of psyche, flight of the soul. To illustrate: It has been said that the sociopath (APD), the psychotic, and the victim of possession are virtually immune to any touch of therapy. Why? We must look to the *absence of self* for the answer. That is what we will do in this chapter.

This approach also gives us a handle on the remarkable similarities that exist between multiples, somnambules, narcissists, obsessives, autistics, psychics, sociopaths, and so forth (as discussed in the introduction). While it is standard practice to label these as "dissociative" states—which is true enough—dissociation, taken one step further, boils down to separation from self. This of course is what we mean by self-in-abeyance. And this field, this arena outside of self, turns out to have its own distinctive features (like the tunnel), accounting for the *similarities* between all these assorted states of altered consciousness. Indeed, they are all the hallmarks of displaced psyche.

When the persona begins to break down and ASCs take over, psyche conforms to a new set of realities. No, not *inner* realities, but stuff that exists in the External Unseen. And this is exactly why so much behavior that is *ab*normal also appears to be *para*normal. In fact,

---

*It seems also that acute or chronic *under*stimulation (say, locked in the closet by a psychotic caretaker or even just plain chronic neglect) can breed yet another kind of ASC, the mind deranged by isolation and the reduction of normal sensory input. Example: serial killer Ed Kemper, as a child, was locked up in a dark basement where he "saw the devil's face for the first time."

we might drop the clinical-sounding "altered states of consciousness" altogether and replace it with "psychically disturbed." The entire field of human psychology awaits that moment of truth when the psychic faculty leads the way. Hasten the day.

Meanwhile, the experts continue to use bland and sterile labels like "nonlocality of consciousness," safely avoiding the whole matter, most notably the central question of what that other locality is. When we compare notes from those who have been "in the tunnel," a common picture emerges:

- The victim of possession: the girl named Anneliese (of whom we will hear more) describes the peculiar sensation of "being hurled into a dark pit" (Goodman 1981, 21); the enlargement of her pupils seems to vouch for her description.
- Trauma: The victim of severe burns, who stayed in shock for a week, remembers "escaping into this dark void . . . just tumbling through space" (Keyes 1981).
- The multiple (MPD): driven away by pure terror, she finds herself in a place that is "still and dark and completely outside of time" (Castle and Bechtel 1989, 235). Similarly, the supermultiple Truddi Chase "heard the thoughts of another . . . from deep in the Tunnel" (Chase 1987, 104).
- The serial killer (Arthur Shawcross) tried to describe the moment of the crime: "It's just like the light was closing into that one spot. A tunnel going dark . . . I'm in a daze . . . it's just like something closes in on me." That tunnel, that close space, is the all-purpose metaphor used also by scores of persons to describe the OBE undergone at the point of death.

Anneliese's enlarged pupils remind us of the criminals whose eyes are described as all black, meaning all pupil—completely dilated—from spending time in that dark tunnel. Like Gwen Graham, nursing home murderess, with "two totally separate personalities . . . saintly and possessed"; entering a spell, "her face turned red and her pupils dilated" (Cauffiel 1992, 336, 64, 441). Or like Ted Bundy: While Bundy was in Florida under the alias Chris, a neighbor noticed that he would look real different sometimes—his eyes would become very dark, the pupils huge. Bundy had light eyes setting off a handsome, intelligent face; but they became dark at times. It was extreme dilation, or enlargement, of the pupils, that darkened his eyes. With Anneliese, the hapless German maiden whom the exorcists could not save from her ruinous possessors, it was the same. Father Alt, one of her exorcists, perceived a shadow behind the college girl on one occasion as the predatory spirit approached. "I am being molested," she told the priest who watched as "her eyes darkened and she became absent" (Goodman 1981, 48).

The same thing happens with certain psychoactive drugs like LSD. It is among the keenest clues, those enlarged pupils. But Anneliese, whose blue eyes turned black, and Bundy with his hazel eyes were not on LSD. *Without* drugs, spontaneously, their organism fell prey to the dark side of ASC, the perils of the tunnel. Those darkened eyes crop up also in MPD: Sybil, with sixteen alters, went white in the face and "the pupils of her eyes became dilated" when Peggy (an alter) took the spot. And when Vicky showed up (another alter), the eyes dilated again. "What happened?" Sybil asked her therapist. "Another fugue?" At such times, "her pupils were the size of the irises themselves." Halfway around the world, in the crazed state known to Indonesians and Malaysians as *amok,* "darkened eyes" (*mata gelap*) is the term used to refer to the frenzied individual gone postal, freely acknowledged as a form of spirit possession. It is the same in Haitian possession: the subject becomes completely stiff limbed and the pupils of the eyes dilate.

But there is much more than those dark eyes that alert us to psyche gone Elsewhere; I am referring to the stark absence of self. The flight of the soul leaves behind the impression of empty persona, a shell, a void. Nobody home. This abeyance is so fundamental, so universal, we encounter it in almost every kind of mental illness. Table 2.1 illustrates this.

TABLE 2.1. NOBODY HOME

Condition	Subject	Description
OCD	patients	make statements like "I am nothing," "I feel like there's nobody inside"
Bulimia	patients	are trying to "fill an emptiness"
Bipolar	Betsey	"I felt like I wasn't really there" (Duke and Hochman 1992, 84)
Spirit possession	Jersey	"would suddenly absent herself" (Peck 2005, 80)
Satanic victim	Michelle	"I was all gone . . . just floated away" (M. Smith and Pazder 1980, 17)
Mediumship	undeveloped medium	"her mind was in a vacuum state" (Scott and Norman 1985, 303)
Mediumship	developed (voluntary)	"My mind seemed blank" (Oahspe Addendum, 908)
MPD	multiple	"like a garage without a car" (Mayer 1989, 172)
Autism	autist	"I was an invisible non-entity . . . a gray void" (Stillman 2006)
Hysteria	self	"my mind [was] completely in abeyance" (Fortune 1981, 15–16)

The "nonperson" is a constant in criminal psychopathy. David Berkowitz, the Son of Sam, was called "a nondescript person with no real identity." But the key to our analysis can be found in David's own evaluation in which he, significantly, paints himself as "an empty vacuum . . . your life void of many things . . . the unclean spirits will fill the very same void" (Klausner 1981, 363). This is the vehicle running on empty. Self in abeyance. What follows inevitably is the drawing power of a vacuum. Filling the void.

"It's like I was void of thought. Like I left for a little while."
BOBBY JOE LONG, SERIAL KILLER
(MORRISON 2004, 167)

Adrift in a nameless limbo, psyche is set to attract "homeless" entities. The same applies to the phony persona: John Kappler's persona was all veneer, all show—a surface self. The biographer of this crazed killer calls it "the armor of his false self." Inside was a void—prey to usurping entities; Kappler's empty vessel of self had attracted negative controls.

The same kind of force found its way into the mind of Arthur Shawcross, one of New York's most notorious random killers. "I knew something was coming over me that I couldn't control." "No matter what I do, it ain't right," Arthur recalled of his youth. His mother-from-hell called him stupid, dummy, dumb bastard, and the like. Arthur began running away from home at six. *His real self also ran away,* into the void of abeyance. The real problem—*absent self* (Olsen 1993, 52, 487).

> *"Art? Arthur? Is anybody home?"*
>
> A SCHOOLTEACHER

Killer Eric Chapman felt as though he "lacked an ego . . . felt hollow and invisible" (Markman and Bosco 1989, 303–4). Hollow: When the mind goes blank it becomes like a slate, a tabula rasa; as when mediums perform automatic writing in a totally relaxed, even blank, state of mind, independent of their volition. William Howitt performed automatic drawing "without a thought of my own." George Russell (1918, 58–59) wrote that "once in an idle interval in my work, I sat with my face pressed in my hands, and in that dimness, pictures began flicking in my brain. . . . While I was in [this] vacant mood, my companion [co-worker] had been thinking of his home, and his quickened memories invaded my own mind." In fact, others offering tips on how to develop your own psychic powers have said the key is to practice detachment, forgetting self and making one's mind completely blank. A state of emptiness, really.

But it has its downside: Just as "the chief characteristic of obsessional patients is a sense of emptiness" (Levenkron 1991, 83), so it goes with the multiple, like Jenny who wrote in her journal, "Is there a *me?*" (Spencer 1989, 79), or like Katherine, whose therapist said, "it was not she who was being raped. It was someone else" (Castle and Bechtel 1989, 217).

In other words, to avoid the pain and trauma, the multiple simply absents herself—or himself: "I just closed my eyes and went away,"* said Billy Milligan, describing how he reacted to being sodomized by his stepdaddy at age eight. And whenever Billy "went away" and an alter took his place, Billy had no idea what the alter had done. "I don't remember what they said I did. I don't know anything." No feint; Billy simply did not remember that he raped three women. No, he wasn't faking memory loss. "His amnesia was legitimate. . . . [His] memory was poor, with long periods blanked out" (Keyes 1981, xii, 131, 117, 28, 148, 361). Throughout his childhood, Billy was constantly losing time.

With the soul in flight, lost time is as typical of OCD—"I cannot remember very many events" (Rapoport 1989, 54)—as it is of MPD, where the host loses all awareness of his actions. The famous multiple Eve had blackouts followed by periods of which she had absolutely no memory or knowledge. Her husband was going crazy, accusing her of stunts she didn't know a thing about—filling his shoes with water, sewing the cuffs of his trouser legs, watering his whiskey, spilling ink in the house (typical pranks of the mischievous alter).

She slays and her hands are not bloody.

SWINBURNE

MPD: "No wonder I got in trouble when I did not do anything—or so I thought. No wonder it seemed I had not learned major chunks of material at school. Perhaps, too, this was why some of my friends would stop talking to me and in some instances end our friendship" (Cohen et al. 1991, 87).

Absent self, by definition, is empty self, resulting in what psychiatrists call *flat affect*. The term designates a notable lack of emotion—often due to a "nurturance vacuum" back in early life. Think of the apathetic individual, the opposite of affectionate: undemonstrative,

---

*The phrasing is identical to Jimmy's: "I just go away." Like Billy, Jimmy was sexually abused by his father—who he finally stabbed to death (Mones 1991, 38).

doesn't care, dull. Feelings are almost entirely in abeyance. Self is some-where else. You can't get a rise out of 'em. "They're locked in this limbo. . . . They say, 'If only I could cry, I'd feel better.' Or, 'I should have feel-ings, but I don't'" (Duke and Hochman 1992, 41). A surefire giveaway of abeyant self, flat affect has been noted in the unresponsive antisocial personality (APD) as well as the remorseless criminal offender. Mark Hofmann, the Mormon bomber, for example, bore "a blank stare . . . empty of emotion" (Lindsey 1988, 166, 2).

Again and again, it is emptiness—even more than viciousness—that is perceived in the look of the most dangerous culprits. "Most of the time," says forensic psychologist Barbara Kirwin speaking of New York's prolific killer Joel Rifkin, "he seemed utterly absent, as if his self had long since left his body behind"; she mentions his "vacant, glazed eyes . . . expressionless"; the press had depicted him as "detached, bored." He spoke in a "droning monotone . . . no emotion at all" (Kirwin 1997, 42–43, 49–51). Similarly, the mother of one of Eric Napoletano's victims remarked that "there was something in the way he looked, in his eyes . . . I saw emptiness" (Pienciak 1996, 69, 383). Indeed, in the course of Eric's trial, the judge was "sickened" by the young man's lack of remorse.

"I have no remorse. I don't feel sorry for anybody"—admitted John Wayne Gacy, Illinois killer of teen boys, whose response on TAT was "an essential lack of feeling for other individuals." Psychiatrists found that he "had no feeling for any of the people he killed" (Morrison 2004. 104).

"His expression hardly ever changed," commented Gordon Burn (1985, 35) of Peter Sutcliffe, England's notorious Yorkshire Ripper, who was thought to possess an "abnormal lack of emotion." There was that same flat tone when the BTK killer, Dennis Rader, told the story of his extensive crimes to detectives. And in the fascinating case of the Green Beret and Army physician, Jeff MacDonald, it was the same—no "semblance of feeling or emotion" as he described the crime (familicide), no "sense of guilt." Flat affect, in point of fact, is nearly universal among violent psychopaths, as a quick searchlight* reveals:

Searchlight meaning a summary of the salient points or array of relevant cases; I will use this term and method throughout the book.

- M. Romand (familicide/France) was a "robot deprived of all capacity to feel."
- Ted Bundy, "cold and calculating," evinced a "nonemotional demeanor" (Rule 1986, 45, 392).
- John Hinckley Jr. (wannabe presidential assassin) was noted for his inability to feel or express emotions.
- John List (familicide) was "cold and impassive," aloof—a "cold fish." Taciturn and calculating, he spoke characteristically in a "deep monotone" (Sharkey 1990, 19, 23, 270).
- Bobby Joe Long could not understand his own "blank feeling" of disorientation and confusion. His mother said she'd not even seen him cry since he was hit by the car at age seven; he became "so cold and indifferent" (Morrison 2004, 166, 181).
- Robert Berdella tortured and killed merely as "experiments, nothing more." The interviewer found him "bereft of most human emotion" (Morrison 2004, 194).
- Dennis Sweeney, shooter of politician Allard Lowenstein (1980) was "emotionally flat."
- Lawrence Bittaker, a murderous sociopath, "displayed no outward expression or emotion" (Markman and Bosco 1989, 269).
- Diane Downs, child killer, was diagnosed with "superficial affect."

Yes, there is overwhelming evidence of flat affect among irrational killers, but it's not much help when the forensic psychiatrist explains that this person has "a piece missing" or is "unfettered by conscience" (Blinder 1985, 151). This *emotional robot,* as some have termed it, has more than a piece missing. Psyche itself has become unhinged and wandered off. This is the crux of the dissociated state: self in abeyance, emotions in abeyance, conscience in abeyance. Spiritually void, this shell of a person has been a loner *for the same reason:* lack of feeling for others. Court psychiatrist Dr. Martin Blinder interviewed a prisoner named Ken who, he observed, had "managed to get through almost three decades without connecting in an emotional way with anyone . . . never a close friend." Murdering left him cold: "I didn't feel anything."

"Unable to identify or empathize with others," says Blinder, "he kills casually, without remorse" (Blinder 1985, 146, 149, 151).

Discussing the killing spree of Gary Tison, Dr. Robert Hare (1993, 209) mentions that Tison's "most striking physical feature was his expressionless eyes." But flat affect is just as typical of the "expressionless" obsessive / OCD—"he spoke in a monotone" (Rapoport 1989, 87)—and even more so among multiples:

Toby "didn't seem to be feeling anything . . . [she] had no feelings" (Mayer 1989, 177).

Eve was colorless, monotonous, inert, sober; her eyes had a vacant look.

Jenny "spoke dispassionately, as if the events had happened . . . to someone else" (Spencer 1989, 172).

"There were no feelings at all" (Cohen et al. 1991, 54), referring to another multiple.

Truddi: "There was nothing . . . no memory, nothing. She had no emotion of her own . . . she did not exist" (Chase 1987, 192).

I might also mention that the extremely conventional person can also become a shell, a cliché, a poster boy of normalcy—but a blank of a real person, to the point that he is perceived by discarnates as an empty vehicle. This was the case with Danny S.: "He operated entirely on the level of acceptable clichés. . . . It was as if he had no personality of his own" (Naifeh and Smith 1995, 335).

Beat the Box

As one forensic pathologist put it, "If you have someone with a very flat affect, the lie detector test doesn't work very well" (Glatt 2002, 151). Superagent and behavioral analyst Robert Ressler (1992, 192, 154) has expressed a similar point of view: "True psychopaths are frequently able to beat the box"; some, so dissociated that they truly believe in their innocence, actually volunteer to take the test—and pass it, too. The polygraph "will not register as much as a blip" (Markman and Bosco 1989, 93). Mark Hofmann, the Mormon bomber, passed the test with flying colors, later admitting that he had become expert at "concealing his emotions" (Lindsey 1988, 249, 381). Forensic analysts know that "many hardcore criminals, particularly psychopaths devoid of conscience, can defeat the polygraph at will" (Newton 1998, 175, 69). The robotic, empty "nice guy" can "beat the box" no sweat— difficult for a person with a normal ego and superego to do. No tells or twinges of conscience are there to betray the detached mind, the dissociated self. He flatlines; he beats the box. After his second homicide, David Meierhofer volunteered to take a lie-detector test and to be given truth serum. He passed both tests. Gary Ridgway, the manhunted Green River Killer, passed two polygraphs. California's Zodiac serial killer stood his "lie detector [test] on its head" (Graysmith 1987, 58).

Abeyance has yet another earmark peculiar to absent self: inexhaustible funds of energy. It may seem surprising that we can find this abundance of energy in such disparate categories as bipolarism, astral projection, OBE, and MPD. But not really, once we realize that retired self is a well-rested organism. The astral projectionist is "transported on a wind of ether . . . [whose] currents revitalize the traveler, so that he returns to the physical body feeling overcharged with vital energy. . . . Outside of phenomenal time . . . fatigue is non-existent. There is no expenditure of energy" (Battersby 1979, 88, 91).

"Don't you ever get tired?" one doctor asked the multiple Truddi Chase. Even her shrink did not know what to make of her "enormous energy highs. . . . She slept very little" (Chase 1987, 17, 133, 305). For the multiple, whose lost time is spent "resting" in the tunnel—while his alters, who "keep him asleep" run the show—slumber is all but redundant. In her secondary state, the woman called Felida "moved swiftly from one household task to another, seeming to possess enormous physical energy" (Crabtree 1985, 40); at fourteen, she had fallen into "a deep sleep," awakening as her alter. Even the alter personalities "seemed, as they surfaced, to be rested, as if they had been in the deep relaxation of a trance state. The overall effect was the presentation of a tireless client" (Spencer 1989, 213).

The same lack of fatigue is evident in the hyper or manic phase of the bipolar personality—and for the same reason. When she is "up," Dorothy (bipolar) "can get along on almost no sleep." Other bipolars like Max "never felt tired." Betsey, another, "slept little," while Patty Duke herself could go "two weeks without sleep." Now the experts suggest that lack of sleep "may precipitate mania" (Duke and Hochman 1992, 34, 46, 84, 12, 95–97). But that makes no sense. Isn't it the other way around? Isn't mania (see chapter 7) an ASC dominated by a restless, tireless, *secondary* personality? Let me put it this way: rather than sleeplessness causing the mania, it is probably just the opposite—too *much* sleep (in the tunnel) triggers the mania. Here's how: during the low/depressed part of the bipolar cycle, the person tends to do nothing or sleep a lot and/or be "out of it" most of the time. Being "out of it" *quite literally*, self is diminished to the point of vacuity. Nature abhors a vacuum, and other (alter) beings step in. Longing for excitement and eager for action, they are full of energy. Vacant self is easy prey to the incorporeal intruder; in fact, the intruder (alter) often lends just that vitality that the host has forsaken.

Empty self, in short, is a veritable magnet for spirit intrusion.

What has been made empty may be filled by the biblical seven devils.

ARTHUR GUIRDHAM,
THE PSYCHIC DIMENSIONS OF MENTAL HEALTH

The excursion of the soul leaves an empty house behind, which may attract a parasitic tenant.

ARTHUR CONAN DOYLE,
THE EDGE OF THE UNKNOWN

With the body-house vacated, that tempting vacuum presents a fine opportunity for wandering spirits. "If there are spirits nearby waiting for bodies to enter, they slip right in" (Fiore 1987, 115). "The devil plays in the empty pocket" is an old German saying. Also German is the word *poltergeist* (literally, "noisy ghost"), which we have adopted in the English language to cover the bizarre displacement of things, usually household objects, spontaneously moving or breaking all by themselves. Such cases lend themselves to a spiritual interpretation involving the abeyance (passivity) of a human subject; that person or focal agent, as case studies indicate, is usually an adolescent. In fact, it is believed that he or she is actually the human battery for the phenomenon.

The youngster is "used to supply power for the ghostly activities" (S. Smith 1968, 106). Once deep analysis is undertaken, the child or teenager is usually found to be in a classic passive-aggressive state. It was quite a remarkable discovery that most of these children (focal agents) are not living with their natural parents, and they are overwhelmed by a seething resentment and hostility. Yet all that anger is denied, suppressed, bottled up.

And yes, it is the bottling that makes for the human battery. One of the best documented cases is the Miami Poltergeist (1967). Julio, the focal agent in this case, was a nineteen-year-old Cuban, unhappily separated from his mother (who remained in Cuba) and experiencing severe problems with his stateside stepmother. At the Miami warehouse where Julio was employed, bottles of shoe polish began to fly off the shelves. A cigar box sailed across the room. Whole shelves toppled over of their own accord. No one was hurt, but with the phenomena ongoing, there was a lot of damage.

When the mayhem was traced to Julio (not his actions but his mere presence), some of America's top paranormalists got on the case. The young man, they found, typified the focal agent profile:

A bundle of repressed resentments and denial. Check.
Harbored feelings of rejection and worthlessness. Check.
Inability to express feelings, especially rage; impotent defiance. Check.

Utter passivity (withdrawn); seemingly detached. Check.
Deep sadness. Check.

Isn't it interesting that Julio admitted that the breakages in the warehouse "made me feel happy. I don't know why." But the parapsychologists understood: somehow the breakages also "broke the tension" pent up inside Julio. The poltergeistery, say these experts, was the boy's way of striking out, the "tension directed into his physical environment" (Roll 2004, 153, 158). Left unsaid, however, is exactly how that works. Taken on faith is the wrong assumption that inanimate objects can just come to life in the presence of a troubled youth. I don't think that is how it works. Something is missing in this pat formula. But of course! The spiritual interpretation must be left out, that is, if you still want to be counted among the "experts."

> *The unpleasant but sometimes spectacular poltergeist phenomena are so regularly reported from all quarters of the globe, but so airily shrugged off [by] the modern scientist . . . camouflaging it in psychological clichés.*
> AUGUSTINE CAHILL, *DARKNESS, DAWN, AND DESTINY*

Careful scrutiny has uncovered definite psi faculties, like clairvoyance and precognition, among these young focal agents. As Susy Smith saw it, Julio "is a latent medium" (S. Smith 1968, 167). He was prone to trance, and like other psychically disturbed people, he was given to nightmares and suicidal thoughts. In his case, the last straw, the stressor, the trigger, may have been the case of measles, mumps, and chickenpox—all in quick succession—that Julio suffered just prior to the weird breakout at the Miami warehouse.

The "middleman" left out of most of the experts' equations is the spiritual entity accompanying Julio. When a psychic medium was called in to the warehouse, he detected a spirit presence (Roll 2004, 121), probably on the order of the rebellious angels who "rushed in . . . on the mortals, gaining power sufficient to hurl clubs and stones and boards.

Roused, the mortal occupants [saw] things tumble about by some unseen power" (Oahspe, Book of Wars 20:10).

In the Muslim world, the unseen power in such instances were known as *jinns* (a rough equivalent of English "genie"). The Lebanese adept "was able to summon djinns to his assistance," causing an egg in a saucepan to "spring suddenly out" or a jug to "move around without being touched" (Inglis 1992, 288). In Morocco, a similar class of spirits (known by the variant *jnun*) are credited with "capricious and revengeful" acts (Crapanzano and Garrison 1977, 44). These jinns have an unsavory hold on the people; their story comes to life in Tahir Shah's astounding narrative:

> "The house is full of them . . . infested with Jinns, hundreds of them.
> You can't imagine their [the people's] fear. . . . An empty house is a
> magnet. . . . Leave a place empty for a few weeks . . . and it's full
> from the floor to rafters with an invisible legion of Jinns. . . . They
> go by various names—Jinns, Genies, Jnun—and are believed by all
> to share the earth with us. . . . Invisible to humans, they can take
> almost any form they wish . . . disguised as cats, dogs, or scorpions.
> . . . Nothing gives them greater pleasure than injuring humans. . . .
> They are all around us. Their world shapes our own. . . . If they
> could they would slit our throats. . . . Jinns were also known for
> stealing human children . . . substituting a Jinn-child in place
> of the one they take. . . . Everyday mishaps were . . . put down to
> the work of supernatural forces, with the Jinns at the center of the
> belief system. . . . When she dropped a glass vase, she said it was
> the Jinns. . . . They were a back door by which all blame could be
> neatly side-stepped. . . . The explanation was always the same: 'It was
> not my fault. It was the work of the Jinns.' . . . I said, 'Superstitious
> thought is crippling them [the people]'". . . . [The man replied]:
> "The Jinns are at the heart of [our] culture. Pretending they don't
> exist won't help you." (Shah 2006, 14–15, 112–13, 171)

Leave the West, the so-called First World, and such mischievous wraiths inhabit the memory and lore of every traditional society known to man. In these lands, the disruptive poltergeist is no mystery. Nor is it puzzling when the "noisy ghost" comes to afflict the family whose tensions and suppressed anger have reached the boiling point.

> *Uri Geller complained that most parapsychologists misunderstood the true sources of the mysterious force. "They keep talking about my mind," he said. In his opinion, psychic power didn't emanate from his mind at all but from other minds—entities who were telepathically channeling the power through him for their own purpose.*
>
> HUNT AND MCMAHON, *THE NEW SPIRITUALITY*

Another psychic-sensitive, England's Wilma Davidson (2006, 104), asserts that there are actually "a higher number of earthbound spirits in the West, compared to the East. . . . The only explanation I can find is that more people in the East are aware . . . that life carries on after death." Awareness alone is a big part of the solution. Because the *problem* is reinforced when denial drives us deeper into darkness: Spiritual forces thrive most readily on buried emotions. "Neither was aware," comments Dr. Blinder on two of the murderers he analyzed, "of any hostility towards the victims." And in another case brought to Blinder, a Mrs. Williams—who shot her husband in cold blood—was "almost entirely unaware of any hostile feelings." Afterward, she could not believe she shot her husband. Predictably, her own shut-down personality (shaped by strict and highly proper churchy parents) was shy, demure, inhibited, naive, and highly controlled (Blinder 1985, 128).

Clearly, when suppression of true self becomes chronic, there is a disintegration of persona and very little left of native self to assert against wandering spirits of darkness. "The person simply does not have the strength to ward off the intruder" (Maurey 1988, 76).

Poltergeistery, as we have seen, tends to shed light on these conundrums, as in the "massive repression and denial" noted by Scott Rogo (1979, 106–7) in the case of young Arnold, a poltergeist focal agent. In this 1961 case, Arnold's extremely traumatic childhood was uncovered, including brutal foster care, real mother often in jail—a mother, incidentally, who once tried to kill her husband. "Arnold used denial to handle all these conflicts"; he was never able to verbalize his anger. Significantly, his general approach to life was "passive and submissive," which is how he tried, unsuccessfully, to cope with feelings of aggression.

> *The dying embers of a man's repressed pain have the unwieldy habit of catching fire, spreading underground, and burning down everything nearby.*
> KEITH ABLOW, *COMPULSION*

Repression, chronic denial—and subsequent self-estrangement—are the key, not only to poltergeistery, but to a raft of equally distressing problems. In OCD, for example, "Zach was dealing with his obsessions and compulsions with total denial" (Rapoport 1989, 51). And as for phobia: Most phobics were unusually timid or shy as children, wouldn't-hurt-a-fly types (yet they do have a strange fear of harming others!). Often it is the child in the "nurturance vacuum" who has no one in the family to turn to, no one to depend on, who withdraws with his fears, repressing his hostile feelings to parents, and further alienating himself from himself. This sets him up for intrusion.

Multiples, too: The multiple Jennifer "had almost completely dissociated herself from her depression and rage" (Schoenewolf 1991, 20). The famous Eve was "bound by propriety and inhibition," mousy, timid, diffident, docile, passive, meek, and weak (Thigpen and Cleckley 1957, 27). So repressed, conventional, and self-effacing, Eve stifled her resentments to the point of erasing self.

With nothing to mitigate these vicissitudes, the "demon" of spirit possession is free to enter and draw the needed spark of energy from those strongly in denial. It has been found that the greater the repressed rage, the more horrendous the entity that finds lodging therein. Some demoniacs are so perverse, they encourage the host to take his or her own life. This business deserves a chapter of its own. So on we go.

3

THE BLACK DOG UNLEASHED

I heard the whispering . . .

DANNY S., QUOTED IN NAIFEH AND SMITH,
A STRANGER IN THE FAMILY

After Danny S. slit both of his wrists while in prison (he survived), he remarked, "It really wasn't a suicide attempt. It was much more than that." Was he trying to eliminate *himself?*—or *Him,* the word he used for the presence, the "separate mind," the whispering one, the somebody, the voice that "was coming from inside" (Naifeh and Smith 1995, 279, 134, 328)? Even the title of Danny's outstanding 400-page biography, *A Stranger in the Family* (by Steven Naifeh and G. W. Smith) hints broadly at the alien self that intruded upon this golden boy from a "perfect" family. Imprisoned for serial rape and one murder, Danny, a personable and intelligent young man, had been given to "unexplained absences," typical of the vacated self that we pinpointed in our survey of abeyance. "I was a zombie." Just before the onset of one of his blackouts or brownouts, "he would get a distant blank look in his eyes . . . dark and hollow" (Naifeh and Smith 1995, 178, 113, 158).

Probing abeyance, we saw at the tip of the iceberg evidence of massive suppression and denial. Denial / dismissal remains the most common line of defense: In Danny's case, "he not only refused to admit that he had killed her—he denied that she was dead." His was "a wall of silence, sometimes a wall of frenetic, disjointed denial, sometimes a wall of evasive non sequiturs; but always a wall" (Naifeh and Smith 1995, 368).

The passionate language of his biographers says it all: "Denial. Denial. Denial. All roads led back to denial. . . . Evil isn't so much Satan and demons as it is just the little lies we tell each other." The denial, of course, went beyond Danny himself. His parents "had lived emotionally estranged for much of Danny's childhood yet covered it up with pretending: pretending they had the perfect marriage, pretending they had the perfect family. Growing up with denial like that, Danny didn't need to be abused. . . . Having to live this massive lie of perfection—perfect son, perfect parents, perfect family—was more of a burden than any beating or molestation could ever be" (Naifeh and Smith 1995, 380–81).

Gary Gilmore also slit his wrists in jail.* So did serial killers Henry Lee Lucas (who had been diagnosed passive-aggressive) and Ed Kemper (seven kills). Other suicidal serial killers (whose random crimes are known as "stranger murders") include: Chikatilo (the Red Ripper), Richard Ramirez (the Night Stalker), Richard Speck (nurse killer), Richard Chase (the Vampire Killer), Dr. John Cavaness (Chief of Surgery), Eric Napoletano (Mama's Boy), Joe Kallinger (the Shoemaker), Arthur Shawcross (Nice Guy), George Grossman (cannibal killer), Harvey Glatman (rope killer). What else do these psychopathic killers have in common?

John Kappler (Dr. Death) was an established anesthesiologist in California who emerged from a childhood of denial and abuse as a nonperson, ultimately diagnosed schizophrenic and passive-dependent. It is the passive / void personality that most interests us. That void made him wide open to usurping entities whose dictates were later identified by experts as "command hallucinations." But they were not hallucinations, not imagined, for Kappler's empty vessel had attracted

---

*Until the time of Gary's execution by firing squad (his choice) in Utah in 1977, the capital punishment moratorium had been in force in the United States for more than ten years. Gary had killed two Mormons.

negative controls. The voices arousing him to murder and mayhem began instructing him to administer the *wrong medicine* to his patients; one of his victims, a mother in labor, suffered brain damage from his handiwork. "I attempted to kill three patients," Kappler later confessed.

As a *passive* personality, please note, everything depended on what people thought of him; rising as he did from a lower social milieu to a prestigious one, Kappler's persona was all veneer, all show—a surface self, an empty suit. His biographer, Dr. Keith Ablow, calls it "the armor of his false self." Deceiving spirits spoke to Kappler, urging him as he got in his car, to *kill himself* in an accident. The so-called hallucination also commanded him to commit vehicular homicide; two tragic deaths did result. He felt possessed. "It was as if the car was being driven by someone else." He was told to "hit and run." Said Kappler, "I felt like it was a duty to perform, and I performed it"* (Ablow 1994, 67, 31, 37, 52, 41, 77, 89, 10). Who but a pliable patsy would obey such a command?

Ken Bianchi, California's Hillside Strangler (ten murders in 1977–78) also attempted suicide twice (while in prison). Patterns of abeyance are striking in the case history of this disarming con man ("oozing sincerity") whose friends were "certain he was incapable of violence." Nevertheless, his lost time, or "amnesic periods" ("I can't envision myself killing anybody") and the "blank spots in [his] life," as well as his petit mal seizures (which were not epilepsy—see introduction) and "massive dissociation" are all well-known signs of a captured self (O'Brien 1985, 260–61, 156–57). Ken's abeyant self also manifested in incontinence, "trouble concentrating," arrested development (learning problems), and immaturity (irresponsibility).

Plus denial—Ken was in total denial about his (mentally disturbed) mother's cruelty (in addition to beatings,† she had punished him by putting his hands over the gas burner). She dominated both her husband and her son. It is most interesting that Ken's alter personality,

---

*Kappler, a Korean War vet, may also have had PTSD; see discussion toward the end of this chapter.

†The beatings, it seems, were for things done by Steve, his alter ego, not Ken. Steve "said he could come into my body . . . do terrible things, and then leave me to take the blame."

named Steve, hated Ken's mom and hated Ken for not standing up to her and for being such a "nice guy." (Another alter was little Billy, a frightened nine year old.) *It was Steve who urged Ken to commit suicide.* But the law, for its own reasons, does not recognize MPD or even the amnesic episodes so common among such offenders. Be that as it may, both Drs. John Watkins and Ralph Ellison did diagnose MPD, with a violent alter. In Watkins's words, "Ken is a true and very complete MP [multiple personality] . . . However, legal precedent doesn't know really how to deal with such a case" (O'Brien 1985, 261).

Ken himself struggled for an explanation: "I'm not a normal person. . . . There's gotta be a reason why I lie, there's gotta be a reason why I steal. There's gotta be a reason for some of the things that I've done" (O'Brien 1985, 157).

There is a reason.

> *Our knowledge of the . . . psychodynamic roots of violence has barely scratched the surface.*
> CANDICE DeLONG, FBI PROFILER

> *There's often a pretty clear logic behind madness.*
> JO NESBO, *THE SNOWMAN*

As we go on, breaking this "logic" down to its elements, we will zoom in on the clues, diagnostic clues, that can alert us to the devastation of psyche. Ken Bianchi exhibited several of them, including

- Migraines
- Nightmare
- Head injury in childhood
- Phobias
- Logorrhea (nonstop speaking)

One more clue: exposure to pain and death; Ken worked for two years as an ambulance tech. In a different case, another emergency medical technician came to Dr. M. Gibson with "intense suicidal thoughts and depression. I saw several entities around him that had died by suicide. They were entreating him to join them.* I told him [what I saw] and he was shocked ... [Finally] we persuaded the entities to leave" (Gibson 2008, 8).

Dr. Kappler, we remember, was an *anesthesiologist*. Here, too, were hidden occupational hazards.

> *When a patient has been given a general anesthetic for a surgical operation, he may find upon resuming consciousness, that he has one or more extra personalities on board. ... Pain will also drive out a possessing spirit. Many dentists become possessed. ... The pain induced by the drilling clears the patient, but results in the spirit finding a new home with the dentist! ... The two professions having the highest suicide rate are the dentists and psychiatrists ... the dentist with his drill and the psychiatrist using the electrode for shock treatment ... [and these] possessing spirits often urge their host to commit suicide.*
>
> EUGENE MAUREY, *EXORCISM*

Even so, it is not the *happy* well-adjusted dentist or the happy psychiatrist who succumbs to the possessing spirit, but the unhappy or depressed one. Later on we will take a closer look at the factors that make a person a likely target for entity obsession. But for now, let's consider the question of depression. Unaware that he is attracting a morbid influence with his depressed thoughts or hidden feelings of self-loathing, such a person may become an easy mark for parasitic entities. Some, though, *are* aware: "I have been aware of other persons in me," wrote novelist Jack London, a suicide, in *The Star Rover*. Another author, William Styron, himself a depressive, wrote extensively about other writers and

---

*Similar entreaties in the literature include Susy Smith's (1970b, 154) report on an acquaintance bothered by an "external entity who began to talk to her in her mind. He told her he loved her and wanted her with him ... that he would make her kill herself so that she would be in his sphere."

artists prone to depression "which, in its graver . . . manifestation takes upward of twenty percent of its victims by way of suicide. Just a few of these fallen artists, all modern, make up a sad but scintillant roll call: Hart Crane, Vincent van Gogh, Virginia Woolf, Arshile Gorky, Cesar Pavese, Romain Gary, Vachel Lindsay, Sylvia Plath, Henry de Montherlant, Mark Rothko, John Berryman, Jack London, Ernest Hemingway, William Inge, Diane Arbus" (Styron 1990, 35).

The wording of Styron's description of his own severe depression gives us pause; he calls it "a *trance** [emphasis added] of supreme discomfort . . . helpless stupor . . . unfocused dread." Styron's cryptic phrasing seems to correspond to that of another artist, the actress Patty Duke: "Most of the time I didn't know why I was depressed." In other words, the enigmatic play of depression suggests an unseen cause, or as Duke put it, "there is something—I don't know what the name of it is—that takes over, and there isn't anything you could have done." She adds, "I can't even remember how many times I tried to kill myself. . . . A couple of times I tried to jump out of a moving car" (Duke and Hochman 1992, 10–11, 111). That Something that takes over must be a product of ASCs: Prone to dissociative states, Duke experienced dramatic mood swings (bipolar), violent outbursts, obsessions, suicidal urges ("demons inside me"), precognitions, phobia, and OBEs. OBEs? Betsey, another manic-depressive who tried to kill herself with pills, averred, "when I was depressed, I felt like I was looking at myself from the outside" (Duke and Hochman 1992, 84–85).

All this brings us full circle on abeyant self, the involuntary OBE easily inviting psi effects, like foreknowledge and even stirring inspiration: An abundance of talent/creativity is definitely one perk among those who are "open." Charismatic entertainers are blessed with it, but the price may be exorbitant. Writing about actor Robin Williams's suicide, his friend Dick Cavett asked, "Why does the gift for great performance seem to go hand in hand with unshakable depression?" (Cavett 2014, 54).

---

*Every suicide attempt by G. (a Swiss girl) was made while she was in a *trance* (Naegeli-Osjord 1988, 83).

It is in their openness that we will find the answer to that question. Not in brain chemistry: Cavett, like so many who hope for a *medical* breakthrough, speculates that "there [may be] something in the brain chemistry of the performer that produces this woeful result. . . . Will some chemical link be found?"

Well, okay, certain links are known: low levels of serotonin, for example, have been found in the autopsied brains of some suicides as well as in depressives and those with impulse disorders. Mind and body work together, so the question really is: Is the serotonin level a cause *or an effect* of depression? The "black dog" of depression (Winston Churchill's phrase) is so potent and unremitting that people have come to regard its cause as physical, like, say, diabetes or asthma. "Depression is a chemical imbalance in the brain," say medical experts; but we are also told, "the science of understanding the human brain is still in its infancy. . . . It is very difficult . . . to make good mental health diagnoses. The best experts in the world have trouble in this area" (Lysiak 2013, 224–25).

Sure they have trouble. The deeper they delve into the *physical* for answers about the *mind,* the further they stray from the real but intangible realm of psyche. Out-and-out psychic sensitives, like Darrin Owens, who are open to the Invisibles and their negative ambiance, may not know exactly where the influence is coming from, but they can *feel* it. Darrin, whose psychism probably began at birth, had suicidal impulses at age fifteen. He prayed to God for understanding: "God, listen . . . I don't know what's going on. . . . Why am I different? Why do these weird things happen to me? . . . I mean it, God: I'm going to kill myself . . . so show me your truth!" (He planned an overdose of pills) (Owens 2006, 14).

Like Darrin, many autistic children are exquisitely sensitive; ASCs and paranormal incidents are often second nature: prophetic dreams, mind reading, foreknowledge, communing with angels, hyperesthesia, crisis telepathy. Some of these children are ghost seers (the hovering spirit, for some reason, is often a deceased grandfather). William Stillman, author and autism advocate, has stressed that it is not unusual for many young adults with autism or Asperger's to reach the "dark place" and entertain suicidal thoughts.

Other folks, simply experimenting with ASCs, have inadvertently landed in that dark place. Sitting in circle (séance), a psychic medium is suddenly "seized with a desire to rush away to the rapids and throw myself into the [Cayahoga] river" (Fodor 1966, 266). Even seemingly benign pursuits like transcendental meditation and other mind-altering techniques of the New Age have been known to trigger "bizarre disturbances . . . 'bad trips' . . . psychosis and suicide." Shouldn't we, then, think twice before trying to "blow open and knock down barriers that God has placed in the human spirit to prevent a takeover by demonic beings" (Hunt and McMahon 1988, 51–52, 267)? That God-given barrier has indeed been severely breached in the condition known as MPD (aka DID). Black depressions and suicidal attempts are all too common among multiples. Examples are too numerous to mention.*

One case, though, is worth mentioning—the multiple Billy Milligan, whose own father, an *entertainer* (comedian) had killed himself. Does a suicidal strain run in families? Yes, it does, but not genetically nor through brain chemistry. Nurture, not nature, points the way. Patty Duke, bipolar and suicidal (as mentioned above), learned all about suicide from her mom. An explosive and depressive personality, the mother was given to suicidal threats, once actually "turning on the gas jets and vowing to kill herself and all of her children" (Duke and Hochman 1992, viii).

In another family drama, the mother of a twenty-four-year-old daughter who had killed herself over a failed relationship, in turn tried to take her own life. She hoped to join her daughter. Instead, "she found herself in what appeared to be hell, being jostled up and down [by] . . . two satanic beings" (Rawlings 1978, 95–96). Maurice Rawlings relates this to a similar case of a demon-inspired suicide: a fourteen-year-old girl

---

*The interested reader can follow up with a few such cases in Spencer 1989, 86; Thigpen and Cleckley 1957, 88; Schoenewolfe 1991, 7; and Keyes 1981, 19, 23.

became despondent over a bad report card. Her parents had totally focused on her inability to measure up to her sister's grades—and her looks. They always compared the two. The girl committed suicide—or tried. Her stomach was pumped and as she came out of a coma, she cried, "Make them let go of me . . . those demons in hell!"

We opened this chapter with a brief rundown of suicidal killers, noting a certain pattern of passive-aggressive behavior. This, too, is a family affair. Poke around their family histories and soon you find the makings of a loser, a criminal, a suicide. Take James Ruppert for example. This man killed eleven of his relatives. In his late teens, James had tried to hang himself. Even this was a failure, though he remained suicidal for decades to come. Reviled by both parents, James, who later proved to be sexually impotent, was an outcast in his own family, the son of a violent, cold, and rejecting father and a "mistake" according to his mother who had wanted a girl. She beat and taunted the boy while showering love on his older brother—himself a sadistic person who locked James in the closet, tied him with rope, beat him with a hose, and sat on his head.

Grisly family histories among suicidal offenders are not unusual but the norm. Arthur Jackson, a murderous stalker and would-be assassin, had tried to kill himself on his twenty-first birthday. He was the son of an alcoholic father and schizophrenic mother. The mother of Joe Kallinger, another suicidal killer, flogged him with a whip, beat him with a hammer, burned him on the stove, and threatened to castrate him.

There are about 40,000 suicides in the United States per annum— and probably more attempts. Among the most common stressors are depression,* anguish, hopeless despondency or dejection, unbearable stress or guilt, trauma, grief, crushing disillusionment, defeat, or dis-

---

*Underplayed are so-called antidepressive and other medicines like ADHD drugs that may actually trigger suicidal urges. William Styron (1990, 70–71) was "convinced that this tranquilizer [Halcion] is responsible for exaggerating to an intolerable point the suicidal ideas that had possessed me." Soon after he was taken off it, "my suicidal notions dwindled then disappeared."

grace. *Group* suicide* is another matter, possibly delusional or mission oriented, for example, the 1996 mass suicide of the members of the Heaven's Gate cult, who thought a spaceship was coming to collect their souls and take them to a better life.

Let us not underestimate the demonic power: One modern satanic priest, who turned from his wicked ways and wrote a book about it, speaks about his work in "raising a demon" (Warnke 1972, 67–69): "As members of the Brotherhood, we probably understood demons better than most people, because we used them to accomplish our evil deeds. . . . There are legions of demons . . . [who can be used to] inflict disease, possess men, possess animals, oppose spiritual growth, disseminate false doctrine, torment people. . . . [They] talk or cry with a loud voice, using the tongues and lips of humans. They can tell lies . . . when embodied in a human being. They can . . . cause suicides."

I do not doubt that human malevolence can raise a demon or summon dark angels who are all too eager for mischief and mayhem or to fulfill a curse. Before being hanged, H. H. Holmes, the notorious multicide of "Murder Castle" (in the 1890s), hurled curses upon everyone who had played a part in his conviction. Shortly after Holmes's execution, his attorney died and the superintendent at Holmes's prison committed suicide. The coroner who had testified against Holmes at the trial also met a gruesome death, as did the priest who attended Holmes at the gallows and the foreman of his jury.

Nandor Fodor (1964, 71) once wrote that he has "personally known several people who claimed to possess a demonic power that made people drop dead. . . . [One] rather unsavory character I have observed . . . was a drunkard and a criminal. . . . [He had] an accomplice who could have given him away. . . . He wished, with a fierce concentration that his partner-in-crime would commit suicide. He did

---

*In Mesolithic times, "vagabond spirits . . . persuaded mortals to suicide . . . and they killed themselves by thousands and tens of thousands" (Oahspe, Book of Thor 6:14). In the archaeological record, human bones, arranged in a circle, have been found, suggesting ritual suicide in compact.

commit suicide . . . carrying out the telepathic suggestion. . . . If ever there was a psychic murder, this was it."

A more recent case of an all-too-effective imprecation involved Pat M., a 1970s TV personality who had offended an occultist (tarot reader) whose talents extended into the Crafte, the black arts. No sooner did he place a vehement curse upon the pretty, happy-go-lucky celebrity than things began to go wrong, very wrong. Friends slipped on her stairs (felt pushed) and were in auto accidents, her boyfriend tried to choke her, and *two close friends committed suicide*. Too, her private secretary died mysteriously in Pat's mansion, in a baffling fire.

The vivacious Pat was determined to get to the root of the problem and managed to uncover the ghosts-in-the-closet, which may have served as excellent *proxies* for the evil-minded tarot master. In addition, her street, as it turned out, had in the nineteenth century been the site of public hangings. The mansion itself was a graveyard of sorrows and crimes, its tenant history riddled with acrimonious divorce, alcoholism, sickness, accidents, murder, and suicide—"a miasma of horrors." Were these unhappy dead recruited by the hostile sorcerer (Montandon 1975, 35, 162, 183, 186, 150, 132, 171)?

When actor Robin Williams took his own life, many asked, "how he could do it when he had everything: fame, wealth, adulation, family love . . . and plenty of work" (Cavett 2014, 54). Well, the unseen cause remains hidden. Maybe he had *too much* of a good thing, arousing the fiend of jealousy. Let me illustrate this point with a case from Dr. Wickland's files: One suicide, Mrs. X, who came through Mrs. Wickland (the medium), declared that "evil spirits had been attracted to me by the *jealous* [emphasis added] thoughts of other persons." Mrs. X, though extremely happy, had hanged herself in a bizarre fit of mania. Her spirit later explained: "As soon as I found myself out of my body, I saw at once the cause for my rash act." It seems that many were jealous of her lovely family.

What's more, "I did not know at that time that I was a psychic— because I belonged to the Baptist Church. . . . [Something] got hold of me. I did not know what I was doing . . . I remember feeling very strange, as if somebody had taken complete hold of me . . . made me kill myself, because they wanted to break up our happy home." Reviewing the case, Dr. Wickland would comment, "A great number of unaccountable suicides are due to the obsessing or possessing influence of earthbound spirits, some of [whom] are actuated by a desire to torment their victims" (Wickland 1974, 132).

> Wandering spirits . . . pursued evil for evil's sake . . . persuading mortals to suicide and to all manner of wickedness. . . . [Others] know not themselves who they are. . . . Neither can they go away from the mortals to whom they are bound.
>
> OAHSPE, BOOK OF FRAGAPATTI 37:3 AND 35:7

Sometimes the possessing entity finds himself stuck in a mortal's body, becoming enraged because he cannot get out of it. In such circumstances the only solution is to convince the host to commit suicide. Eugene Maurey, exorcist extraordinaire, offers this explanation for a person who "attempts suicide without obvious or known reason: All too often the possessing entity tries to kill the host body . . . [simply because] the invading spirit becomes tired of living in the body he has chosen. . . . The entity apparently finds himself trapped. . . . He wants out . . . [and] convinces his host to commit suicide" (Maurey 1988, 147–48, 63). Psychiatry, however, calls such urgings command hallucinations, the delusional voices of schizophrenics. No ghosts need apply.

Yet, given the number of hauntings* and poltergeist cases that involve a suicide (remember that Julio, the focal agent of the Miami Poltergeist was suicidal), no amount of hallucination can cause stones

---

*A good number of irrational suicides have been linked to *haunted* places where, indeed, an earlier suicide had taken place. Spooky Old England is full of such tales. In one, an army officer visiting an English country house "had no reason at all to be contemplating suicide" (Archer 1967, 92–93). Nevertheless, "horrible thoughts began to enter his mind, followed by a feeling of despair and an urge to kill himself." Some irresistible compulsion found him climbing out the window to get to the pond. Shaken, he turned away in time. But later, a maid, in the middle of cleaning, went out and did actually drown herself in the pond. There was no apparent motive for her act. Consulting public records, it was found that since the reign of James I, a large number of suicides had occurred at that pond.

to fly about, eggs to be thrown of themselves, bricks falling inside the house out of nowhere, crockery smashing, mirrors tearing off the wall, furniture moving. All this and more occurred during the Jabuticabal poltergeist event (in Brazil in the 1960s). The focal agent was an eleven-year-old girl named Maria, "a natural medium." The poltergeist was vicious, penetrating Maria's flesh with needles, attempting to smother her, setting her clothing on fire. "Perhaps her unseen attackers somehow administered the final blow. . . . In 1970, she was found dead of apparent suicide. She had consumed a soft drink laced with pesticide" (Guiley 2000, 198–99).

Suicide, in fact, is not unusual in cases of possession where the poor victim feels it is her only hope for release from the torment of intrusion. June Smith, a psychotic, hacked herself to death after setting fires in her house to "combat an evil spirit" (Michaud 1998, 135). The "rapid cycling" (see chapter 9) seen in other victims of possession often entails suicidal attempts during the low end of the cycle (Duke and Hochman 1992, 37); in the same way, MPD victims not infrequently find themselves at the mercy of a suicidal alter.

Several years ago, a colleague of mine shared with me a most compelling (unpublished) account of "demonic oppression." He sent me a transcript of the victim's own testimony in which she declares that the "unseen fiend . . . tried to block and stop anything and everything in my life . . . *it is constantly telling me to commit suicide* [emphasis added] . . . it is constantly trying to *merge* [emphasis added] with my mind." She explained that it all began decades ago when she, young and naive, stayed at an ashram in India that was centered around a certain guru (who had instructed his followers "to merge with him"). For reference's sake, I will call her FD, meaning "former devotee." FD, who claims that the guru was actually a phony and pedophile, wrote, "I am sending this letter anonymously because of fanatics in [his] ranks who harass people (or worse) who tell the truth about their experiences."

How like the biting poltergeist was the "unseen force" that assailed FD! "I have been beaten, bitten, punched, and kicked by something unseen. All of a sudden after I touched his [guru's] feet, I was . . . hearing a male voice calling me filthy names and demanding that I obey it or it would hurt me." Later, there was "a horrendous malevolent presence in my room . . . [and] odd noises in my home . . . I have been sexually assaulted by something unseen. I have been stung, burned, and been given excruciating pain throughout my body. . . . *It often tells me that the only way I can stop the pain is to commit suicide* [emphasis added] . . . I hear that there are suicides associated with him. How many [others] had the situation that I have been faced with for so many years and felt such deep guilt and shame that they could not tell anyone what they were suffering?" (personal communication).

The most urgent message that I want to convey in this chapter is that suicide does *not* "end it all." In fact, negative conditions are actually *magnified* in the nonphysical state—without a body to anchor these miseries. "How more helpless is a deranged spirit than a mortal! . . . They float on their own wild thoughts" (Oahspe, Book of Fragapatti 29:5 and 33:18). Of all Mrs. Piper's (mediumistic) messages, those who had died by suicide were the most confused, desperate, muddled, miserable—and lost.

> *Some people remained in the void, especially if they had committed suicide.*
>
> MELVIN MORSE, *CLOSER TO THE LIGHT*

With the multiple Jenny, "the threat of suicide was constant. . . . She spoke about wanting to die. Death, she said, was the only way out of the pain and confusion. In death she would find peace" (Spencer 1989, 255). What a delusion!

> *And life is indestructible.*
>
> JACK LONDON-X, SUICIDE

Mrs. X, if you recall, was a sensitive, but didn't know it. She came through Mrs. Wickland to explain her sorry tale (suicide by hanging) as compelled by jealous spirits. Still bound to the earth sphere, she related through the medium "the indescribable mental hell she was in . . . 'Oh, what horrors of despair and remorse I have gone through!'" Dr. Wickland's comment: "Those who have ended their physical existence as suicides find themselves still alive, and, having no knowledge of a spirit world, labor under the delusion that their self-destructive attempts have failed and continue their suicidal efforts. When they come in contact with mortal sensitives, they mistake their physical bodies for their own, and impress the sensitives with morbid thoughts and instigate them to deeds of self-destruction. The fate of a suicide is invariably one of deepest misery, his rash act holding him to the earth sphere" (Wickland 1974, 132–33).

The suicide, in other words, is literally anchored to the Earth he hopes to escape! In ethnographic accounts, one finds many examples of these earthbound (EB) spirits. Iberian and Russian traditions held that the fairies are spirits of the dead, or more precisely, of the premature dead; for example, the nixes are girls who committed suicide because of a broken heart. Like ghosts of the departed, they can make themselves visible to humans, but usually only to those with clairvoyant sight.

In Jewish tradition, the mentally imbalanced may become a target for a *dybbuk,* an invading spirit. A girl (Esther) was deranged of mind; the obsessing spirit was a man who had committed suicide by drowning himself. How did he invade Esther? "The occasion was propitious. He knew that Esther had illicit relations with a young man, and watched for the moment when she *abandoned herself* [emphasis added] to his embraces." At that instant he entered her aura (Oesterreich 1935). In another case reported by T. Oesterreich (1935, 10), a boy was possessed by "an evil and lying demon." The mother was upset that her son didn't even have his own voice, nor did the boy recognize her. When the demon spoke through his mouth, he "declared that he is the spirit of a man *killed in war* [emphasis added]."

This brings us to the psychic toll of war, and inevitably, military suicide. Cpl. James Jenkins fought bravely in the ferocious fifty-five-hour battle of Najaf (Iraq 2004) and was awarded a Bronze Star. But after his second tour in Iraq, he could not sleep, and if he did, the nightmares were horrible. Jenkins, depressed and full of remorse, was unable to be intimate with his fiancée. He told his mother, "I killed 213 people, Mom . . . I can't live like this" (Dobie 2008, 14). He cried like a baby. Later he shot himself fatally in the right temple.

The twenty-three-year-old African American, like so many other young Marines, was suffering from untreated PTSD, post-traumatic stress disorder. They called it shell shock in the First World War, then battle fatigue in the Second. Increasingly euphemistic, it became operational exhaustion in Korea, and finally PTSD in Vietnam. In the early nineties they called it Gulf War syndrome. No matter what you call it, combat trauma involves devastating and even mysterious symptoms, which may include

- nightmares
- flashbacks
- panic attacks
- paranoia, hypervigilance
- racing thoughts
- memory loss
- guilt

- depression
- exhaustion and insomnia
- rashes
- balance disturbances
- trembling
- palpitations
- seizures

Have I left anything out? Yes, the syndrome (sometimes in delayed response) entails behavioral problems on the home front, which, as the cases pile up, involve

- substance abuse
- domestic violence, impotence, and/or divorce
- personal isolation, detachment, edginess
- helplessness, hopelessness, joblessness, homelessness
- vehicular homicide
- crime
- suicide

*Everybody's lives are shitholes. . . . All of us have the same
problems.*

SGT. P. ULOTH, MARINE CORPS VET WITH
PTSD AND SEIZURES (QUOTED IN DOBIE 2008)

"The estimates are conservative," reported the Associated Press on
June 30, 2004, referring to a sharp rise in PTSD and military suicides. "Why do the numbers keep going up? We cannot tell you," said
an Army spokesman disingenuously* at the height of the war in Iraq
(Jelinek and Hefling 2009). It was a turning point: prior to 2008,
Defense officials had not disclosed the number of PTSD cases from Iraq
and Afghanistan. But then the announcement came: records showed
about 40,000 troops diagnosed with the illness known as PTSD.† If the
official military count was originally one out of six, that figure now
doubled, once the spotlight was thrown on it (Dobie 2008, 12).

By 2012, the sorry facts emerged: *even more than combat casualties,*
"self-harm is now the leading cause of death for members of the Army,
which has seen its suicide rate double since 2004" (Dokoupil 2012, 42).
Plus, *active-duty* suicides (numbering about 260 in 2013) were scant
compared to the number of veterans who took their lives after coming
back home. "Every month nearly 1,000 of them [discharged veterans]
attempt to take their own lives. That's more than three attempts every
90 minutes" (Dokoupil 2012, 42). Thus, more vets were dying at home
than soldiers in combat missions abroad. Back in '08, the VA put the
suicide rate of vets at five thousand a year (Randall 2008, 4).

When Corporal Jenkins (suicided hero of Najaf) went to Division
Psychology for help with his depression, they diagnosed him with
adjustment disorder rather than PTSD. They gave him Ambien to help

---

*The obvious was not mentioned: increased exposure of troops to combat, thanks
largely to President Bush's troop buildup; more deaths than in previous years; violence
increased in Afghanistan with the Taliban insurgence; more troops serving a second,
third, or fourth tour of duty; tour lengths extended from twelve to fifteen months.
†As of April 2015, a half million troops who served in Afghanistan and Iraq were
diagnosed with PTSD.

him sleep and Ativan, an antianxiety drug. Then they declared him fit for duty. But the Ambien didn't help and neither did the Ativan.

And now the little hide-and-seek game with PTSD was on. Could the mounting problem be contained by *changing the name,* by moving cases over to a more innocuous diagnostic label? Like "adjustment disorder"? One psychologist advised her staff, "Given that we are having more and more compensation-seeking veterans, I'd like to suggest that you refrain from giving a diagnosis of PTSD straight out." Instead she suggested that a diagnosis of adjustment disorder be made, since she and her colleagues "really don't have time to do the extensive testing that should be done to determine PTSD" (Randall 2008, 4). The ploy became endemic: one PTSD Marine, for example, had to wait months for an appointment with the regimental psychologist and when he finally got one, "the doctor tried to talk him out of his symptoms" (Dobie 2008, 15).

But this approach was short-lived, and so the next gambit was to suppose a *pre-existing* personality disorder. This was how SPC J. Town was sent packing. Town, who served for seven years, ended up suicidal with PTSD, traumatic brain injury, and loss of hearing after a rocket blew up above his head. "I was kind of flying and then there was a fireball behind me," he recounted. He bled from his ears and fell unconscious (Randall 2008, 5). But with the label of "pre-existing personality disorder," the Army was able to discharge him with no benefits; even though Town did not have any history of mental problems. Indeed, it was around this time that investigative reporters discovered that "the majority of [soldiers] who committed suicide did not have known histories of mental disorders" (Jelinek and Hefling 2009, A3).

By 2009, with the problem refusing to go away and tactical dodges proving ineffective, assorted treatment strategies for PTSD hove into view. Embarrassingly banal were their clinical programs offering two-bit psychobabble, emphasizing "education, compassion, and forgiveness" (Dokoupil 2012, 43). Then some geniuses decided to appeal to the victims' macho pride, so they sent in a "former corporate coach" whose version of stress management would emphasize "warrior resilience" and "sucking it up" (Gomez 2009, 1). By 2014, the experts were saying that fear was the key to unlock the closed door of PTSD. Then, in 2015, they changed that to guilt.

As pathetic as these pseudo-solutions were, the hardcore hypocrisy came from the science stronghold itself. "Scientists," according to the most recent pseudo-breakthrough, may "soon be able to erase our most traumatic memories" using a (mice-tested!) inhibitor drug called HDAC, which helps "brain cells to form new connections" (Conniff 2014, 14). And aren't we the poor saps who are so easily seduced by any scientific announcement with the word *brain* in it! The latest and greatest (April 2015) hit us with "the nation's first ever brain bank for post-traumatic stress disorder." The donated brains, in this macabre development, will hopefully yield "important biological insights that might improve care for the hundreds of thousands of people who suffer from it [PTSD]." But even if they do find the hoped-for "structural changes associated with PTSD"—so what? Bully for science. The carrot that it "could reshape treatment for military veterans," I'll wager, is an empty promise (Thompson 2015, 41–43). I'll stand with the reader who commented, "I am no scientist, but they don't need a brain bank to find one cause of PTSD." Thus wrote Robert Brudno of Washington, whose brother had been a POW for over seven years in North Vietnam, in a letter to the editor of *Time* on April 13, 2015. Brudno's brother took his own life after only four months of freedom, having "endured the horrors of war, only to return to a country that blamed the war on the warriors. I leave the physiology of PTSD to the scientists, but they won't find the marks . . . in the brain. Those wounds were in the heart" (6).

It was not Corporal Jenkins's brain but his "untreated PTSD [that] led to his suicide. . . . When he most needed help from the military, the military failed him. . . . Denied benefits, [Jenkins was] left with only a bitter sense of betrayal." It is in that emotion (sense of betrayal) that we begin to see the outlines of a passive-aggressive pattern. Jenkins's downward drift, on the aggressive side of the equation, involved gambling, bad checks, the brig. On the passive side was his "unswerving devotion to duty" (Dobie 2008, 14–16). It is the same formula that we see in countless cases of mental breakdown: Trauma + Denial = Disaster.

Decades ago (1971) John Kerry spoke of "the feelings these men carry with them after coming back from Vietnam. The country doesn't know it yet, but it's created a monster . . . in the form of millions of men who have been taught to deal . . . in violence and who are given the chance to die for the biggest nothing in history."* The "passive-dependent" (or passive-aggressive) type is marked by an identity void, a personality vacuum, self having been robbed, in most cases, under the strict, hectoring, or domineering rule of an enforcer-type parent. Many killers are of the passive-aggressive type, most raised by an overbearing, rejecting parent with a zealous agenda.

> *Brainwashing in whatever form is the ultimate passive-oriented experience.*
>
> ALAN WEISMAN, *WE IMMORTALS*

Hypocrisy lies at psyche's bedrock. In this comparison, the "parent" is the military, and the "child" is the trusting recruit who loses himself in the illogical crime of war. In Iraq, thousands of soldiers were disillusioned by the change of mission from liberation to occupation. The soldier's soul, now awakening from the American Dream, informs him it has been a nightmare.

Shock and trauma can unhinge the mind. Flight of the soul is the next best thing to actual flight from the horrid scene. PTSD clinicians often hear lines like "Nothing can prepare you for what it's really like . . . some say, It feels like I've lost my soul." It is the familiar tale of disintegrating vets (Dokoupil 2012, 44).

This is the pathology that the great psychoanalyst Nandor Fodor had in mind when he wrote—"I began to wonder whether indeed a devastating shock might not produce a kind of psychic lobotomy, tearing loose part of the mental system and leaving it floating free, like a disembodied entity" (quoted in Rogo 1979, 241).

---

*A transcript of this speech can be found at "John Kerry: Statement before the Senate Foreign Relations Committee," on the American Rhetoric website, updated April 19, 2017.

Though combat neurosis or PTSD has as many varieties as it has victims, one common denominator of the war experience is shock. In 'Nam, it was mortar fire, foxholes and the dread tunnels, hand-to-hand combat, shrapnel, malaria, jungle rot, fear of the night, or seeing "all those bodies stacked along the side of the road" (Blinder 1985, 30); this was Dan White's testimony. White, who murdered San Francisco's mayor in 1978, had been a paratrooper in Vietnam.

Nothing unseats psyche as efficiently as trauma and witness to violence. In Iraq, "two in three [soldiers] handled or uncovered dead bodies; and the same ratio saw wounded and sick women and children they couldn't help. Nearly 80 percent had lost a friend or had a friend wounded" (Dokoupil 2012, 43). Vets also tell us about the constant threat of surprise attack, while surveys confirm that 95 percent of Marines have been shot at.

Army SPC J. P. Dwyer, a medic, became a hero when he was photographed running through a battle zone carrying a small boy named Ali. The picture ran in newspapers across America, hailed as a portrait of the "heart" behind the U.S. military machine. But "Doc" Dwyer was haunted by memories of his experiences in combat. During the first three weeks that his unit was in Iraq, seventeen of those days included gun battles. The day before the famous picture was taken, his Humvee was hit by a rocket. Back home, he struggled with PTSD: depression, check; lawlessness, check; drugs, check; paranoia, check; divorce, check. Doc Dwyer died alone at age thirty-one of a drug mishap tantamount to suicide.

Authorities stick to the disingenuous sound bites: "The military isn't really sure what's causing the suicides" (Gomez 2009, 1). Besides suicide-by-drugs,* there's always suicide-by-cop. "Deeply paranoid and suicidal" since back in New Jersey, former Army SPC German Sanabria was a different, harder man when he returned from his second tour of duty in Iraq. When the twenty-six-year-old vet was caught in the act of stabbing his stepfather, police shot Sanabria to death (February 2008).

---

*Dwyer died after "huffing" (inhaling the fumes of an aerosol can) and taking "some pills."

One attorney, representing an Iraqi combat vet charged with manslaughter, termed it a hole in their souls. In the science of psyche, that hole is the equivalent of void self; and once the soul has absconded (from the frightful trauma), who carries on—and how? What exactly is the thing that takes over? I am convinced there is only one path that leads to an answer: ASCs—especially those that manifest as memory loss, detachment, paranoia, panic attacks, seizures, nightmares, inexplicable crimes—and suicide.

There is one more verse to the rhyming "hole in the soul":

The hole
In the soul
Means a loss
Of control

This is PTSD. It is an ASC. One is no longer in control. Something can "take over."

In the upcoming chapter we dive right into the psychic side of crime. But we are not quite finished with the scars of war—or with Vietnam stress syndrome, for we have only looked at the damage wrought on the mortal side of life. What about the actual casualties? More than fifty thousand Americans died in Vietnam—mostly young guys who had barely begun adult life. They, too, left the war with PTSD—*but on the Other Side.* Slain in war, their spirits are in chaos, unable to move on, tormented and hard bound to the earth in fury and frenzy.

Spirits in chaos, millions of them, fasten themselves on to the battlefields, still battling; or fasten themselves on mortals, obsessing them to madness and death.

OAHSPE, BOOK OF SETHANTES 3:36

Known as chaotics or deranged angels, these obsessing spirits fill the lower heavens and remain helplessly anchored to the living, delighting in darkness, quarrels, and crime. Among them are the entities behind spirit possession, though often unwittingly, not even knowing where they are. "There are millions of souls in heaven slain in war . . . not knowing that they themselves are dead. . . . They have not wisdom or strength to go more than one length away from the mortal they inhabit" (Oahspe, Book of God's Word 7:11, and Book of Lika 21:12). And their mortal hosts may be "driven to nameless deeds of horrors" (Oahspe, Book of Wars 54:18).

It is time, then, to plunge into the dark side. However grisly and gruesome, it is in the depths of sociopathy—the world of the predator—that we may uncover the most telling features of psyche and the genesis of soul murder.

4
SOUL MURDER

> Those who seek to do evil, who seek to make others unhappy, who delight in crime and pollution . . . shall, if spirits, be called drujas . . . and there are hundreds of millions [of them].
>
> OAHSPE, BOOK OF JUDGMENT 6:10

The term "soul murder" is occasionally used by psychologists to indicate the sort of emotional abuse that robs a child of ripening self. We find it in forensic psychiatrist Keith Ablow's book *Inside the Mind of Scott Peterson.* Convicted in 2004 for the murder of his pregnant

A   B

Figs. 4.1a and 4.1b. Signs of (a) druj (rhymes with stooge) and (b) druk, its mortal counterpart. One of the most ancient words for wandering spirits of the lowest grade is drujas. *In Persia, the word has been retained, signifying spirit of falsehood; in India, it means lost spirit, while the Eastern European word* dracu *(as in Dracula) probably has the same origin.*

As there are on earth paupers and vagrants and beggars and criminals, so are there in hada [hades] spirits that are a great trial to both mortals and angels.

> OAHSPE, BOOK OF LIKA 21:2

wife Laci, the all-American Peterson, it soon became clear, had a piece missing. Though ambulatory and superficially normal, Scott, as Ablow's probing revealed, carried murder and child abandonment in his deep family history. In the final analysis, though, it was his own upbringing—"emotionally strangled" (Ablow 2005, 22)—that turned him into a (dangerous) nonperson. (Gary Gilmore's brother once remarked that Gary was "murdered emotionally.")

Nonperson is a suitable catch-all for vacant self, hollow man, and is in fact the translation of the Russian word for sociopath / psychopath.* There are two basic ways to become a nonperson, and they represent the two extremes of parenting. In a nutshell (we will soon expand on the subject), there is, on the one hand, the overbearing, perfectionist, spoiling, "helicopter" (hovering) type of parent. On the other hand, at the opposite end of the spectrum is the cruel, neglectful, trashy, abusive, rejecting type of parent. Either extreme, it seems, can engender a psychically damaged child, with no real sense of self.

"My son has done nothing wrong"—mother of Scott Peterson (Ablow 2005, 96). Scott Peterson, a child of the first type, was raised by a mother who would "suffocate him psychologically, strangle everything that was uniquely *him,* gold-plate her trophy son, and entomb him in her vision . . . of the perfect child. . . . Anything but the perfect child would not be tolerated by his parents. . . . [He] would have to be nearly invisible" to avoid their wrath. "There are myriad and subtle ways a mother can tell her son that he must cease to exist as a person, that his true self must essentially disappear" (Ablow 2005, 63–64).

Before going further, let me say this: Nothing stated in this chapter is meant as an excuse for crime. We only want to understand. Early trouble doesn't get anyone off the hook, it isn't a get-out-of-jail-free card, we are not bleeding hearts, and we certainly do not want to let lethally dangerous offenders back on the streets. Our only purpose is to enlighten. What the legal system does with such damaged goods is a separate, though related, matter.

---

*Russia may be the only country with a higher murder rate than the United States.

That said, we may plunge into our investigation of these psychic badlands. "Teetering on the brink of nonexistence . . . Scott Peterson was absent, buried inside himself . . . a gaping black hole" (Ablow 2005, 97, 107, 147), in short, an abeyant self—which may prove to be an open door to the most unsavory class of discarnates, drujas, the loose cannons of lower heaven (hada). And this is why I would differ with Ablow's statement that Scott was "spiritually dead" (2005, 22). Far from it, he was "very easily led"; indeed, his void self was a magnet for disembodied entities.

> It's the fashion, in modern New Age philosophies, to deny the very existence of . . . entities dedicated to committing evil in all its guises. . . . New Agers readily embrace various concepts of benevolent incorporeal entities—guardian angels, guides, transcendental masters, a Supreme Cosmic Intellect, etc.—but deny the possible existence of any malevolent ones.
>
> ROBERT H. CODDINGTON,
> EARTHBOUND: CONVERSATIONS WITH GHOSTS

In our general naïveté (or is it denial?), we speak of Spiritualism strictly as a realm of love and light. Spiritology, though, frankly encompasses both the dark and the light. Isn't it time for the vaunted consciousness revolution to include (or at least acknowledge) *both* sides, the light and the dark, of human potential?

> Obsessors are mostly earthbound spirits. . . . Some of them may commit acts of revenge or do other harm. . . . And if an evil personality gets into control, the obsessed may be driven to criminal, insane acts.
>
> NANDOR FODOR, BETWEEN TWO WORLDS

"The dragon of vengeance," as the late great Paul Lindsay (author and FBI veteran) phrased it, operates from Both Sides. In Polynesia

(Marquesan Islands), for example, "returning spirits of the dead wandered in the country to avenge themselves . . . [returning from] hades, the kingdom of the dead . . . [in] posthumous vengeance . . . to persecute and torture another hated person" (Williamson 1933, 2:45).

"I will be more dangerous when I die."

ANGEL MATURINO RESENDEZ,
THE RAILWAY KILLER

Evil spirits are both yourselves and the dead. Whom ye have slain [death penalty] still live to torment you in spirit. . . . Though their bodies be dead, they obsess you to deeds of wickedness. . . . For even as mortals delight in vengeance, so can the talent grow until its feast lieth in the fruit of hell [hada]. . . . Think not that by slaying a man thou art rid of him. . . . Millions of angels who in mortal life were . . . tortured or put to death . . . take delight in evil . . . wandering about sometimes in gangs of hundreds or even thousands.

OAHSPE, BOOK OF FRAGAPATTI 19:10 AND 37:4,
BOOK OF GOD'S WORD 18:4, AND
BOOK OF JUDGMENT 32:16–17

When spirit mentors were asked "What are evil spirits?" (Newbrough 1874), the answer came: "Perverse creatures who led evil lives and who, being born into the spirit world . . . [still] grope about on earth, leading men and women into crimes. Some were murderers on earth and you hanged them, and thought you got rid of them. . . . This was a crime in you, for these hangings are visited back upon your society . . . for spirits influence people to criminal acts." We see this in serial killers who (randomly) steal lives, just as their discarnate hosts were or feel they were cheated out of their own life.

History is full of homicidal lunatics with psyche sufficiently compromised to hear the Voice, or the talk of spirits. But knowing nothing of the unseen world and its inhabitants, they jump to the grandiose conclusion that that voice is God himself—or the very devil! "Satan gets into people and makes them do things they don't want to do," declared Herbert Mullin (thirteen kills) (Vronsky 2004, 155). They have called their wicked spirit familiars everything from Divine Inspiration to Satan. More likely, these men are the dupes, the stooges, of highly negative entities, some of whom themselves were criminals in life and seek vengeance or "desire to experience riotous living again . . . [by finding] a host body to continue their career of crime" (Maurey 1988, 102).

Fig. 4.2. A lithograph of John Wilkes Booth by J. L. Magee, illustrator of "America's most lurid disaster scenes."

Among most psychologists, it is a knee-jerk reaction to label the hearer of voices a (paranoid) schizophrenic. It is not so much the label that bothers me as the assumption that those voices are *hallucinated*. In fact, the visions and voices of the criminal psychopath may be a form of depraved clairvoyance or clairaudience verging on (demonic) possession. Surveying the most extreme, the most wicked, crimes, we find at least half of them involve some nefarious clairaudience. Here are some examples in table 4.1.

TABLE 4.1. MURDER AND THE VOICE

Killer's name	Crime	Experience	Source
Ameenah	killed her children	"heard the voice of Allah ordering her to sacrifice her children"	Kirwin 1997, 254
David Berkowitz	6 semirandom kills	"voices, thousands of them . . . urged him to act"	Klausner 1981, 195
Ken Bianchi	strangled 10 women	the spirit "said he could come into my body . . . and do terrible things"	O'Brien 1985, 182
Orlando Camacho	cut off his wife's head	God, saints, and gangsters talk to him and read his thoughts	Markman and Bosco 1989, 24–27
Eric Chapman	killed grandmother	Ordered by a voice to kill someone in the family	Markman and Bosco 1989, 302–8
Richard Chase	6 (vampire) kills	conversed with "invisible people"	Markman and Bosco 1989, 162
John Wayne Gacy	sodomized and killed 33 young men	"He could hear the Other Guy [disembodied] screaming"	T. Cahill 1987, 197
Ed Gein	serial killer	his dead mother spoke to him	Douglas and Olshaker 1998, 371
Gary Gilmore	2 senseless murders	"he heard voices coming through the jail vents"	Gilmore 1994, 250

Killer's name	Crime	Experience	Source
Joe Kallinger	3 homicides, including his own son	commanded by "voice of the demon" as well as by "God of the Universe"	Schreiber 1984, 85, 118
Dr. John Kappler	manslaughter and several medical-homicide attempts	"heard voices . . . inside his head . . . commanding him to commit violent acts"	Ablow 1994, 6, 111
Herb Mullin	10 kills including a priest	killed "at the urging of voices"	Ressler 1992, 20, 146
Abdul Oman	deadly assault and attempted homicide	voices told him the doctor was the devil	Kirwin 1997, 96
Joel Rifkin	strangled and/or dismembered 17 prostitutes	voices led him to his victims	Kirwin 1997, 51–52
Arthur Shawcross	killed and mutilated 15 people plus 2 children	"he hears voices commanding him to do certain things"	Olsen 1993, 117
John Shrank	shot at Theodore Roosevelt in 1912	a voice instructed him to thus avenge the McKinley assassination	Donovan 1962, 102
Norman Simons	sodomized and strangled 9 boys	"a very dominating and serious" voice urged him on	Ressler 1997, 180–81
June Smith	arson and suicide	voices in the dark called to her: "I want you"	Michaud 1998, 134–35
Danny Starrett	serial rape, 1 homicide	"I heard somebody whispering . . . inside [me]"	Naifeh and Smith 1995, 134
Dennis Sweeney	killed New York Representative Allard Lowenstein	"constantly harassed by voices inside his head"	Kirwin 1997, 247
Peter Sutcliffe	13 kills, mostly prostitutes	"I heard . . . God's voice"; "he heard the voice hundreds of times"	Morrison 2004, 134; Burn 1985, 247

> *That insurgent horror . . . lay caged in his flesh, where he*
> *heard it mutter.*
>
> ROBERT LOUIS STEVENSON,
> *THE STRANGE CASE OF DR. JEKYLL AND MR. HYDE*

In a similarly strange case, *The Strange Case of Dr. Kappler*, Keith Ablow, a decade before tackling the Scott Peterson saga, took on the harrowing story (and mind) of Dr. John Kappler, the California anesthesiologist previously discussed. The sinister voices arousing Kappler had instructed him to administer the *wrong medicine* to his patients; "I attempted to kill three patients" Kappler later confessed. Spirits also urged him to "jump in front of a bus," or, as he got in his car, to kill himself in an accident. The (so-called) hallucination commanded him to "commit mayhem." Only the percipient knows how powerful, authoritative, those commands can be. Driving along, he heard voices and felt possessed. "It was as if the car was being driven by someone else."* He was told to "hit and run" (Ablow 1994, 10–12, 77).

Remembered by a schoolmate as "sort of a nonperson," Kappler emerged from a terrifying childhood; his home life, violent and alcoholic, manipulative and unstable, held secrets and shame, denial and abuse (Ablow 1994, 29, 67, 31). Kappler had been conceived out of wedlock to two teenagers in tenth grade. It was a big family secret that caused him lifelong shame and turmoil. It didn't help that both parents drank and fought—fisticuffs, dishes flying, constant screaming, or that the only child they beat (there were three) was John. All this set the stage for devastated self.

> *Humiliation obliterates him [a man].*
>
> JAMES BALDWIN,
> *THE EVIDENCE OF THINGS NOT SEEN*

---

*Serial killer, Richard Macek also had "a car with a mind of its own" (Morrison 2004, 24).

Inside was a void—prey to usurping entities whose dictates psychiatrists label "command hallucinations." But were they? Or had Kappler's empty vessel of self attracted negative controls, his own persona "enemy-occupied territory," invaded now by "a destructive agency"—what Ablow called a "dark domain of demons." Kappler was in the grip of a force he could not shake: "Do I have to do it? . . . I was begging the voice not to make me do it" (Ablow 1994, 111, 52–54, 41, 89). The voices were "inside his head" and, as John himself put it, "I don't go through any thought process—I just do what it says." As Manfred Guttmacher (1960, 59) put it, "the usual role of thinking . . . [is] conspicuously absent in these cases."

> *While under control, their [mediums'] own will is set aside.*
> *. . . They are as helpless as the subject of the mesmerist.*
>
> HENRY S. OLCOTT,
> *PEOPLE FROM THE OTHER WORLD*

Who knows, may not all men be as automatons, some in the hands of Gods, and some in the hands of devils?

OAHSPE, KA'YU (AKA CONFUCIUS), BOOK OF ESKRA 36:47

We know quite a bit about the automatisms performed by the fully entranced medium, who produces, say, automatic writing or automatic drawing "without a thought of my own" (William Howitt, in Fodor 1966), or by the sleepwalker or the person speaking in tongues. We need also to understand the deranged automatisms of the criminal.

Instances of criminals' automatisms include

- David Berkowitz, serial killer: total change of handwriting; seen also in the Zodiac—Allen's "handprinting did not match Zodiac's" (Graysmith 1987, 209); also seen in the MPD case of Henry Hawksworth whose alter, Dana, wrote in "handwriting different than his own" (Hawksworth 1977, 229)

- Fred Coe, serial rapist: "he was like a robot" (Olsen 1983, 77). (I also found the word *robot* in descriptions of other killers: John List, Joe Kallinger, Ted Bundy, Arthur Shawcross, Gary Ridgway.)
- J. W. Gacy, serial killer: "It was not his voice"; Gacy was a sleepwalker and hyperpraxic (Morrison 2004, 82, 85). Several sleepwalking homicides were labeled "non-insane automatism" (Kirwin 1997, 137)
- Joe Kallinger, homicide: "Something is speaking through you"; there were also strange "automatic movements"; from him also came "another laugh completely different from his" (Schreiber 1984, 134–35, 338, 84)
- Richard Macek, serial killer: described as a "zombie"; hyperpraxic; exhibited a "robotic kind of cruelty" (Morrison 2004, 43)
- Gary Ridgway, Green River Killer: "Anyone who observed Gary would remember—the automaton, the robot" (Rule 2004, 650)
- Danny Starrett, rape/homicide: automatic drawing (Naifeh and Smith 1995, 126, 178)
- Dan White, homicide: "It was like a reflex . . . I wasn't thinking" (Blinder 1985, 44)

The element of overshadowing, moreover, is betrayed by the baffling lack of motive—it was done without a reason; Kappler's victims taken at random. His murderous acts were "completely irrational, purposeless and motiveless . . . [he] was incapable of controlling his conduct" (Ablow 1994, 134). In any other place or time, this would be called possession. In fact, according to the guidelines laid out for the priestly rites of exorcism, John Kappler exhibited unmistakable signs of demonic possession: voices, spells of unusually rapid speech, coprolalia ("screaming obscenities"), and exaggerated grimacing (Ablow 1994, 59, 106, 53). Concerning the latter, some have counted facial distortion as the first sign of possession. This, according to psychiatrist M. Scott Peck, can only be "described as Satanic . . . an incredibly contemptuous grin of hostile malevolence . . . a ghastly expression . . . blazing [with] hatred" (Peck 1983, 184, 188). Compare this to the grisly grimaces and "crocodile smile" of Russia's Red Ripper (fifty-three kills) or our own homegrown rapist/murderer Joe Kallinger (the Shoemaker) whose face would become "distorted [by] weird expressions . . . facial grimaces" (Schreiber 1984, 90, 95, 371). Though old-school Christians blamed the devil himself for "distorting the face into a strange demonic cast" (Christiani 1961, 70), the more modern exorcist recognizes this kind of grimacing as "the ghastly paranormal expression" (Peck 2005, 114) of a possessing entity.

Whatever the automatisms that may erupt, it is their involuntary nature that interests us most. This is particularly relevant to the seemingly motiveless crime. Such cases remain unsolved to this extent: the *motive* is still in shadow. The usual reasons are just not there: jealousy, rage, revenge, greed, rivalry.

> *The motive thing was a real headscratcher.*
> Tim Cahill, *Buried Dreams*

Not only are the experts at a loss for motive or reason—"there can be no rational explanation" (Olsen 1983, 70)—but the killer himself often does not know what moves him to such violence. "It's senseless," Chris Longo replied when asked to explain the motive of his crime (familicide), adding, "It should never have happened & I'm fighting every day to . . . figure that out. I don't think that I'll ever know" (Finkel 2005, 304).

> *What the hell is wrong with him?*
> Arthur Shawcross's psychiatrist
> (Olsen 1993, 456)

Arthur Shawcross, with that strange, blank innocence that we sometimes see in the bearing of the human monster, cannot account for his own crimes. This was no self-serving legal feint. Asked what he was thinking when he strangled those prostitutes in Rochester, New York: "I don't know . . . I was, you know, in a fog." In prison, the former fishing buff and do-gooder was genuinely tormented—"why I did it." Interviewed by numerous specialists, some driving hard for an explanation, the brown-eyed killer with the puppy-dog look could only say "it just happened . . . I just lost control of everything around me" (Olsen 1993, 467, 484).

"I had no reason to commit the murders," Robert Ressler quotes John Wayne Gacy. As far as Agent Ressler was concerned, "the emotional components of stranger murder seem incomprehensible . . . beyond rational understanding" (Ressler 1997, 46). Well then, if we can't find a rational cause, let's look for an irrational one. Where is the rule that says sociopaths act rationally? As one detective said, "You can't use logic to tell you what these people are thinking" (Barer 2002, 128).

The perpetrator himself may be the most baffled of all. Let's take the time to searchlight this:

- Bobby Joe Long: "I could never kill anyone"(Morrison 2004, 165, 168) (he killed eight people). "I killed a bunch of sluts and whores and I don't even know—why?"
- Arthur Shawcross: "How could anybody think I'd hurt a kid?" (Arthur's first two kills were children).
- Ken Bianchi's alter said, "He couldn't figure out what he had done and why. . . . I wouldn't let him remember" (O'Brien 1985, 145).
- Richard Ivers: "I don't know that I have done it" (Archer 1967, 100).
- The I-5 Killer: "I am not a violent person" (Rule 1988a, 130).
- Albert DeSalvo, the Boston Strangler: "What really happened to me? . . . I want them to find out why I did these things" (Frank 1966, 340, 317).
- John Wayne Gacy: "the idea that I am a homosexual thrill killer and all that—that garbage . . . that I stalked young boys and slaughtered them. Hell, if you could see my work schedule, you'd know damn well that I was never out there" (Ressler 1997). Sure, Gacy was a workaholic; but he found the time (lost time) to kill thirty-three boys.

Then, when overwhelming evidence of their crimes is before them, or flashbacks break through, the same murderers are at a loss to explain their acts:

- Bobby Joe Long: "I couldn't stop myself" (Vronsky 2004, 287).
- Shawcross: "I don't know why I butchered her" (Olsen 1993, 484).
- DeSalvo: "Why I done it, I don't really understand" (Frank 1966, 283).
- Gacy: searching for a motive was like "looking into a fog . . . like working a jigsaw puzzle" (T. Cahill 1987, 174).
- Joel Rifkin: he had "no idea why he killed" (Kirwin 1997, 65).
- Henry Lee Lucas: "I don't know why I committed this crime" (Cox 1991, 51).
- Solly (wife killer): "I know I did what I did, but I don't believe it. It makes no sense" (Blinder 1985, 16).

When you come right down to it, most of these senseless crimes are committed during *lost time*. Blanked out. A fog. No memory; even "ordinary" crimes of passion are frequently committed in lost time. A British study estimates that in as much as 60 percent of murders, the accused was amnesic for the event, what psychology calls *fugue* or temporary dissociation. Victim of multiple head injuries, Ken Bianchi, for example, was prone to the fugue state. "He simply cannot accept, understand, remember or believe that he (such a good boy) could possibly do such crimes. . . . Ken knows nothing of the crimes" (O'Brien 1985, 261).

Ken was supposedly epileptic in childhood. A small temporal lobe cyst showed up on the MRI of Arthur Shawcross. At his trial, Dr. Dorothy Lewis argued that his cyst indicates a form of epilepsy, called partial complex seizure state, causing Arthur to fall into the fugue state. Note that Gacy, Danny S., Ramirez, Bianchi, and others were all thought to be epileptic as children. But were their seizures really epilepsy? Or did they fall into the Void, the outer zone just beyond the physical? In favoring a paranormal interpretation of epilepsy (as discussed in the introduction and elsewhere), we see a link to certain automatisms that accompany the seizure. Hyperpraxia, for example, as in Gacy's case: as a teenager he was put on Phenobarb and Dilantin to medicate his "epilepsy." His doctors told him that when he had a seizure, he became immensely powerful.

Without factoring ASCs—and their automatisms—into the equation, we cannot understand the blackouts, amnesia, and loss of control that are standard fare in the brutal sociopathic personality. Fight or flight: given the childhood of killers who were abused and/or overcontrolled, is it any wonder that the flight option so often results in the fugue state? ASCs are common in those who have not survived their toxic upbringing very well, and that includes Dan White, John List, Richard Ramirez, Arthur Shawcross, Albert DeSalvo, John Wayne Gacy, Henry Lee Lucas, Dean Corll, Joe Kallinger, Diane Downs, Ken Bianchi—and many more given to altered states—all terribly susceptible to that Elsewhereness that puts one in the orbit of the disembodied world. The Outer Darkness.

With altered states, loss of control and of memory are typical as we survey the fractured world of the psychopath. But since our legal system of punishment demands a psychiatric verdict of sanity (knowing right from wrong) in order to convict them, these offenders *must be considered in control of themselves.* And this is precisely why FBI profilers and forensic psychiatrists argue (incorrectly) that the violent predator is primarily motivated by a conscious desire for complete control over his victim: "If you commit violent crimes, you do so by choice. . . . Killing becomes the ultimate act of control" say Douglas and Olshaker in *Obsession* (1998, 34).

"Manipulation-domination-control" is now the mantra of profilers who make a point of quoting such celebrated predators as Ted Bundy who confessed his need to wholly control and dominate women. Nevertheless, during the manhunt for Bundy, "psychiatrists were more inclined to believe that the killer was a man obsessed by a terrible *compulsion* [emphasis added] that forced him to hunt down and kill the same type of woman over and over and over again" (Rule 1986, 131). Bundy himself explained on death row that "he received no pleasure from harming . . . his victims"; in fact, his crimes filled him with "disgust, repulsion, fear and wonder" (Vronsky 2004, 120, 318).

Certainly the accoutrements of bondage (ropes, handcuffs, gagging) deployed in some of these vicious assaults display the most venal kind of subjugation. Granted, the quest for power and command seems to be foremost in all such crimes. But if we scratch the surface, it becomes clear that the so-called thrill, the passion for domination, "the godlike rush of power over another person" (Markman and Bosco 1989, 44) is not really *enjoyed;* rather, it comes unbidden. This is the nature of dissociative acts. Commenting on killer Richard Macek, Dr. Morrison notes "that Macek had very little internal self-control" (2004, 34–35).

> For heavens
> SAke cAtch Me
> BeFore I Kill More
> I cannot control myself
>
> —*words scrawled on wall, with the lipstick of one of*
> *William Heirens' victims.*
> (from Douglas and Olshaker, *Mindhunter,* 126)

"I kept praying someone would see the [license plate] number and call the police," Danny S. admitted after his crimes, which he described as—"feeling myself losing control . . . it was something else taking over control of my body. . . . I get that panicky feeling . . . I could no more stop it than I could stop my heart from beating" (Naifeh and Smith 1995, 331, 144, 365).

"Don't let me out. I know I'll kill again," declaimed Henry Lee Lucas, the one-eyed drifter killer; while yet another, John Joubert, acted "as if by rote" during his murderous forays. He "was glad that he had been apprehended, for he was sure that he would have killed again. . . . He could not restrain his impulses"; indeed, he was diagnosed "301.20" meaning schizoid with *compulsive* features (Ressler 1992, 120–22). Peter Kuerten, Germany's Jack the Ripper, could not remember most of his killings; upon his capture, "he seemed almost grateful to the police, saying 'If you had not arrested me when you did, I know I would have had to take another life'" (Archer 1967, 94). Chikatilo, the Russian Ripper who took fifty-three lives, said, "Everything I have done makes me tremble . . . I feel only gratitude that they captured me" (Conradi 1992, 101). Is it any surprise then that Chris Longo (familicide) described his capture as "a big weight off my shoulders"; while Arthur Shawcross, who "seemed to have the impulse control of a barracuda," would admit (while anticipating his parole hearing) his biggest fear was that he would "get out and kill another child" (Olsen 1993, 149). Some, in fact, turn themselves in for this very reason, as did Ed Kemper, California's Co-ed Killer, after murdering and beheading his own mother.

Given our punitive, retaliatory code of justice, maybe it soothes our conscience to assume that the assailant is having a good time of it, feeding his pleasure principle, "getting his pleasure from rape and torture and death" (Douglas and Olshaker 1998, 34). Think of how much harder it would be to *punish* a perpetrator whose actions are actually "driven by forces beyond his control" (Depue 2005, 135). This inconvenient fact is generally passed over at the same time that the bogus gratification principle is given top billing: a spree killer, for example, is described as "getting the thrill of the hunt, the thrill of the kill" (Michaud 1998, 23); depicting these madmen as *relishing* their handiwork makes it almost easy for us, in turn, to relish the full extent of their punishment at the hands of the state.

The killer, as the official portrait is sketched, has an immense appetite for ravishment, which the act of devastation satisfies; he commits these crimes, according to a leading expert, "for the same reasons anyone repeats pleasurable behavior" (Barer 2002, 129). "They are seeking emotional satisfaction," echoes FBI profiler Ressler (1992, 32). The pleasure theory then ostensibly provides an explanation of *why* the crime was committed. It fails, though, to address the many crimes whose perpetrators simply *do not know* why they acted as they did. "Thank God it's finally over," said Eddie James, captured after a senseless and brutal double homicide. "I don't know what prompted it. That's a blank" (Walsh 1998, 47). Jerry Brudos, Oregon's shoe-fetish killer, was yet another who was under the "influence of an urge that even he himself could not . . . define." The judge wanted to know if the attacks were *deliberate.* "I really don't know. It just happened" (Rule 1988b, 179).

And what about Harvey Glatman, the Jewish rope killer who "takes no pleasure in the killing . . . he feels like vomiting" (Newton 1998, 11, 180)? "I really didn't like to kill," said Glatman.

> *"It's a mystery . . . It [sic] hard to control myself. . . . Where*
> *this monster enter my brain I will never know. . . . I can't*
> *stop it."*
> BTK (Wenzl et al. 2007, 28, 307, 501)

Still, these predators "do enjoy their crimes," according to Agent Douglas, this time in reference to David Berkowitz, New York's Son of Sam killer. But it did not make him feel good; Berkowitz was a compulsive killer. "I thought of it as a job. I never was real happy," admitted the chubby, blue-eyed shooter. "I couldn't wait for it all to end." Indeed, the mother— *the grieving mother*—of one of Berkowitz's victims may have grasped the situation with greater insight than any of the experts, when she came to realize that the Son of Sam was "a sick man . . . needed help. I thought he himself wanted to be caught" (Klausner 1981, 365, 316, 64).

To the experts, though, David's case "was just one more example of manipulation, domination, and control" (Douglas and Olshaker 1998, 35–38). For his part, David felt he could never convince the agent—or the psychiatrists—of the phantoms that had invaded his mind.

> *"What can I do? How can I make people understand? . . .*
> *Nobody listened. . . . There is no doubt in my mind that a*
> *demon has been living in me since birth."*
> From David Berkowitz's prison diary
> (Klausner 1981, 170)

Rather than being a "notorious manipulator," the Son of Sam was actually the manipula*tee*; in his own words—"these demons . . . wanted people to die. That's it. Pretty simple. . . . Me? I never needed or wanted it" (Klausner 1981, 83).

It is unwise to apply the standards of normal self-control or free will to a psyche that has gone out of orbit, gone haywire. When analysts make this mistake, saying, for example, that psychopaths "*choose* to follow their own base urges*" (Depue 2005, 8) or that they "*choose* to listen to [a devil]" (Kirwin 1997, 36), they are overextending the great principle of Free Will and choice, which can only apply to the *sound mind*.

It simply does not apply to the unsound mind. In the annals of irrational crime, we come across a thousand ways in which the precious gift of free will is *lost*. Indeed, the reflexive, obsessive, almost robotic drift of the unhinged mind wanders far, far away from any place where pleasure or enjoyment or even choosing is a possibility. At the bottom of the pit is a person *divested* of his free will and of his personal power. Powerless. From Dr. Blinder's criminal casebook alone come many attestations of this loss of power and self-direction: "feelings of utter impotence . . . devoid of any ability to influence the course of her life"; "powerlessness, dissociation with suppression of anger" (Blinder 1985, 75, 79, 154).

> *In the idiopathic [cause unknown] type of aggressive outburst, there is a complete loss of control, the actor is himself bewildered and often seeks to learn what occurred and why he has done what he did. . . . [There are] indications of severe ego deficiency which permits impulse to flow.*
> MANFRED GUTTMACHER, *MIND OF THE MURDERER*

"Severe ego deficiency" is a long-winded way of saying *nonperson*, which we are already familiar with in the form of void, abeyant, or passive self. The spiritual vacuum virtually sucks in other personas; the vehicle running on empty draws power from Elsewhere to fill the void. Here are some key phrases describing this murderous nonperson:

- Ted Bundy: "non-emotional," "removed," "the void of his soul" (Rule 1986, 392, 116)
- Richard Chase: "nonverbal . . . withdrawn," "no emotion or feelings," "blank look" (Markman and Bosco 1989, 167, 184, 174)
- Chikatilo: "arrest of development" (Conradi 1992, 253)
- Fred Coe: "he was barren," "seemed to lack emotion," "he's a shell . . . there's nothing there" (Olsen 1983, 270, 348, 87)
- John Wayne Gacy: "there was no feeling," "lacked an independent identity" (T. Cahill 1987, 307, 109)
- Joe Kallinger: he was his parents' "obedient robot," "he didn't know who he was," "Joe was treated as a nonperson" (Schreiber 1984, 45, 51, 362)
- Bobby Joe Long: "lacking in emotion, rang hollow," "never matured emotionally beyond infancy" (Morrison 2004, 157, 180)
- Henry Lee Lucas: "almost infantile manner" (Cox 1991, 57)
- Charles Manson: "I was truly a nothing" (Emmons 1986, 222)
- Marie Noe: "There was nothing behind her blue eyes," "total lack of emotion" (Glatt 2002, 20, 3)
- Joel Rifkin: "He seemed utterly absent . . . as if his self had long since left his body" (Kirwin 1997, 42, 49)
- Arthur Shawcross: "he never grew up," "broken down ego functioning" (Olsen 1993, 286, 193)
- Peter Sutcliffe: "It was possible to walk into a room in which Peter was sitting and not even notice he was there" (Burn 1985, 32)
- Dan White: "a virtual nonperson" (Blinder 1985, 50)
- Randy Woodfield: "no emotion there at all . . . just emptiness" (Rule 1988a, 474)
- R. L. Yates: behind the window of his eyes, "there wasn't a soul home. . . . His eyes were dead" (Barer 2002, 106, 33)

[He] can mimic the human personality perfectly.

KEITH ABLOW,
INSIDE THE MIND OF SCOTT PETERSON

Peter Vronsky (2004, 160–61) reports on an intriguing though macabre episode in the college days of Ted Kaczynski, the notorious Unabomber, an episode that points to another way that the nonperson may take shape. As a young man, in 1959, Kaczynski survived "a series of brutal personality-breaking" experiments conducted at Harvard and similar to CIA trials, testing brainwashing, mind control, and other intelligence techniques. How well, for example, could recruits withstand "interrogation designed to break down their personalities"? What personality types would be best suited for clandestine work? Ted was only seventeen when he became a test subject, a lab rat, for this protocol that made "surprise attacks" on subjects' belief systems. Harvard's records of Kaczynski's involvement in the program were quickly sealed when the story leaked in 2000. "Some of the other participants, however, recall the experiments as being devastating of their . . . personalities."

> *"I would like to get revenge on the whole scientific and bureaucratic establishment."*
>
> TED KACZYNSKI

Let's not be fooled by appearances: lacking a true self, the nonperson may easily slip into any role, often appearing to all the world as a compliant, clean-cut, respectable fellow. The astute profiler is well aware of this veneer of politeness; some offenders are even courteous or helpful to a fault, like Scott Peterson, remembered by acquaintances as "respectful and serious" (Ablow 2005, 104); or like Chris Longo (familicide), regarded by church mates as "a model for other men"— polite and charming; or like David Meierhofer (kidnapper-killer), so well mannered and considerate.

Logic: A child raised in the school of deceit and pretense, counterfeit and cover-up, himself becomes perforce a master of imposture, a genius (well taught) of guile, an artiste extraordinaire of craft and camouflage. We often find the Big Lie or the Big Secret lurking in the family background of the psychopath. David Berkowitz's adoptive parents told the boy that his mother had died in childbirth, which gave him a heavy feeling of guilt. But it was a lie; she merely had had him illegitimately. (Eventually he did reunite with his mother and sister—with mixed results.) John Kappler (Dr. Death), as we saw, was also conceived out of wedlock. It was a big family secret. Ted Bundy also grew up inside the bubble of a big family secret. Because his young mother conceived out of wedlock, the family pretended she was his *sister,* not his mother. There was another big secret in Ted's family: daddy/grandfather, a church deacon, kept a large collection of pornography, which little Ted found and studied.

Mark Hofmann, the Mormon bomber (1985) was a piece of work who held a shameful family secret—his grandmother's polygamous marriage that postdated the 1890 Mormon decree against plural wives. "It was a secret that members of Mark's family seldom discussed" (Lindsey 1988, 29). Mark, in turn, would become one of the biggest deceivers and frauds the Saints had ever known.

There were "terrible secrets" and hypocrisy in Gary Gilmore's weird family, as well as mysteries, death of children, abandonment. His mother once tried to smother his baby brother—and Gary witnessed it.

The Big Secret was also imposed on Richard Ramirez, the Tex-Mex Night Stalker, serial killer, after witnessing a murder at age fourteen: While visiting his older, favorite, cousin Mike, Richard watched his cousin shoot his wife to death in cold blood. Richard was then instructed never to say what he had seen.

Though Diane Downs (who murdered one of her children and attempted to murder the others) had been molested by her father at age twelve, their secret was never once discussed. Her father was an influential man, after all.

It was not until the trial of Spokane's prostitute snuffer, Robert Lee Yates Jr., that a childhood secret came out: Yates had been repeatedly molested by a neighbor at the age of six. "This has remained a deep secret for him throughout his life" (Barer 2002, 287). Oh, another little long-held Yates family secret emerged around that time: Yates' grandmother had killed his grandfather with an ax.

The big lie or big secret is perfected in the school of deceit and hypocrisy whose unwitting students then fit the passive-aggressive mold. They are, according to Malachi Martin, "hostages to the devil" animated by "a peculiar fascination with the negative," thus drawing the dark side to one's aura. On the other hand, some households merely enjoined conformity, but too often through unyielding rigidity and uncommon strictness—centered on a religious ideal and in the absence of true affection. "I was truly the chattel of an Irish Catholic mother" averred Dr. John Kappler (Ablow 1994, 35).

When sociopaths come from a family where there has been no overt abuse, look instead for this uncompromising agenda or for the Great Pretense or for the charade of a "good home." Diagnosed passive-aggressive as well as obsessive-compulsive, John Hinckley Jr. wrote, "I continue to grovel for normalcy." During his trial (for the shooting of President Reagan and others) reporters dubbed his syndrome "dementia suburbia." He came, of course, from a "good" and prosperous home. No abuse, but pressures "to keep up with the rest of a successful family" (Caplan 1987, 63, 91–92, 80–85). The Hinckley saga was not unlike that of Lyle Menendez (Beverly Hills parricide), "smothered by his parents" who were "fixated on perfection"; the father had drilled superiority into his sons, was controlling and demanding; yet the boys were, at the same time, very spoiled.

The term *soul murder* was also used by psychiatrist Dr. Robert Mayer for the sort of *emotional* abuse that robs the youngster of ripening self. Artie Shawcross's mother was an extremely abusive and controlling woman—bossy, jealous, a martinet—who thoroughly intimidated her son. A screamer and screecher who dominated her family, she used every four-letter word in the book to dress down her slightly retarded son. Still, the experts concluded that Artie's "inner workings are probably completely beyond comprehension." *Duh.*

Didn't Roy Hazelwood's study of serial rapists find that 76 percent had indeed been "victimized as youngsters" (Depue 2005, 286)? This fact—and it is a fact—is not incomprehensible. But whitewashing the Great American Family is a stubborn old habit; few are eager to learn that *parenting*—American-style—has a seriously ugly side.

12 STEPS
TO RAISE A DELINQUENT CHILD

1 Begin with infancy to give the child everything he wants. In this way he will grow up to believe the world owes him a living.

2 When he picks up bad words, laugh at him. This will make him think he's cute.

3 Never give him any spiritual training. Wait until he is twenty-one and then let "him decide for himself."

4 Avoid the use of "wrong." He may develop a guilt complex. This will condition him to believe later, when he is arrested for stealing a car, that society is against him and he is being persecuted.

5 Pick up everything he leaves lying around. Do everything for him so that he will be experienced in throwing all responsibility on others.

6 Let him read any printed matter he can get his hands on. Be careful that the silverware and drinking glasses are sterilized but let his mind feast on garbage.

7 Quarrel frequently in the presence of your children. In this way they won't be so shocked when the home is broken up later.

8 Give a child all the spending money he wants. Never let him earn his own.

9 Satisfy his every craving for food, drink, and comfort. See that his every sensual desire is gratified.

10 Take his part against neighbors, teachers, and policemen. They are all prejudiced against your child.

11 When he gets into real trouble, apologize for yourself by saying, "I could never do anything with him."

12 Prepare for a life of grief. You will be likely to have it.

Taken from the pamphlet entitled Twelve Rules for Raising Delinquent Children distributed by the Houston Police Department

Fig. 4.3. Poster distributed by the Houston Police Department

The unmaking of self begins at home. The nonperson is made, not born. Forensic psychiatrists readily observe the criminal's need to humiliate and degrade, yet are reluctant to trace this to the parents who taught them this very behavior in their "sponge" years. *Lousy parenting*—criticism, debasement, belittlement—*is the kindergarten of crime.*

Studies have also shown that for 47 percent of serial killers, the father had left the home before the boy was twelve. That leaves mom. "The harm you [mother] did can never be undone"—Ted Kaczynski, Unabomber (quoted in Douglas and Olshaker 1999, 287). Some are weak or masochistic women (who attract the sadistic husband/boyfriend). Some are jailbirds or alcoholic. Some turn tricks. But most rule the roost: two out of three serial killers were raised by a domineering mother. Quite a few of these moms are sociopaths themselves; others are schizophrenic. Some are possessed. Some are perfectionists. Some are provocative, seductive—serial wives, marrying and divorcing in steady succession. Some are overly possessive. Some are explosive, and some are downright scary.

Profilers, we know, have whittled the homicidal formula down to control and domination. But killers do not come into the world with these urges. They were taught it. Usually by their parents. We are so quick to identify the beast of dominance in these deviants, but so reluctant to acknowledge its creator: parents, caregivers, like the overpowering alcoholic father who practically enslaves his sons. Bondage, bindings, and all such evil accoutrements do not come out of thin air but are learned early—in the school of entrapment. Enter the serial killer: rope fetishists like Harvey Glatman, whippers like Henry Lee Lucas, sadistic control freaks like Eric Napoletano—all with a hostile or highly domineering parent. The mothers of gynocidal men (for many if not most serial killers prey upon *females*) are controllers. Matricides (Ed Gein, Henry Lee Lucas, John List, Ed Kemper) are usually the product of an overbearing mother, Kemper remembering his own as "a damned manipulating, controlling beast" (Vronsky 2004, 261). (The reader interested in criminology may consider the especially disturbed mothers of Ken Bianchi, Joe Kallinger, Jerry Brudos, Richard Chase, John Joubert,

Bobby Joe Long, Dean Corll, Fred Coe, Arthur Shawcross, to name a few.) In short, the sponge of a young mind forged with the *imprint of control* is most easily lost to *itself.* And when consciousness is somewhere else, the unseen controller can step in.

* * *

A bright and handsome paranoid schizophrenic named Herb Mullin killed both men and women at the urging of voices that directed him to make blood sacrifices for the sake of the environment! Mullin had a fierce delusion about preventing earthquakes in California: they could be avoided, according to his telepathic voices, by taking some lives (final count: ten). When he was a small boy he had argued, "Jesus could not possibly fit into the communion wafer." Later, he spoke of "lies designed to induce naïveté and gullibility in young children . . . thereby making them susceptible to receive and carry out telepathic orders."

The child shaped and trained to submit to fixed ideas remains predisposed to the controlling touch. He is like wax to the unseen powers in search of a host. Psychic research, for well over a hundred years, has been geared toward identifying those entities that come into a person's presence—whether that person is schizophrenic, psychopathic, mediumistic, or simply harassed by a spiritual parasite. "Such an entity," avers Eugene Maurey (1988, 120), if strongly negative, may "urge the victim to commit . . . murder." Otherwise put, Dr. Wickland viewed this encroachment as capable of resulting in "bestiality, atrocities, and other forms of criminality" (Wickland 1974, 20).

The case of Dennis Rader (BTK killer) is instructive. Once captured, he tried to explain: "You don't understand these things because you're not under the influence of Factor X, the same thing that made Son of Sam, Jack the Ripper, Harvey Glatman, Boston Strangler . . . Hillside Strangler, Ted of the West Coast [kill] . . . which seems senseless; but we cannot help it." When asked to explain Factor X, Rader replied, "I just know it . . . kind of controls me. . . . How can a guy like me—a church member, raised a family—go out and do these sorts of things? . . . I actually think it's demons inside me" (Wenzl et al. 2007, 66, 308).

Where spirits usurp the corporeal body . . . holding the native spirit in abeyance, such spirits shall be known as damons.

OAHSPE, BOOK OF BON 14:9

Demons? Although demonology went out of fashion a long time ago in the civilized West* (apart from horror movies), its nonexistence, really, can be attributed more to political correctness than to the evidence at hand. Those we rely on for expert opinions have come up with sterile labels (like paranoid schizophrenia or episodic dyscontrol) that only distance us from the psychogenesis of lunacy. And when it comes to explaining immensely brutal and irrational crimes, the veneer of expertise breaks down entirely, our flustered analyst now washing his hands of the problem by calling it subhuman behavior: "[Such persons] are completely, utterly inhuman" (Morrison 2004, 3). "The depths to which human beings can sink . . . suggest subhuman forces" (Markman and Bosco 1989, 192). "This guy goes beyond the study of human behavior" (Lavergne 1997, 7; quoting a psychiatrist's comment on Ken McDuff, Texas serial killer). Said a prosecutor in another homicide case, "There are some people who are just outside humanity. . . . This is not a human being" (Naifeh and Smith 1995, 286).

But even the man-on-the-street can do better than that. In fact, the offenders themselves have had extraordinary flashes of insight that the "experts" have chalked up to self-serving vindication. For example, when Danny S. told his lawyer that he "entertained the thought that I was possessed by demons," his lawyer said, "Cut the bull, Danny" (Naifeh and Smith 1995, 135). David Berkowitz (Son of Sam) wrote that "people feel a certain eeriness about me—something cold, inhuman, monsterous [*sic*]. This is the power and personality of the demons."

David emerged from childhood with "overwhelming feelings of rejection." Given that the absence or depletion of self becomes a standing invitation to the Unseen Ones, we can better understand David's state-

---

*Demonic possession is still recognized today in 360 out of 488 societies surveyed (Davis 1985, 215).

ment that "unclean spirits will fill the void" (Klausner 1981, 363, 57). "Might it be possible," David asked, "to convince the world about the dark spirit forces that live on earth? I will die for this cause!"* (from his prison diaries, shown in his own neat handwriting in Lawrence Klausner's book *Son of Sam*).

"Phantoms," David wrote, "came into my head." The voices urged, "Get her. Kill her." "Demons were clamoring for blood . . . wicked, wicked demons" (Klausner 1981, 83, 106, 170). Berkowitz's prison diary also declared, "I am possessed . . . I am a person who has been visited by an alien force or being . . . I was doing nothing more than what the demon voices commanded. . . . The demons ran amok in my apartment." Insightfully, he wrote, "I know that if the police set up a 'Demon Task Force' then a tremendous step would be taken. . . . Society [also] needs to erect a 'Demon Hospital' in which suspected cases of demon possession could be treated" (Klausner 1981, 15, 46).

> *I want to be sent to a Mental Hospital to get the evil out of me.*
>
> ARTHUR SHAWCROSS, QUOTED IN OLSEN,
> *THE MISBEGOTTEN SON*, 441

We might recall the case of Susan A. who strangled her own eight-month-old baby. She had presumably "developed delusional ideas about being possessed by demons" (Lunde 1976, 99). Was it really delusional? Not according to the likes of the Vatican and its time-honored rite of exorcism, the *Rituale Romanum*. In 1970, after the arrest of Dean Corll (the deranged Texas multicide with twenty-seven kills), the Vatican's daily *L'Osservatore Romano* commented on the case: "We are in the domain of demons . . . an evil force . . . monstrous . . ." The editorial's reference to the "dissolution of a man" seems to tally with Corll's nonperson of a self. An unwanted child, he grew up into a young

---

*Truman Capote and F. Lee Bailey are among an enlightened minority proposing that serial killers be studied—not executed.

man shrouded in "a cloud of silence" and casting the blank stare of the psychopath, "like the walkin' dead." Elements of his story have a familiar ring: helpful and polite, isolated, severe childhood illness and subsequent blackouts, arrested cognitive development ("semiliterate"). His mother, married and divorced five times, was at once a religious fanatic and flashy dame; though critical and demeaning of her son, her reaction to his crimes amounted to a wall of denial: "I will never believe these terrible accusations"* (Olsen 1975, 261, 214, 82, 212).

Something as simple as inappropriate laugher may be a clue to derangement, a tell, especially if it comes unbidden. Joe Kallinger (the Shoemaker) tried to shut out his uproarious laughter "by holding his hand over his mouth, but . . . [it] had a personality of its own. . . . He wondered whether the laughter was a part of the demon." That horselaugh of his "gushed forth without outside provocation and it was accompanied by convulsiveness . . . it just took over." Joe said, "A force was manipulating me—I didn't know what it was but it had to be something other than myself" (Schreiber 1984, 84–85, 151, 169).

Clearly an automatism, the same bizarre gales of laughter came from Peter Sutcliffe (the Yorkshire Ripper) who'd erupt into spells of "laughing uncontrollably . . . [he] couldn't stop . . . [it was] a ten-minute job." His Teddy-boy friends noticed: "You'd j^{u}st say summat an' he'd bust out in *hysterical* laughter, really f---n' loud, almost rollin' on floor. . . . It were one of them laughs where it screeches out; he'd shout out like a right shrill shriek an' the whole pub'd look round" (Burn 1985, 37, 43, 58).

Ken McDuff, a Texas serial killer, also issued "maniacal laughter at things no one else thought were funny" (Lavergne 1997, 16). Sometimes it's the multiple/MPD who does this, like Alex whose "laughter was weird and inappropriate and never touching his eyes" (C. Smith 1998, 116). Martin Ebon (1974, 72) has noted that "one who talks loudly or laughs long may be possessed." The diabolical laugh, in fact, is so often met with, we will have to condense our findings in summary form in table 4.2.

---

*This denial is not uncommon. Arthur Shawcross's mother-from-hell declared, "There's nothing wrong with my son" (even though he killed fifteen people). The Boston Strangler's mother: "I don't think he could hurt anybody" (Frank 1966, 315).

TABLE 4.2. MALIGN LAUGHTER

Who	Crime	Description
Dr. Dale Cavaness	killed his son	"big laugh," especially in connection with his practical (read: sadistic) jokes. Dale would "burst into his loud laugh, a kind of rippling guffaw, haw-haw-haw-haw. . . . He doubled up with laughter" (O'Brien 1989)
Andrew Cunanan	4 homicides	"an extremely boisterous laugh . . . so obnoxious . . . [you could] hear that braying cackle for blocks away" (Walsh 1998, 214–15)
Diane Downs	shot her children in cold blood	laughed at inappropriate moments, e.g., all through her trial. Friends could not help but notice her near-hysterical laugh
Paul Keller	arsonist	his father described Paul's "inappropriate behavior . . . such as laughing when another child fell down and hurt himself" (Douglas and Olshaker 1999, 60)
Eric Napoletano	serial killer	"laughed heartily" while torturing women and also in court during his sentencing (Pienciak 1996, 177)
Dennis Rader	BTK killer	he emitted a "sharp, high-pitched cackle" as he described a kill to the cops (Wenzl et al. 2007, 275)
Richard Ramirez	Night Stalker	everyone noticed the "high-pitched hyena-cackle" he let out right in court (one victim recalls Ramirez, after setting her free, letting loose with an "eerie laugh")
Gary Ridgway	Green River Killer	as he was "beating her . . . with the rifle's butt . . . he started laughing maniacally" (Rule 2004, 472)
"Oddie" Shawcross	serial killer	"for no apparent reason, he threw his head back and emit[ted] a high cackle, trailing off in a low, loonlike warble" (Olsen 1993, 176)
Cathy Wood	nursing home murders	her aunt remembered her "outbursts of extreme laughter" (Cauffiel 1992, 431)

When John List (familicide) laughed, "it was, like, strange. . . . He was, you might say, programmed"; John himself admitted, "It's like I had no control all the while I was doing it [laughing] . . . like some force . . . something beyond my control"; as for the killing, he said, "Once I started, I was like on auto-drive" (Sharkey 1990, 237, 302). And in the case of Ed Gein (whose story inspired the book and movie *Psycho*), even as a boy he was in the habit of laughing at weirdly inappropriate times. Gein, stalker/killer, was raised by an abusive alcoholic father and a crabby, impatient, domineering mother, "a bible-obsessed religious zealot who created a willing religious captive in Gein" (Morrison 2004, 51). Her "strong ideas about religion and morality . . . [were] fanatically impressed upon Ed and his brother, Henry. . . . Neither Ed nor Henry ever married [or] had sex" (Douglas and Olshaker 1998, 366–71). Gein, incidentally, could not recall the killings, said he was "in a daze," felt he was driven to his ghoulish activities by an irresistible force that he said invaded his mind from someplace outside himself (see table 4.1, Ed Gein, on page 84).

> *It's hard, it is very hard to be possessed by unknown forces.*
> NORMAN SIMONS, SOUTH AFRICA'S
> "STATION STRANGLER" (RESSLER 1997, 180–81)

One finds a similar description of the haunting of Gary Gilmore: "There was now a terrible spirit living inside [him]. . . . That awful ghost . . . had somehow gotten inside him" (Gilmore 1994, 115). Indeed, the metaphor of choice, Dr. Jekyll and Mr. Hyde, pops up regularly whenever an unknown force emerges as Factor X in a crime. California's sadistic sex killer Zodiac, for example, "seemed to change into yet another personality, like Jekyll and Hyde" (Graysmith 1987, 210). Harvey Glatman's lawyer used the same comparison for the madness "burning inside him" (Newton 1998, 280). Dr. Markman (1989, 146) recounts that the wife of another killer "came to think of her husband as a Jekyll and Hyde," so sweet and charming— *sometimes*. Gary Ridgway (Green River Killer) "was a totally different person" (Rule 2004, 597) when he began to molest her (the one girl who actually got away). Of Arthur Shawcross, nice guy and do-gooder with violent mood swings, it was said, "All his misbehaviors seemed to follow from unknown forces." Arthur himself wondered "if I have been living two different lives. . . . One of the psychiatrists said I was a Mister Jekly and Mister Hide [sic] two people in one body" (Olsen 1993, 442, 490). The otherwise mild-mannered and sensitive Danny Starrett was "transformed . . . into a Dr. Jekyll and Mr. Hyde," his defense declared. Danny himself wrote, "I started picking up somebody else's thoughts. . . . They simply were not my thoughts. More and more, I began to view them as belonging to another person." He called that other person *Him*. "There was no stopping HIM. . . . The head turns . . . but I'm not turning the head. When the head turns, I can see the girl . . . sitting in the car in the next lane. If the girl turns off the freeway, HE pulls in behind her and starts following her" (Naifeh and Smith 1995, 328–29).

Template of the charming but deadly "lady-killer," Ted Bundy described himself as a "very non-violent person" (who nonetheless killed dozens of girls in his cross-country rampage). Apparently "there was a hidden Bundy—the 'entity,' as Ted first described him to me: a deviant killer who collected and preserved his victims' severed heads. . . . It was the 'entity' who sought credit for the murders, even as the public Ted indignantly disclaimed them" (Michaud 1998, 3–4). In his prison revelations Ted always spoke of himself in the third person. Sirhan Sirhan, the paranoid schizophrenic who shot Robert Kennedy (as commanded by "a voice"), always "referred to himself in the third person" (Ressler 1992, 42). Likewise did a possessed woman (in India) "speak of herself in the third person" (Oesterreich 1935, 213). Dissociated people can do this; Marie Noe (child killer) "seemed as though she was talking about somebody else" while describing her own "monstrous actions" (Glatt 2002, 185).

"He should be studied, not buried," said Albert DeSalvo, speaking dissociatively of the Boston Strangler—himself (Frank 1966, 252)! Dennis Rader (BTK) "was a Jekyll and Hyde"; during the manhunt, he wrote a letter speaking of the guilty one: "*he* [emphasis added] has already chosen his next victims and I don't know who they are yet. . . . The pressure is great and some-times he run the game to his liking. Maybe you can stop him. I can't" (Wenzl 2007, 322, 29).

I'd like to mention one curious cluster of behaviors that frequently forerun the homicidal career. The combination, starting in pre-adolescence, of bedwetting, animal torture, and fire setting is a strong foresign of escalating violence. It is known as the MacDonald Triad or the "homicidal triad." More than a half century before crime analysts identified the homicidal triad, the scriptures of Oahspe homed in on those unholy discarnates pulling the strings: "Vampire angels nestle in the atmosphere of mortals . . . [while] evil angels obsess mortals for murder's sake, to make mortals *burn houses and torture helpless creatures* [emphasis added]" (Oahspe, Book of Cpenta-Armij 2:2). "Evil angels" in this quotation refers to ex-mortals, members of the human race who have passed into spirit, but who return "to mortals purposely to inflict them with pain or misfortune" (Oahspe, Book of Bon 14:16).

The prosecutorial phrase "personification of evil" may be more apt than we realize: lacking physical bodies, evil spirits must find a mortal outlet, latch on, and "possess human beings. These earthbound spirits are the supposed devils of all ages—by-products of human selfishness, false teachings, and ignorance" (Wickland 1974, 18). Roger Depue, one-time chief of the FBI's Behavioral Science Unit, thought that "evil is more than a vague notion. It is an entity. . . . It has reflexes and intuition. . . . Those who do not believe the devil walks this earth have not seen the things that I have seen" (Depue 2005, 7).

When juvenile records are sealed, we may lose all evidence of the homicidal triad. This is unfortunate, as it is the keenest of warning signs. Nevertheless, we are now aware of other symptoms of malign invasion, portents that serve as harbinger of an obsessing entity.* Be on the lookout for

- the darkened eyes
- the malevolent laugh
- copious grimacing

---

*Exorcist Eugene Maurey would add one more indicator to this list—a certain stench: "The terrible odor indicated the presence of a strong killer entity, extremely dangerous" (Maurey 1988, 120–21). The inhabitants of hell "carried the foulness of their hells with them" (Oahspe, Book of Lika 14:7).

- coprolalia: streams of obscenities
- logorrhea: rapid, effusive, nonstop speech

The presence of a spiritual parasite may also be gleaned by what I can only call the unnatural gait. The FBI is not unaware of this warning sign and have, on a few occasions, included it in their profiles. Example: In 1992, while tracking down career criminal and serial killer James Wood (in Idaho), investigators put together a quick profile with the help of behavioral experts at Quantico. Our man would be a loner, strange and compulsive, possessed of a beer belly, driving a beater, and possibly walking with a limp.

The limp, though, may be different from the physical deformity suggested by the profilers. It may not be organic at all, but more like the "slight limp" noticed in Chikatilo, Russia's Red Ripper (Conradi 1992, 94), or the perplexing, painful limp acquired by Danny Starrett. The *dissociative* limp: it had started for Danny in childhood, along with other symptoms of overshadowing—headaches, dizziness, blackouts, "whisperings," and obsessive (automatic) drawing of sadistic scenes. No amount of doctors or tests could explain any of it. Most alarming was that the leg, which would slip out from under him (his left leg), was not growing as fast as the other one. The situation may be comparable to Dr. Crabtree's obsessed patient Karen, an adolescent whose limp was also without medical cause.* Like Danny S., she experienced both pain in, and shortening of, the left leg; fortunately for Karen, an exorcism was performed; Danny was not so lucky.

Accounts of crippling caused by spirit interference stretch from biblical times (Luke 13:11) to the casebook of Dr. Pierre Janet who preceded Dr. Freud and in fact coined the word *dissociation*. In one of Janet's cases it was reported that "the demon twisted his [patient's] arms and legs." And in the sad German case (1970s) of the possessed

---

*This difficulty is comparable to cases of hysterical lameness, so common in the nineteenth century. In 1857, for example, a patient named Betsey Cook, unable to walk, was brought before a healer / medium, having been diagnosed with nervous spasms (hysteria). The healer did her magic and Miss Cook got up and walked.

college girl, Anneliese Michel, her "limbs contorted in a grotesque way"; at other times, her legs would become stiff like sticks (Goodman 1981, 162). Similarly, in Haiti, participants in the trance-possession cult are known to go completely stiff limbed. FD (see page 68), also possessed, stated, "I have been told by both priests and psychiatrists that I had a case of demonic possession. . . . It somehow is able to injure me physically . . . so bad that I have been barely able to walk."

In every part of the world, "problems with the locomotive faculties . . . [have been] observed among the possessed" (Crapanzano and Garrison 1977, 94). This mysterious dysfunction also turns up among OCs (obsessive compulsives), like Darrel who, for some reason walked "stiffly" (Rapoport 1989, 87). Among autistic kids, too, are those who exhibit robotlike movements, or who feel like "cement," or who coordinate their limbs only with the most extreme and willful effort. Most significantly, autistics regularly report feeling "disconnected" from their bodies.

Some of the most compelling instances of the dissociative limp come from case studies in MPD. On several occasions, Billy Milligan (with twenty-four different personalities on board) was unable to walk without assistance. Another male multiple, Henry Hawksworth had an alter with a "peculiar walk." Dr. Crabtree's multiple patient Maria "was unable to walk normally." The multiple Kit C., with seven alters, also had trouble moving her legs.

We have reason to believe that any form of *spirit control* may affect the organism—limbs in particular. A poltergeist focal agent (age sixteen) is found to have a "funny walk." And back in the day when home séances were popular, "sitters" for physical phenomena and PK (psychokinesis) sometimes reacted with spasmodic jerks of the limbs. The jerking, it was believed, was caused by a reaction in their bodies, the sitters now harnessed as hosts for the materialization.

And the same sort of spasms are noticeable among psychopaths. Coincidence? I don't think so. For example, something was wrong with the Shoemaker's walk, his unsteady "shuffling"; "he walked with strange, jerky movements" (Schreiber 1984, 323, 371).

Let us take a moment to searchlight this unique clue—the overshadowed gait:

- Richard Chase, "The Vampire of Sacramento," moved "unsteadily from place to place . . . shuffling and dragging one foot" (Markman and Bosco 1989, 188, 170).
- Cho, the Virginia Tech shooter (2007), had undiagnosable trouble with his legs.
- One girlfriend of Fred Coe, compulsive rapist, noticed "the slight ungainliness in his rolling walk" (Olsen 1983, 61).
- California's notorious Zodiac lumbered along "like a bear."
- John List, familicide, had a "bouncy, awkward gait" (Sharkey 1990, 288).
- Jeff MacDonald, also familicide, "shuffled like an old man" (McGinnis 1983, 376).
- Melvin Rees, Maryland area serial killer (nine victims), had a "strange gait"; he waddled like a duck.
- Timothy McVeigh had an "awkward strut."
- Arthur Shawcross, at age ten, had come down with "a mysterious malady . . . crippl[ing] his legs" (Olsen 1993, 445).
- Peter Sutcliffe, the Yorkshire Ripper, had "a stiff walk" (Burn 1985, 48).
- Peter Woodcock, Toronto serial killer, had "a strange walk."

Our country is the world capital of serial killers, taking second place for rapes. When the world's emerging nations were polled to identify the biggest problems facing their country, crime scored the highest at 83 percent. Dr. Arthur Guirdham, a British psychiatrist with decades of experience treating the neurotic, the psychotic, the obsessed and possessed, spoke openly of the "enormous increase in acts of senseless violence . . . as we wade through the wreckage of civilization." Much of it, as he came to believe, is due to "the influence of malignant discarnates. . . . Generally speaking, the seemingly pointless crimes are due to possession" (Guirdham 1982, 209).

Let's face it, "tough on crime" posturing is more the vote-grabbing strategy than any kind of answer or solution. Neither are the system's "hired guns" (court psychiatrists) making any progress toward a solution. Working hand-in-glove with the powers that be, the so-called experts are only too happy to play the game, feeding us disingenuous adjectives—like *delusional* or *incomprehensible* or *subhuman*—instead of coming to grips with the decidedly paranormal aspects of mental illness and of crime. It costs, after all, a great deal more to care for mentally ill prisoners than "healthy," "sane" ones. But calling rabid crime an "ultimately unexplainable evil" (Douglas and Olshaker 2000, 464) is equivocation of the first order. It is only unexplainable when we refuse to explore Factor X.

Soul murder starts at home, and that's strong medicine—for any of us. But leave psyche out of the picture and we'll keep spinning our wheels, spinning yarns about the human mind that suit the status quo and enable nothing but a self-serving agenda.

> *The denial of the existence of spirit beings could have serious consequences.*
>
> DAVE HUNT AND T. A. MCMAHON,
> *THE NEW SPIRITUALITY*

* * *

Having once planned an entire book on "psi crime," I find myself swamped with material too copious for a single chapter. Lists and tables have helped me to compress some of these observations and main ideas; yet, so much more remains to be discussed! We have only skimmed the surface of parenting and toxic households. Other issues and problems may be just as critical. A significant portion of serial killers—Ramirez, Sutcliffe, Berkowitz, Gacy, Bianchi, Hofmann, Gein, and others—underwent excessive exposure to the dead as young men (in cemeteries, mortuaries, and the like). This is taken up in appendix B. In addition, appendix C covers the all-important role of early trauma—especially head trauma—in the unleashing of madness and mayhem.

5

"I SHALL WALK THE SKY"

There are other worlds and dimensions, and this should be taught in our schools as part of our general education.

ENA TWIGG, *ENA TWIGG: MEDIUM*

A dialogue between two infants in the womb concerning the state of this world might handsomely illustrate our ignorance of the next.

THOMAS BROWNE, 1605–1682

*Those of us who think
That death is an evil
Are in error.*

SOCRATES

The great soul Henry David Thoreau was only forty-five when, stricken with TB, he passed into spirit. "This is a beautiful world," he said, "but I shall see a fairer." His last words were, "The winter is coming when I shall walk the sky." Afterward, his sister said, "I feel as if something beautiful has happened—not death."

It is fitting, in this new era of enlightenment* that our understanding

---

*This New Dawn of Light is the subject of my book *Time of the Quickening* and my work-in-progress *The Kosmon Brief.*

of eternity should open up and all the myths and fables of the afterlife should melt away like a baffling dream of the night.

MYTH #1 — R.I.P.

Rest in peace?

> O man, beware of angels who say: When thou diest thy spirit shall enter paradise and dwell in perpetual ease and glory, or, who say: Heaven is an endless summer land, with silvery rivers and golden boats for all.
>
> OAHSPE, BOOK OF DISCIPLINE 3:22–3

When the great writer Herman Melville stayed in Polynesia, he heard the Taipii version of Paradise, with its never-ending supply of bananas and breadfruit, a place where "souls rested through eternity upon mats finer than those of the Taipii, and every day bathed their glowing limbs in rivers of coconut oil" (Williamson 1933, 2:44). Fanciful though it sounds, this is not too different from our own vision of "eternal rest," which the Victorian era so fondly but ineptly termed "the long silence." Even today theology teaches that the soul goes to sleep at the time of death and remains quiescent until the Last Judgment. This must be why people assume that death brings peace and rest. The departed, some think, lie in the earth in the "sleep of death" until their Savior comes; or the good Christian who dies goes immediately to be with her Lord (2 Corinthians 5:1–9, Philippians 1:21).

But is the afterdeath really such a placid existence—filled only by meaningless repose? Do we go to some far-off star and there dwell in peace ever after? Who invented this fairy tale?

> Who shall tell the story of heaven!... Can a man describe a million men, women and children? A hundred million! A billion! Five billion! ... And yet this is only the lower heaven! ... A strange voice rises up from the earth, saying: Have they anything to do in heaven? O

you Gods! ... And the countless millions who know little more than the beasts of the field! Yet mortals are falsely taught that the[y] would skip off to paradise and possess great learning in the hour of death!

OAHSPE, BOOK OF OSIRIS 7:1–3

The universe contains a principle of growth and development:
. . . We go not to some heaven of everlasting contemplation
and inertia. We have work to do—that is why we were born!
. . . Every human soul reaches perfection in time.
AUGUSTINE CAHILL, *DARKNESS, DAWN, AND DESTINY*

MYTH #2 — RICH REWARDS

Beware of angels who say: Eat, drink and enjoy yourself . . . for when you are dead your path shall be straight to glory.

OAHSPE, BOOK OF DISCIPLINE 3:24

Dr. J. B. Newbrough, amanuensis of the Oahspe bible (1882), had these thoughts on the Christian heaven: "Those who have been devout worshippers of Christ are expected to receive rich rewards. But in what shape has never been explained," except to say that "after a person has

Fig. 5.1. John Ballou Newbrough, 1828–1891

become sufficiently pure, he rises up and sits by Jesus . . . on the right hand of the Father . . . and a dove sits at the foot of the throne. . . . The purified have nothing more to do but sing and pray all their eternal lives . . . bowing and smiling forever" (quoted in Martinez 2009, appendix D).

MYTH #3
IN THE TWINKLING OF AN EYE

Think not that great wisdom cometh suddenly by dying . . . [yet] with faith in thy soul, thou shalt die and enter heaven fearlessly.

OAHSPE, BOOK OF JUDGMENT 20:19, 20:21

Somewhere along the line, someone started teaching that death, in the twinkling of an eye, endows us with universal knowledge or instantly improves our being in some important way. But as Chiang-X (Psychics 1972, 103) put it, "Because we are in another dimension, many people think that we are all-seeing and all-knowing. But that is not true . . . I am [only] a helper . . . and each of you has a helper* in our world who seeks to light a little path that is so often fraught with difficulties."

Death causes no change in the human spirit.

ARTHUR CONAN DOYLE,
THE EDGE OF THE UNKNOWN

Major General Alfred Drayson, a friend of Doyle's and scholar in his own right, held the same view, that is that every spirit passes over to the next world exactly as it is, with no change whatever. This world is full of wise or foolish people. So is the next.

---

*The progress of spirits depends on "extending helping hands to those on planes of life below . . . [simply because] no man can lift himself by his own bootstraps; each needs help" (Titus 1971, 117).

The next world is but an extension of this one, and whatever
we are here so shall we be there. Whatever possibilities we
have latent now shall be developed then.

AUGUSTINE CAHILL,
DARKNESS, DAWN, AND DESTINY

In recent years the psi literature has filled up with ADCs (after death communications) that offer sober, sometimes detailed, accounts of the change called death. As one soul newly arrived in the spirit world related, "Transition from the physical body to the ethereal body occupies only a matter of moments . . . I feel no different. Nothing angelic. . . . What do we do [here]? We do everything for which we are fitted" (Fuller 1986, 80). In other words, spirits "are apportioned to different [places] . . . according to their development, and proper officers and teachers are provided unto them" (Oahspe, Book of Thor 4:10). "You gravitate to a place you are fitted for," communicated a young man who had died in World War I; "there's no judge or jury, you just gravitate, like to like."

Each finds his place, each writes his own destiny. Robert Monroe called it a homing device: familiar with the outer regions from his own extensive OBEs, Monroe thought that "your destination in heaven (or hell) . . . seems to be grounded within the framework of your deepest *constant* motivations, emotions, and personality [which] act as your homing device when you enter this realm" (Monroe 1971, 121).

MYTH #4 — ANGELS

In Western society, one thinks of angels as beings of some separate or higher evolution—bouncy little cherubic creatures with wings, haloes, and pale beatific faces. Yet angels are nothing more than the souls of the dead, of the departed. The wise Cicero underscored this point: "Is not almost all heaven filled with the human? Those very gods themselves had their original [sic] here below, and ascended from hence into heaven" (Wickland 1974). And this is why the earthborn gods call themselves, simply, Elder Brother.

A human being on the physical plane is called a corporean and on the spiritual plane, an essean, an angel. As Dr. Betty explained, "We are one kind of being, and spirits are another. We are visible and they are not. We are subject to the laws of physics and they are not. We have physical bodies and they do not. Yet they are as conscious as we are, as individual as we are" (Betty 2012, 28).

Jehovih said: On corpor, bring | forth man into life, and | give him a corporeal body, which is a womb for the spirit to dwell in;* and when | deliver him from this womb he becometh an inhabitant of atmospherea. . . . Man | gave a corporeal body that he might learn corporeal things; but death | made that he might rise in spirit and inhabit my etherean worlds. . . . My heavens are for raising the soul upward, for ever and ever!

OAHSPE, BOOK OF SAPHAH: OSIRIS 121,

AND BOOK OF KNOWLEDGE

All men go to spirit at death and become angels—but angels are of all characters and grades, including guardian angels (*ashars*), matchmaking angels (*loo'is*), materializing angels (*sargis*), and others who work for the upliftment of souls; as well as bad angels (*daevas*), lusters (angels of secret vice), chaotics (deranged angels), and drujas. The ashars' job is to make a record of every mortal, of the grade of his wisdom and goodness, and when that mortal dies and his spirit is delivered, his record is delivered with him to the Es world.

The grade of a man—or for that matter of a nation—can be measured on a scale from 1 to 99, the latter being the highest possible grade, while grade 1 is the lowest. All the great prophets, from Zarathustra to Joshu (Jesus), were above grade 90. As Justin Titus

---

*The Eloist Brothers put it this way: "Just as a fetus resides in a womb, which is the ideal environment in which to grow until it is strong enough to subsist on its own, our spirit is at first housed in a corporeal body, until it is strong enough to subsist on its own in the eternal world of Spirit. . . . Angelic beings are not a separate order in creation, but once-mortals like us" (Oahspe Eloist Edition, xvi–iii).

Fig. 5.2. Icon of Es, the unseen world, where angels live. Es, in Aramaic, meant "spirit." Es encompasses all that is beyond. The gaps in the circle represent openings for light to reach us, coming from the higher (emancipated) heavens.

(1971, 148, 31) put it, "the elevator to heaven is not running, take the stairs—the grades. . . . Eventually every man must climb those grades and develop strength, purity, love and power through the exertion that comes through climbing." Though many factors combine to establish one's personal grade, the scheme is essentially a measure of goodness, of benevolence, of service to others: grade 1 represents complete selfishness, while grade 99 represents the highest degree of selflessness. In fact, the Tetracts of the ancients defined sa'tan (Satan) as the most pernicious of man's inclinations, and its oldest translation was "selfishness per se."

There is nothing complicated or abstract or metaphysical in this philosophy. It is as straightforward as a simple act of kindness—or malice. Crime analysts "believe the psychopath is fundamentally a self-absorbed person . . . [motivated by] a global attitude of selfishness" (Kirwin 1997, 88). Selfishness is, according to Dr. Nandor Fodor, the ultimate key to malign overshadowing, for he defines "possession [as] an invasion of the living by a disincarnated spirit . . . for the purpose of selfish [emphasis added] gratification by the spirit." As one overshadowed individual experienced it, the entity harassing her "doesn't feel malicious, just selfish" (Sagan 1997, 17). And by the same token, one

Fig. 5.3. Ancient sign of selfishness. "The more a man's Spirit is wrapped up in his own materiality, the more is he influenced by the spirits of darkness" (Howard 1971, 136).

criminologist explained that women who kill their own children "are all self-involved. The babies mean nothing." Like Marie Noe who killed eight of her own babies: "The baby cried all the time and was getting on her nerves" (Glatt 2002, 169, 67).

The same philosophy moves our smartest psychic researchers to declare that "spiritual growth is synonymous with service to others" (Maurey 1988, 66). Again, there is nothing mystical about it. "As these grades are on earth, so [they are] in the heavens thereof and in all cases [they] depend on *what one does for others*" (emphasis added) (Oahspe, Book of Judgment 9:16). We ourselves determine our rank in the here and hereafter—according to our capacity to unfold others, to lift them up, to give joy or comfort.

Self-improvement, self-realization, and all personal enhance-

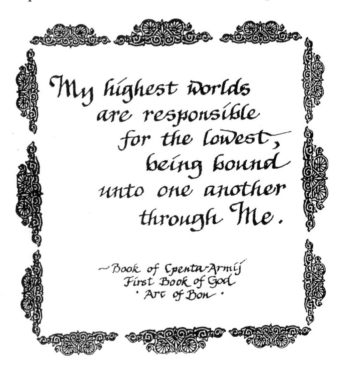

Fig. 5.4. Another verse that amplifies the meaning:

Inasmuch as ye raise up them that are beneath you, so will I send them who are above down to you, to raise you up also.

OAHSPE, BOOK OF FRAGAPATTI 15:14

ment may be ideals of the New Age—but, being almost exclusively *self-absorbed,* have little to do with the soul's actual progress. Indeed, among the highest grades, responsibility is felt for all who are beneath. "Did not the Great Spirit make all things by giving?" said Confucius, aka Ka'yu (Oahspe, Book of Saphah: Tablet of Biene 16).

> *I believe that a life well lived is a journey toward selflessness.*
> *It begins with the importance of self, and ends with the*
> *importance of others.*
> ROGER DEPUE, *BETWEEN GOOD AND EVIL*

"I created man to enter heaven as helpless as he entered earth life, and dependent on those above him, so that he might comprehend the unity between high and low, strong and weak, light and darkness; and I placed him in My mills, where he would learn that even as others grind for him, so should he grind for those beneath him. . . . Because they stoop from their high estate in order to promote My children, are they not becoming more one with Me? . . . And those who follow My example, raising the low to make them have joy in life, are on the road to attain to all power, wisdom and love" (Oahspe, Book of Aph 8:27–9).

"In the spirit world our gospel is good works, and no other. . . . Good works must be done unto others before the spirit can rise" (Newbrough 1874, 48). "Nor have I provided resurrection in this world, or in my heavens above, except by good works done to others . . . and not because of any worship or confessions done before any idols. . . . Nor is there any redemption in heaven to the Brahmins, Buddhists, Kriste'yans or Mohammedans because of their prayers and confessions, but wherever good works have resulted in lifting the people up out of misery and crime" (Oahspe, Book of Judgment 3:24–26).

Thus spake Sakaya (aka Buddha): "Consider, then, what you can do that will raise you in spirit; for this is resurrection. First, to purify yourselves; second, to do all the good you can; and third, to affiliate . . . practicing sharply the convictions of the heart. . . . Without these, there can be no resurrection" (Oahspe, God's Book of Eskra 30:17).

SAKAYA of INDIA

Fig. 5.5. Buddha, aka the prophet Sakaya, circa 500 BCE

"Consider your corporeal body as a ship, in which your spirit is sailing across a wide sea of water. It is better that your spirit learns to acquire strength while it has a corporeal body to ride in. For after death it floats [willy-nilly] in the direction you have shaped it. Neither do you have power to go against the current" (Oahspe, Book of Judgment 13:33). And there are perks to learning this lesson early: "Whatsoever service he did in mortal life . . . shall stand to his credit two-fold in spirit" (Oahspe, Book of Divinity 5:8). The perks are also in the here and now; as W. E. Butler (1978, 227) once observed, "Most people find that to be able to help others . . . gives them an increased pleasure in living . . . [howsoever] this basic urge in man is often smothered beneath a code of selfishness and egotism. But every now and then it shows itself."

Souls, in short, rise (resurrect) in accordance with their own efforts. And their progress is ever upward, from one heaven to the next. These heavens above the Earth extend outward on higher and higher plateaus, separate belts, as it were, some a thousand miles high. The ongoing journey has been called Eternal Progression; hence the hidden meaning of Jacob's Ladder and the staircase glyph so often seen in ancient pictographs. Indeed, the afterlife, the heaven world, is stratified, hierarchical, consisting of separate spheres.* One newly arrived in the first sphere happened to send an ADC (posthumous message) to his loved ones. He said, "there are other places to visit in the spirit world. It is not like heaven as one would think. It seems that there are different spheres where people who think alike reside" (Van Praagh 2008, 33).

To explore heaven we must begin at the bottom, the very bottom of the heap. Closest to the earth is the region anciently known as hada (expressed in the Greek word *hades*).

Hada, essentially, is hell—at least fifteen miles above the surface of the earth. Oh, it is a place all right, not just a condition. In his daring out-of-body experiments, Robert Monroe traversed a place he called Locale II, "a gray-black hungry ocean where the slightest motion attracts nibbling and tormenting beings." This, he thought, must be "the borders of hell." Monroe aptly describes the denizens of Locale II as fishlike (and himself as bait), for it is also known as the plateau of animal creation† (Monroe 1971, 120–21). Here abide the lowest grades, the drujas, who wander in

Fig. 5.6. Glyph of hada. No, hell is not down there in the bowels of the earth, but is the first and most disagreeable habitation out from the earth, home to the dregs of humanity, where angels torment one another.

---

*Although modern man has not been schooled in the hierarchy of cosmic administration, anthropologists have observed numerous Third World cultures that subscribe to this layered pattern of the afterworld. Haitian cosmology, for one, has the vodoun pantheon arranged in a "hierarchical order of spirits" (Davis 1985, 44). The same can be said of Malaysian and Brazilian doctrines, which are wonderfully elucidated in Vincent Crapanzano's *Case Studies in Spirit Possession* (1977, 322, 335–40).

†Justin Titus, a Christian then Faithist minister (1976, 34–35), too, thinks that "all undeveloped people . . . are really human animals, and when viewed from higher spiritual light, they appear as animals. . . . Such persons gravitate to the animal plane of life provided by a wise Creator for the maturation of unripe spirit people. The animal plane is a sort of sub-basement kindergarten."

darkness with no understanding of, and less interest in, spiritual things. British-Canadian researcher Joe Fisher inadvertently became acquainted with hada, describing it as the "thickly-peopled 'dead zone' just beyond the frontiers of physical existence . . . the lower astral realm, a gloomy cesspool of the dead, peopled by the spirits of those who have lived base, ignorant, or selfish lives" (Fisher 2001, 272–73).

All this is in contrast to higher locales like the Celestial City, seen by the Eloists: "Its gridwork of Lights are [*sic*] not formed from street lamps but are the soul-lights of millions of consecrated angels set amongst iridescent alabaster libraries and temples and meeting houses that cover the countryside. They are every bit as real, alive and busy as those of any mortal city, but exalted and purified as they lie nestled throughout the many plateaus of the [firmament]" (the Eloist publication *Radiance*, Special Session, April 1985, 28). Others who have ventured into the astral realm have come upon cities. Conan Doyle, for one, in a rare OBE, encountered what he called "a probationary city" with instructors. Just above hada, this is the first resurrection, the place where one receives his primary education in Es—but only when he quits his aimless existence below and voluntarily enlists in the "organic" kingdoms.

Now he is treated like a newborn spirit (an Es'yan), is covered in a comforting birth blanket and attended by celestial nurses and physicians. A few ADCrs have spoken of this awakening; a fellow named Claude passed away and described regaining consciousness inside of some sort of hospital and asking a doctor where he was. The doctor explained that he had left his physical body. Indeed, Oahspe (Aph 9:3 and Lika 23:18) details how "schools and hospitals and nurseries . . . are adapted to receive those of the first resurrection. . . . Teachers and nurses and physicians . . . deliver [them] out of darkness . . .

Fig. 5.7. Sign of Es'yan, infant spirit

yea, every one of them shall become as a star of glory in heaven."

Once restored, the new inhabitant of Es begins his explorations—and his education. He learns the rites and discipline of the intermediate world as well as its amusements, excursions, festivals, sports, concerts, music, dancing, and so on. Depending on his progress, he may spend fifty or five hundred years here, laboring in factories, training at special centers, or attending college.

Granted a peek at the Other Side, clairvoyant John Edward "was shown . . . a college campus: a series of large buildings . . . the largest one referred to as the Hall of Knowledge" (Edward 2004, 152). Other spirit travelers have spoken of "huge systems of education, huge laboratories and institutions" on the Other Side (Fuller 1986). Oahspe exalts "their libraries of records of valorous and holy deeds! A council chamber of half a million souls! Hundreds of departments; thousands! Here a board to select young students to the colleges of messengers. Another board to select students to the colleges of arts. Another to select students to mathematics. Another for prophecy. . . . Another for factories. Another for compounding and dissolving elements. Then come the departments of the cosmogony of the stars; then, of the ethereal worlds; then, the roadways of the firmament" (Oahspe, Book of Osiris 7:1–3).

Apprenticeships run the gamut from the art and science of cosmic travel and food production to painting, marching, and other skills. The student may be trained as craftsman, nurse-assistant, physician-assistant (restoring spirits in chaos and delivering them from the hells of hada); the trainee graduates, in turn, to full-ranking nurse, full rank of physician; then maker of fabrics, transporter of food, then creatif (learning how to create), then science college and architecture. Finally he is eligible to enter the School of Light and Darkness, after which his labor is in building and propelling heavenly boats (Oahspe, Book of Divinity 3:16–29) for short-and long-distance travel.

But it is not all sunshine. Jammed into the first resurrection are the Christian heaven, the Mormon heaven, the Buddhist heaven, and so forth, down to every cult and sect and dogma claiming divinity, salvation, or instant enlightenment. Indeed, the first resurrection is like a huge city, extremely crowded (compared to the upper regions);* most arrive here quite ignorant of a spirit life. "Really, amongst us in the spirit world, there are more of these than the sands of the sea" (Newbrough 1874, Question # 20).

As long as 7,000 years ago, the gods and angels were cautioned: "Be thou careful of too much leniency toward the spirits in the first resurrection. Suffer them not to abide with mortals as teachers. Remember that mortals so love their dead kindred, they would even deprive them of heavenly education, for the sake of having them around . . . [just as] the spirits of the recently dead so love their mortal kindred that they would seek no higher heaven than to linger around them on earth. Which habit groweth upon them, so that in two or three generations they become drujas, worthless to themselves, knowing little of earth and less of heaven" (Oahspe, Book of Fragapatti 34:17).

Not only are the neophytes in these upper kingdoms prohibited from such earthside forays, but a similar prohibition restrains more advanced angels; even guardian angels are not allowed to return to mortals *individually* but only in phalanxes of millions: "nor shall ye ever make yourselves known to him [mortal protégé]" (Oahspe, Bon's Book of Praise 39:8), guiding him only indirectly by such gentle means as dreams, inspirations, and visions. "Thy God cometh not as an individual; neither do my Lords nor holy angels . . . [but they] come in legions of thousands and millions" (Oahspe, Book of Discipline 3:15).

The lower heavens of today are full of spirits informing poor deluded mediums that they are Christ, God, Confucius, Shakespeare, Washington, Lincoln, or any other person who commands the respect of men.

WING ANDERSON,
SEVEN YEARS THAT CHANGED THE WORLD

---

*"Of the wise and good, who strive for continual elevation—how few, compared to the whole! Yet such is the relative proportions of angels of light and angels of darkness . . . and thus hath it ever been" (Oahspe, Book of Discipline 3:14–15).

Likewise comes the sage advice of those who have learned (usually the hard way) to disregard "spirit guides" and other pretenders masquerading as superior intelligences. So-called ascended masters or ancient brotherhoods or benevolent Higher Self or wise beings from Sirius all throw my BS meter into the red zone. These "hyenas" (spiritual phonies) were the bane of the early spirit circles. "This also happens to many . . . they shall imagine themselves controlled by certain angels, when in fact, it is only their own spirit eliminated from the corporeal senses" (Howard 1971, 136).

We have been advised, many times, to beware of spirits claiming such high estate:

- "Few evolved spirits visit the earth. . . . It is simply unwise to attract any discarnate spirit to you" (Maurey 1988, 63, 131).
- "Most [otherworldly] manifestations proceed from a low order of spirits who hover near the earth sphere" (William Stainton, the great medium, in his *Notebook*, Dec. 1872).
- "Mediumship merely invites earthbound spirits" (Fisher 2001, 276).
- "The chances against genuine communication are ten to one. . . . It is wise and sane not to make the attempt" (H. Smith 1919).

Frankly, those excarnates most eager to communicate with the living are usually the least informed, least mature, occupying merely the first rung of the vast firmament. "And it has been shown that the spirits of the dead possess, for a long period of time, the same characteristics and prejudices as when in mortality, and since there is neither harmony nor community of life among mortals, neither is there harmony nor community of life among the angels who manifest to these mortals. For these angels teach one doctrine through one prophet, and another doctrine through another prophet. And it came to pass that the wiser, better angels, weary of the wrangling and deceit of these self-serving Es'yans, departed away to inhabit a heavenly region by themselves. And this was the beginning of the second resurrection" (Oahspe, Book of

Discipline 2:11–12). These deceivers are known to build up their following among mortals by flattery: either by professing great names, like Jean Dixon who told her biographer that "the same spirit that worked through Isaiah and John the Baptist also works through me" (Noorbergen 1976, 114); or by pandering to their hosts' earthly desires for profit or war or marriage or any worldly ambition whatsoever.

> And we came up out of the first resurrection, which may be likened to a great medley, a noise and confusion of a mighty multitude, [and] covenanted to make ourselves orderly, a unit in growth . . . and development, so that the place of the second resurrection would do nothing in common with the first.
>
> OAHSPE, BOOK OF DISCIPLINE 3:2

We need only focus on the words *unit in growth* (meaning collaboration) to understand the power of the second resurrection and why it is called organic. One dreamer, carried aloft until the "earth and the physical realm seemed insignificant . . . a speck of sand," found herself in "a very expansive place" where an ineffable unity bonded "thousands of entities together. . . . We were all one, yet each of us was separate." It is here in the second resurrection that harmony, alliance, and belongingness truly come alive. "They apply themselves not to isolated developments, but to affiliation" (Oahspe, Book of Judgment 24:10). Contrast this with the first resurrection of *individual* striving: "Every spirit in these [lower] heavens hath a philosophy of his own" (Oahspe, Book of Fragapatti 31:7).

"In the Afterdeath," communicated F. W. H. Myers-X, "we become more and more aware of this group-soul as we make progress." Having left personal desires behind, it is natural to attune to each other; thought alone, so fine are these ethers, serves as a universal language. There is no possibility of misunderstanding. One breathes the air of sympathy and rapport. No longer concerned with their own salvation, they are already saved—by their mutual work of upliftment.

"How shall the second resurrection give up its mysteries? . . . How can a man describe a million men and women and children [existing in harmony]?" (Oahspe, Book of Osiris 7:2). Each contributing his unique talent to the greater whole! Spirits who have quit their old haunts and joined organic associations, being enlisted in companies, either for labor or for receiving heavenly instruction, shall be known as being in the second resurrection. "But such spirits as have attained to etherean grades . . . having ascended beyond atmospherea into the etherean worlds, shall be known as being in the third resurrection" (Oahspe, Book of Lika 14:8).

God said: Now behold, O man, I have declared my first and second resurrections to you. And in like manner is the third resurrection, but still higher. And so on, are all the heavens higher and higher, until the inhabitants of them become very Lords and Gods.

OAHSPE, BOOK OF JUDGMENT 32:1

The third resurrection begins the emancipation of the human soul, and it leads to Nirvana.

"I come to prove three worlds to men. First, the earth and its fullness; second, the intermediate world of spirits, where all shall sojourn

Fig. 5.8. Sign of Nirvana. Sakaya (Buddha) said, "The spirits of the lower heavens, like mortals, have multitudes of doctrines; and for the most part they know nothing of the higher heavens, Nirvania, which I proclaim to you" (Oahspe, God's Book of Eskra 30:13). One of the time-honored terms carefully preserved by the Sanskrit sages, Nirvana designates the higher heavens (in etherea), headquarters of the Gods and Goddesses of endless light.

for a season; and third, the Nirvanian worlds beyond Chinvat, where, for the pure and wise, unending paradise awaits" (Oahspe, First Book of God 17:23).

Beyond the Earth and its moon (the frontier known as Chinvat) lies Nirvana, in the Orian realms, populated by all who are gentle and good; it encompasses countless domains, with names like Otaskaka, "World of Shining Waters," and it involves awesome projects such as making roadways for corporeal stars, which labor might employ 90 billion Nirvanians for thousands of years. To him who has attained Nirvana, the past as well as things to come are as an open book; for here one masters attunement with the magnitude of worlds, which condition awaits all men.

> *The day will not be long when you too will be in our realm of spirit and become a co-worker with us, watching the antics of earth life from our side of the great veil you call death.*
>
> A COMMUNICATION RECEIVED BY
> THE ELOISTS IN "SPECIAL SESSION"

The day will come when we will walk these skies—adventuring among their plains and high arches and heavenly caverns amid Orian fields and mountains and crystal fountains—the great visiting places of millions of gods and goddesses, landscapes with bridges and high clefts and seas where course a thousand million ships of light; filled also with farms and roads and cities and valleys—endless places of matchless beauty ripened unto the Boundless Everlasting Creator of All.

Enlightenment awaits every soul. Wisdom came to Bucky Fuller: upon receiving news of a friend's death, he declared, "Whatever life may be it is not physical. I assume all humans to be immortal." He comforted the bereaved, telling them that the news of the deceased, "being no longer temporally available . . . did not alter my sense of their absolute livingness . . . I go right on seeing them. There they are" (Zung 2001, 82).

If all came but to ashes of dung

. . . .

. . . then Alarum! For we are betray'd . . .

. . . .

Do you think I could walk pleasantly and well-suited
    toward annihilation?

. . . .

I swear I think now that every thing without exception
    has an eternal soul!

. . . .

I swear I think there is nothing but immortality!
That the exquisite scheme is for it . . .
And all preparation is for it . . . and life and materials
    are altogether for it!

WALT WHITMAN,
FROM "TO THINK OF TIME"

6

THE UNSEEN GUEST

If you hear voices (out of the blue) you're crazy, right? Hallucinating, psychotic, schizophrenic, a lunatic. Right? Well . . . maybe. Or maybe we all hear a voice from time to time, and there's nothing crazy about it, just a bit mysterious. After all, didn't most of the prophets hear the Voice? Don't mystics honor "the still, small voice"? Psychic-sensitives who can hear spirits are called clairaudient; and the wiser among them, if bothered by pesky voices, simply ignore them. The voices heard by criminal psychopaths (see table 4.1 on page 84) were, unfortunately, not ignored. Indeed, their sadistic commands were taken seriously; they somehow wielded power over their hosts.

If the mystic voice (sometimes called conscience) is peaceful and gentle, bringing inspiration, we are on higher ground. However, when the voice is intrusive or prankish or bullying, we are in the orbit, not only of the paranormal but the abnormal—obsessing earthbound entities who, as we have seen, may even clothe themselves as spirit guides or Higher Self. The woman known as Eve (*The Three Faces of Eve*) heard a voice that "she could not escape . . . a woman's voice . . . often using vulgar phrases" (Thigpen and Cleckley 1957, 23). But the petite and demure Eve did not mention the voice when she first stepped into the psychiatrist's office (back in the early 1950s), having been referred there after neurological examination, X-ray, and laboratory studies disclosed no physical cause of her blinding headaches.

No, it was not the Voice (which she still kept a secret*) that drove her to Dr. Thigpen's office but "the overwhelming pain that seemed to pierce right through the flesh into the bone marrow . . . like a steel hand squeezing your brain" (Lancaster 1958, 41).

Yet the Voice and the pain—and blackouts as well—were inseparable things; just as "the headaches and the voices always came together" for Danny Starrett (Naifeh and Smith 1995, 152). For Eve, first it was the Voice. Then the headache. Then the blackout. She finally told her doctor about the Voice, and having dropped her guard . . . she began to change. At first, she looked dazed; then she stiffened, feeling the familiar tremor in her stomach. Then "utter blankness" followed by a "rippling transformation. . . . She winced as she put her hands to her temples, pressed hard, and twisted them as if to combat sudden pain. A slight shudder passed over her entire body. Then the hands lightly dropped and she relaxed" (Thigpen and Cleckley 1957, 58, 23). It was the first time her doctor would meet Eve Black, her other "self."

"Who are you?" he asked.

"Why, I'm Eve Black," she replied.

There had been times when Eve managed to ignore the Voice, but at the price of a paralyzing headache, often followed by blackout. "She thought she could bottle me up," chortled Eve Black. "Well, I showed her." Later, Eve Black would explain the headaches to the doctor: "She got them from trying to keep me from getting out. She didn't know it, but when she tried to stop me, her head would give her hell. The blackouts, of course, showed she hadn't gotten away with it. They came when I was out" (Lancaster 1958, 41). Though Eve Black was brash and shallow, her insight was canny. Dr. Guirdham, for one, had come to the same conclusion about headaches: "I have seen patients in whom the noises in the head were clear indications that discarnate entities were trying to establish contact. . . . These noises are essentially efforts of his own personality to blur the messages that discarnates wish to transmit" (Guirdham 1982, 104–5).

---

*Many others have been unwilling to discuss the Voice, "fearing to approach a psychiatrist, because he might put her away" (S. Smith 1970b, 154).

Another multiple suffered the same syndrome: "There is too much noise. Headaches are horrendous" (Cohen et al. 1991, 123).

There were times when Eve would literally run away from the headache: she would just take off, attempting to leave the pain behind.* One day she was found unconscious at the foot of a tree, her forehead cut. "She had run full tilt into the tree in one of her blind, agonized flights from the pain of a headache" (Lancaster 1958, 43).

Eve, of course, became the first multiple personality to make big news and ultimately a Hollywood film. Most therapists of that day made a point of saying that the disorder, MPD, was "rare" (so rare, that they had no adequate explanation of it). But this was a self-serving blind; the condition in fact has gotten much more common, if only because psychiatrists have been forced to acknowledge it! Nonetheless, the ultimate significance of the headache remains ignored—by the very profession that presumes to illuminate the human psyche. This chapter takes a closer look at headaches—and nightmares.

> *The person with migraine is par excellence a perceiver of psychic factors, including discarnate entities.*
>
> ARTHUR GUIRDHAM,
> *THE PSYCHIC DIMENSIONS OF MENTAL HEALTH*

If (as I argue, along with Dr. Guirdham) the psychic headache represents the organism's frantic attempt to throw off an uninvited guest (*geist,* ghost), this would explain (1) why no amount of tests reveals any organic cause of the pain, (2) why drugs cannot help, and (3) why the alter, once "out," feels no pain at all. It would also explain why MPs (multiples) are so headache prone. Let's briefly searchlight this:

- "I wish all therapists would understand the physical pain involved with headaches. . . . Physical pain makes functioning

---

*There is a certain parallel here with OCD "exercisers," compulsive walkers or runners who count on physical exertion to distract them from the unholy presence that is worming its way into their mind.

impossible" (Cohen et al. 1991, 122; quoting Reane, an MP).

- Truddi Chase, a supermultiple with ninety-two known personalities (called the Troops), said to her doctor, "Nothing stops them [headaches]. I take Tylenol more for security than relief" (Chase 1987, 25).
- Another famous multiple (with sixteen alters), Sybil (played by Sally Field in the 1976 TV movie), had almost constant pain in her head.
- A female physician was in therapy for almost four years before her alters were discovered: after a confrontation with her doctor she complained of a terrible headache. Very soon after that, her four hidden personalities emerged.
- Helene Smith, a multiple, complained of pain at the base of the skull, in her head, *whenever an alter takes over.*
- A French multiple, Felida, suffered acute pains in various parts of her body; when she had pains in her forehead, she fell into a profound "sleep" from which she awoke as an entirely different person, smiling and gay and feeling no pain (Fodor 1966, 279).

In the case of Jenny (a supermultiple, abused in childhood by Satanists, with not less than 400 personas in her orbit!), the therapist noted that her headaches "often signaled the presence of an alter trying to surface. . . . The headaches were caused by . . . having to hold back another personality" (Spencer 1989, 201, 239, 249). Periods of memory loss—called lost time, in the patois—went hand in hand with Jenny's blackouts: someone else had taken over. Jenny simply wasn't there.

Then there is Alice, a Connecticut housewife who took to using barbiturates, then heroin, "to drown out the voice in her head." She had no idea she was a multiple; there were five alters, as it turned out. Alice "was also losing time . . . [and] had persistent headaches . . . caused by the pressure of the various personalities struggling to gain control" (Mayer 1989, 97).

That takeover is called switching. When one of Cam West's twenty-four alters took over, "my head began to throb and I felt myself falling into the dark zone" (West 1999, 131). Something about that dark zone reminds me of the utter darkness in which some migraine sufferers feel compelled to sequester themselves. An Australian housewife suffering from severe depression perceived a shadow "in her left iliac area." She told the healer, Samuel Sagan, "It just feels dead. Cold. . . . It just likes to be left alone. . . . It likes the dark. Like a cave." Sagan also treated a plumber with an entity attached. It "just wants to be left alone in the dark . . . doesn't want to let the light in" (Sagan 1997, 17, 8).

This mysterious aversion to light may be a sign of hyperesthesia, a baffling condition, sometimes painful, entailing superacuity of the normal senses: an oversensitivity to light, sound, touch, and smell. For the multiple Eve, the simple movement of an eyelid could be an agonizing experience. But no single group has a monopoly on this curious malady; we find it among psychotic criminals (like Richard Speck who had to lie in the dark when his headaches were bad), or among phobics, drug users, and autists, as well as among those suffering nervous breakdown, multiple personality disorder, and spirit possession. In all cases, though, the experience belies an ASC. A paranormal phenomenon. An Elsewhere experience.

For the psychedelic tripper, "the faintest vibrations [were] vastly amplified" (Warnke et al. 1972, 20). The phobic personality may also be acutely sensitive to visual stimuli, touch, and taste; while the OBEr may feel "like a nerve is exposed," the vividness of things "increased a hundredfold" (Battersby 1979, 47). It is as if the person's spirit, detached from his body and hovering at the threshold of etheric space (the rarified nonphysical world) is then jarred by the return to dense matter. In such cases, the sensory pathways are suddenly much too porous.

Occultists call that rarified nonphysical world the astral realm. In one weird case of astral projection, reported by England's H. F. P. Battersby, so acute was the perception of the experiencer that he saw "the molecules of objects . . . [even] the clusters of veins and nerves [of his own body] vibrating like a swarm of luminous living atoms." Another OBEr felt "a snapping pain in her head" so intense it forced her back into her body (Battersby 1979, 50–51). *Anyone* catapulted into the outer zone may endure such parasensory effects.

Migraines seem to be a common complaint among autists, who straddle the precarious frontier of the unseen world. The psychic headache, not surprisingly, is also an occupational hazard among mediums (sensitives). As Nandor Fodor (1966, 294), the great analyst and psi investigator, saw it, "Once we admit the possibility of the soul leaving the body, we have to admit the possibility of another spirit entering it. . . . We are seeing a mind use a brain." In fact, psi research has discovered that the base of the brain is a major point of entry for psychic forces.

A girl named Heather, part of a teen vampire gang, "would struggle for domination of her mind . . . believing she had an alternate personality hidden in her system. Heather's headaches were sometimes so severe, her skin would become tight and her face would take on a faint white color" (Jones 1999, 176). It seems that the more bizarre or villainous the person's behavior, the more wicked the headache. The overshadowing of Danny Starrett (serial rapist) has already been touched on. Despite his crimes, "Danny didn't really fit the classical profile of a serial anything . . . he wasn't a loner. . . . In fact, he appeared to be quite the all-American." Frankly, Danny came off more like a multiple (MPD) than a hard-boiled sex offender—what with his voices, headaches, blackouts, unexplainable absences, and use of the third person—*Him*—when talking of himself. First came the voice (whispering), then the blasting headache. It was "like his whole head is going to explode." Blackouts and lost time followed. Danny explained: "It just starts . . . like my whole brain is engulfed in it . . . I begin to get tense, because I know what's coming next. I get that panicky feeling . . . I'm trying to stop it . . . I feel like I'm going to throw up, and the dull pain in my head [is] getting more intense. And then, for lack of a better description, I feel reality changing" (Naifeh and Smith 1995, 333, 178, 145).

Although each and every case is unique, there is a notable sameness in the symptoms of the criminally obsessed. We saw them hearing the voice; we saw them losing control (chapter 4). Now we see them stricken by the savage headache. Yet these are all part of the same cycle, a single syndrome with all the earmarks of malign invasion. The pattern is so familiar, so common, space allows only a brief summary:

TABLE 6.1.
HEADACHES SIGNAL ENTITY
INTRUSION IN BIZARRE HOMICIDES

Killer's name	Nature of headaches	Signs of overshadowing
Ken Bianchi	recurrent headaches	MPD: had a "twin spirit," logorrhea, and night terrors (O'Brien 1985, 182)
Jerry Brudos	"blinded with pain" for most of his life by migraines, followed by blackouts; "excrutiating pain" (Rule 1988b, 20, 41, 45)	compulsive, hyperpraxic
Eric Chapman	violent headaches, felt a "tight band" around his head	believed he was controlled by people's thoughts; overshadowed by dead uncle
Richard Chase	wrapped his throbbing head in a cloth and stood on his head to get the blood down into it	thought someone was "controlling his mind" (Markman and Bosco 1989, 168)
Ed Gein	constant complaint of headaches	"a force . . . [like] an evil spirit . . . built up in me" (Schecter 1989, 190)
Gary Gilmore	"savage headaches," "lifelong bout with migraines"	hauntings, compulsions, voices; in thrall to "the darkness beyond" (Gilmore 1994, 250, 212, 348)
Gary Heidnik	headaches and dizzy spells	hallucinations, "divine messages" (Douglas and Olshaker 1998, 390)

Killer's name	Nature of headaches	Signs of overshadowing
Joe Kallinger	severe pain in both temples	"I knew I was going out—that is, ceasing to be the normal me—whenever I heard the voice. I'd get a headache . . . then, it was It that controlled me"; he'd end up 70 miles away without knowing how he got there (Schreiber 1984, 101, 145)
Jeff MacDonald	frequent severe headaches	many signs of malign invasion, including "changed personality" just before the attack (McGinnis 1983, 609)
Richard Macek	chronic headaches	hyperpraxia, supernatural blisters, "zombie" (Morrison 2004, 32, 43, 28, 35)*
Jason Nelson	intense migraines that lasted a week	neighbors "attribute his crimes to demonic forces" (Markman and Bosco 1989, 8, 14–16)
Marie Noe	"suffered frequent blackouts with her migraine headaches"; at 14, went temporarily blind with an acute migraine	ASCs plus amnesiac (of killing her children) (Glatt 2002, 58, 37, 222)
Richard Ramirez	"hot-knives-through-the-head migraines" and blackouts	coprolalia, hyperpraxia, suicidal, dual (Carlo 1996, 289)
Arthur Shawcross	sharp headaches	automatisms, fugue, rapid cycling (chapter 9) OBEs, hyperesthesia, voices, coprolalia
"Solly"	pounding headaches	sleepwalking, compulsions, lost time, thought an "intruder" had killed his wife

*Yet forensic psychiatrist Helen Morrison (2004, 32) insists that his chronic headaches were "psychosomatic, perhaps due to overwhelming, disorganized feelings about his crimes or worry about his forthcoming trials." Do we need specialists for this two-bit psychobabble?

To man of the West, headaches are just headaches. But in much of the Third World, ailments of every kind are regarded as provoked by spirits, often their own deceased but restive kin. In the peasant societies surveyed by Crapanzano and Garrison (1977, 289), spiritualist cults are an accepted part of life, and headache sufferers know they can turn to them when all else fails. In one case carefully followed in Sri Lanka, the young woman's headaches and all signs of possession were eradicated when she was exorcised. Similarly, in Puerto Rican culture, an *ataque de obsession* is said to indicate "disembodied spirits that molest the living." When one such entity was identified, he confessed (through the medium of the *espiritualista*) to the various ills he had caused: headaches in the frontal and occipital lobes, stomach problems, pain in the kidneys, clouded vision, and accidents. After the confession, "a protecting spirit of the medium took it [the entity] off to a spiritual school."

In Brazil, a person suffering from headaches, on failing to obtain relief from a medical doctor, may turn to an *Umbanda* spirit for supernatural assistance. Umbandists enjoy citing examples of individuals who were dismissed as incurable by psychologists and were later cured by spiritual means.

Moroccans say "you can only see the *jinn* [a class of spirits] when you're asleep." When a fellow named Mohammed was "struck by a jinn," he held the jinn responsible for his dizziness, his depressions, his dreams, and his headaches. In Senegal, a priestess-to-be (in the cult of ancestral spirits) was stricken with her "initiatory illness"; she felt her "head splitting in two." A rite was then performed and soon after she began to develop her own healing powers. In Egypt, a woman named Aziza became ill soon after the death of her beloved brother: stomach trouble, swollen legs, and headaches that followed bad dreams. "Aziza's case shows general characteristics of possession." The possessor was appearing in her nightmares, running after Aziza, chasing her; then Aziza wakes up with a headache. Whereon, the shaikh recommended a ceremony of reconciliation (*sulha*) and the rite of *zar*—to remove the spirit that had gained access to the host in her weakest moment. Often this means moments of unconsciousness: When Aziza had heard that her brother died, she fainted. It was after that loss of consciousness that she began to have the frightening recurrent dream (Crapanzano and Garrison 1977, 289, 410, 397, 340, 113, 102, 184–85).

Nightmares. The most obvious and pervasive time of unconsciousness is of course during sleep. As Aziza's story unfolded, it was learned that in countries where the zar is practiced (Egypt, Sudan, and Ethiopia), the spirit usually becomes visible only to one who is clairvoyant—or to the dreamer. It is also a fact that in Jordan, people often dream of the jinn; jinn possession via nightmares is well known in that country, and ritual specialists are available to exorcise the disturbing spirits. Jinn in parts of Africa are called *all-edjen-u,* or *ya-ijen-i,* while in Arabic, djinn is the figure to whom trance states are attributed; they speak and act through the entranced subject—which sounds almost like a description of MPD. The multiple Eve (Chris Sizemore) had violent nightmares, followed by sleepwalking episodes. Why do multiples suffer such troublesome dreams? These are the dots that psychology can't or won't connect, leaving the most important questions unanswered. Or giving as a non-answer—*We simply do not know. More research (funding) is needed.* Nevertheless, there is an answer in sight. But only if altered states of consciousness are given full recognition. Perspective is part of this. "Much of the world," observes Stafford Betty (2012, 35), "is mystified by the West's refusal . . . under the spell of scientific materialism . . . to acknowledge the existence of spirits."

One of Henry Hawksworth's alters, Peter, only came out when Henry was *asleep.* Billy Milligan, the multiple with twenty-four alters, was often in a trance as a boy. Dr. Brown observed that Billy's voice was "almost trancelike," sort of robotic. Billy just stared at him. "What are your feelings?" Brown asked him. "Like a dream that comes and goes," Billy replied, "I see lots of things that aren't real. . . . Hey, I'm the only kid who can take a trip without LSD. . . . I get these nightmares that I can't describe . . . my body feels funny, like I'm real light and airy. There are times I think I can fly."—OBE? ASC? Genuinely psychic? Not according to Dr. Brown's diagnosis, which ignored the paranormal component entirely: "Severe hysterical neurosis with conversion reactions—APA Code 300.18" (Keyes 1981, 177). Nice, neat, sterile labels, to file away—but missing the most important point: spiritual overshadowing. Dr. Hartmann (1984, 159, 147) came a little closer to the truth in identifying the nightmare sufferer's "thin or permeable [ego] boundaries." The sense of being a solid self "was less firm in the nightmare subjects, who experienced . . . not quite feeling themselves, not knowing who they were, not feeling their body was their own."

Another multiple, Alex S., had "screaming nightmares that tortured his sleep . . . gory mutilation nightmares accompanied by cold sweats and feelings of immense loneliness . . . [also] plagued by black pictures fast-forwarding through his mind" (C. Smith 1998, 73, 138). Yet another multiple, Toby, complained that nightmares kept her up all night; people were chasing her, hurting her. When Dr. Mayer set out to track down Toby's most reliable alter, he came upon "not one but a trinity. They claimed they were . . . from the spiritual world." Whereon Mayer confessed that he was "no expert on the spiritual world, the afterlife. . . . Quite frankly, the subject confuses me." He would be in his comfort zone with "some scientific explanation for such phenomena." (As if the spirit of man were unscientific!*) Yet, the trinity having surfaced, Mayer wanted to know—Who are you?—"We come from beyond," they replied, "we are not part of her" (i.e., *not* her other selves). The dialogue continued, the trinity asking the doctor—What did he think happened to the soul after the body dies? He could not answer. He admits, "They treated me with patronizing disdain: 'Your spiritual awareness is that of a flea'" (Mayer 1989, 7, 81, 155–57).

Materialist science confidently but falsely asserts that "the dreamer is the author of his dream. . . . He and he alone determines who shall be invited into his dream" (Hall 1953, 30); "the images of the nightmare are only your own thoughtforms." But some dreams—objective ones—are more than just a dream and more than thoughtforms (whatever *that*

---

*"Even though the human soul is as real as the flesh-and-blood body . . . [it] cannot be defined or demonstrated scientifically. . . . Psychology pretends to provide a scientific explanation of human behavior, yet that is clearly impossible" (Hunt and McMahon 1988, 163).

is). Departed loved ones, for example, often come to us in our sleep. So might "the angels [who] talk to him [man] in his sleep, and show him what is for his own good" (Oahspe, Book of Sethantes 10:5).

There is, however, no end to the pretentious twaddle that explains away the dream or the fearsome nightmare: "Nightmares may simply reveal to the dreamer the awesome, transcendent power of the sacred . . . 'beyond good and evil'" (Bulkeley 1995, 48–49, 98; 2008, 270–71). Ah, but it is not beyond evil. In fact, it may well be a direct experience of evil. The same writer I have just quoted, Kelly Bulkeley, analyzes someone's recurrent nightmare "as reflecting the primal glimmers of mortality that have haunted the sleep of children throughout history." Does this elegant bosh mean anything to you? In the end, the same author decides not to fuss over "where they [nightmares] come from" but what their effects are:

> Nightmares function . . . as signals of a disruption in the dreamer's relationship with the sacred. . . . Their nightmares show them [dreamers] the dangers of approaching the sacred without proper caution and respect. (Bulkeley 2008, 50)

Twaddle! Yet isn't it strange that Bulkeley, the author of this sappy guesswork, pushing nightmares off into meaningless metaphysics and sanctimonious New Age babble, quotes from the story of a devout Muslim who helps a demon-infested patient: "Aha," the Muslim concludes, "[It is] a bala/demon that is attacking you." The Muslim then proceeds to do a ritual clearing. And it happens that an onlooking Indian psychoanalyst notes the results of the Muslim's work (the analyst's own therapy on the same patient had been ineffective); he quips, "As far as a quick cure of this particular patient's symptoms is concerned, I must admit that the score stands: demonology 1; psychology 0."

But Bulkeley's specialty is "objectivity," the School of Neutrality— de rigueur in Western science. After providing the reader with a wealth of religious traditions that teach "that during sleep people are vulnerable to attack from malevolent spiritual beings" and also after finding a "close match" between the modern nightmare and the premodern view of "spirit attack" (in sleep)—he slowly begins backing off, in true academic evasion, arguing that we don't have to "get bogged down in debates over natural vs. supernatural causation." But this is precisely the issue that must be reckoned with! "A pragmatic approach like mine," Bulkeley tries to convince us (and himself) "sets aside metaphysical controversies." Cop-out. Instead, he offers the student of life the bland and meaningless alternative of "an empirically based phenomenology of the recurrent forms, functions, and personal meanings of human dream experience." What does this pileup of words really mean? The smarmy argument, moreover, includes the false claim that his view of therapy/ psychology is aimed at healing "the whole person." The *whole* person? Without the Big Picture? Without the gestalt? *Without the soul?* I don't think so. Using the "pragmatic approach" to nightmares, he sets "aside the metaphysical concepts used in different religions" (i.e. the concept of *soul*), pointing instead to some abstract "greater existential self-awareness" (sounds pretty metaphysical to me) as the solution. But no thanks. The School of Neutrality succeeds only in talking its way out of the real issues, a jumble of phrases that signify nothing (Bulkeley 1995, 48–49, 98; 2008, 270–71).

> *The demon theory will have its innings again.*
>
> WILLIAM JAMES

Can we honestly believe that these alleged thoughtforms can come to terrorize us in sleep? That is what psychology is telling us: "The remarkable images *he has crafted* [emphasis added] often defy his under-standing," according to Montague Ullman, on dreamers (1999, 6). But why would human beings, whose basic instinct is supposedly Survival, bother to "craft" these horrendous, threatening images in his sleep? And if they are in fact his own creations, why should they "defy his under-standing"? The alleged Unconscious, dear reader, is not the answer. Thoughtforms are not the answer. "Greater existential self-awareness" is not the answer.

Too many questions are spawned by the "inner world" theory of dreams. More questions than answers. And what about the forgotten *outer* world? Hasn't it already been proven that sleep engenders out-of-body episodes (OBEs), as well as excursions to and from the *Outer Darkness?* Why are we so reluctant to credit ourselves with something more than an inner life and *subjective* dreams? One voice in the wilderness, psychiatrist Arthur Guirdham, speaks of children's nightmares, not as intrinsic, but *ex*trinsic: he vehemently rejects the idea that such dreams are the "flaming imagination of a young child." Rather, they are "a materialization of something which actually has life . . . not simply illusional . . . [but] actual entities perceived by the sensitive child."

As Guirdham reports, many of his young patients suffering nightmares had seen "nasty, grinning, frightening faces which . . . I myself had [seen]" as a child. When Guirdham was about seven years old, he lay in bed one night and was "suddenly aware of a terrifying tension in the air." What he saw next was "an unforgettable figure . . . [with] a satanic grin. . . . Even at that early age I knew myself to be menaced by evil." No, this "was not a Jungian archetype" or a *symbol* of anything or any part of his own mind, but "an invading entity . . . seeking to possess me" (Guirdham 1982, 63–65).

In the moment between wakefulness and slumber, the dreamer sees specters rushing at him.
MACROBIUS, *COMMENTARY ON THE DREAM OF SCIPIO*

We could corroborate Guirdham's opinion by considering the phenomenon of *fratzen,* those unsavory visages that children often "see" at bedtime after the lights have been turned out. I used to see them myself, as a little girl. Young children are by nature sensitive, the psychic channel not yet barricaded, as Guirdham says, "by the iron case of personality." Fratzen, though, can come to anyone—young or old. George Russell once scribbled some thoughts on this interesting phenomenon: "I know from questioning many people that . . . before they sleep [they] see faces while their eyes are closed. . . . These are sometimes the faces of imps who frown at them . . . grin or gibber. Sometimes a figure . . . will be seen which . . . seems endowed with life. To call this imagination or fancy is to explain nothing . . . they have a life of their own" (Russell 1918).

Students who stayed at (the classically haunted) Victorian mansion, Harlaxton Manor in Lincolnshire, England, spoke of disturbed sleep, terrible dreams, and waking to see what looked like a subhuman face close to their own (Underwood 1986, 226–27). Fratzen. In one American haunting, extreme exhaustion had lowered Bill A.'s resistance. He started having nightmares. It didn't help that the house that he and his family had just moved into in Detroit had a "history." Some unhappy spirit was haunting the spare bedroom. That's where the nightmares started: it was so lifelike, Bill woke up gagging and sweating. In one dream, he opened the closet door; propped up against the inside wall was a mutilated, blood-soaked corpse. In addition, a "horrid stench" pervaded the house; also "strange sounds" came from the spare room, and the family dog, a terrier, refused to go anywhere near it. One guest who stayed in the spare room was turned around by "someone" in his bed; and when he saw an apparition and sprang toward it, suddenly all the lights in the house went out—then blinked on again. All this was soon accompanied by an awful wailing sound, like a wounded animal, along with other PK, like the trapdoor near the kitchen opening and slamming shut by itself. Finally, when Bill actually saw the phantom, it was "the most hideous face he could ever imagine." Fratzen. A hissing noise issued from its mouth and a "sewer-like stench oozed from the figure's twisted body." It was "the odor of decomposing flesh" (Scott and Norman 1985, 224–26).

> *In hideous dreams he may even see the very ghost or nightmare-fiend that plagues him.*
>
> EDWARD TYLOR, ETHNOGRAPHER,
> DISCUSSING A POSSESSED MAN
> (QUOTED IN CRAPANZANO AND GARRISON 1977, 5)

Dr. Edith Fiore, in another American case of spirit intrusion, was treating a man named Peter who had apparently attracted "six or more" entities—due not only to his sensitivity (psychic since childhood), but also to his alcoholism. Sometimes when Peter was talking to someone, he would suddenly realize that "another being was speaking through him." Ever since childhood, Fiore notes, "he had recurrent nightmares of a wizened evil man glaring at him." (Under hypnosis, Peter's attaching spirits were located and dislodged [Fiore 1987, 70–71].)

One German case of downright possession will help drive home the reality of fratzen. It was the college girl, Anneliese Michel, who tragically died as a result of overwhelming demonic possession whose story was borrowed for the American film, *The Exorcism of Emily Rose*. Anneliese experienced "repeated visions of grinning, demonic faces." Then she suffered bizarre seizures in which her body would become rigid and *her own face* would be "disfigured in a demonic grimace." "The devil is in me," Anneliese declared. Her face would contort into a ghastly shape similar to the demonic visages that constantly grinned at her (Goodman 1981, 21).

Sleeping fits assailed the boy Robbie (upon whose story the popular movie *The Exorcist* was based). In the presence of his family and two Jesuit priests, Robbie began squirming, thrashing, and shouting in his sleep. "The [Roman] *Ritual*," comments Robbie's biographer, "had warned about this. Sometimes the demons put the demoniac [victim] into an *unnatural sleep* [emphasis added] to keep him from being aware of the exorcism." While in such a sleep, the thirteen-year-old boy would spit on everyone. Once the priest ducked, but Robbie caught him square in the face. "He was an utter marksman at a distance of four or five feet," the priest later marveled; "his eyes were closed and he'd spit right in your face." At intervals, Robbie would wake up—and remember nothing. He was "oblivious to his nightly frenzies." Then he'd fall back into the deep tantrum sleep, and the spitting and shouting would begin again (T. Allen 1994, 135, 122).

Another child, overshadowed (and young enough to be "imprinted" by a strong spirit), became a living conduit for his uncle who had died in a plane crash. So complete was the "take-over" that when the boy awoke from his nightmares he was unable to recognize his own mother.

Jamais vu. Obsessed by the spirit of his uncle, the boy acted "really out of character" when the subject of planes came up, exhibiting an altered, controlled state marked by "uncharacteristic mannerisms, as if he were in a trance . . . as if someone had flipped a switch." Right. The psychic switch—which Robert Monroe called the "valve." The story of this child was recounted by someone who believed it was a case of reincarnation. In fact, reincarnationists have seized upon innumerable instances of overshadowing, calling them instead *memories* of a past life. This confusion will be taken up in chapter 10.

But for now, let us look at one more nightmare scenario that the psychiatrist, himself a believer in reincarnation, interpreted as a past-life memory. Dr. G. believed he himself was the reincarnation of a thirteenth-century Cathar priest who was arrested and died in prison. A few of his patients also began to reveal nightmares of destruction by the Inquisitors and the infamous massacre at Montsegur, in 1243 C.E. One of them, a Miss Mills, had dreamt of being led toward the stake with heaped faggots. She would wake up in the middle of the night with names in her head, Cathar names. Dr. G. then identified those names as connected to the siege of Montsegur and the burning of the heretics (Wilson 1973, 130, 120). Another patient, Mrs. Smith, was also besieged with medieval nightmares of being burned at the stake. Her shrieks were so loud, her husband was afraid she would wake up the neighborhood.

Searching diligently through historical records, Dr. G. was able to identify the names of the long-dead persons mentioned by these patients. Profoundly inspired by the "evidence," he concluded that numerous Cathars had indeed reincarnated in the twentieth century. However, all of them—the doctor, Mills, and Smith—were psychic-sensitives and as such could have attracted the still-unreconciled spirits (or even impersonators) of those tortured heretics. This of course would be overshadowing—not reincarnation. We should not underestimate the drawing power of the mediumistic personality. It would also help to keep in mind that there are, basically, two types of mediums. First, the one who *knows* she is a medium; and second, the person who is indeed mediumistic—but does not realize it.

The clairvoyant who is aware of his powers is also aware of the down-side and finds ways of arming himself or herself against spiritual para-sites and the uninvited guest. However, the psychic who is not aware of his paranormal antennae remains defenseless in the face of the uninvited phantom. For example, most focal agents (in poltergeistery) are of this type. Remember Julio, the focal agent behind the Miami Poltergeist? Julio was a psychically disturbed (negative) medium. He would "fight the demon" in his nightmare. Two months before the startling poltergeistery broke out at the Miami warehouse, Julio, age nineteen, began having nightmares that only got worse in the months to come. In these, he would get killed; sometimes he'd see himself at his own funeral. Around this time, he was so depressed he would go walking down to the train tracks at night, tempting fate. "It was," commented William Roll, "as if some force made him do this." Later, at the Durham Institute for Parapsychology, the only "genuine poltergeist incident" occurred the day after Julio's fight-ing dream. He had awakened disturbed by the nightmare, which was not "just an unpleasant dream," according to Dr. Roll, "but a nightmare in the old and literal sense of the word—since 'nightmare' means 'evil spirit.'" Julio had dreamt that a spirit was trying to get into the house; he then attacked and killed the spirit, but it revived and grabbed a Japanese sword and went after the young Cuban with a vengeance.

Most autists, we know, are also natural psychics, their channel characteristically tuned to the ASC setting. One advocate, William Stillman, has collected hundreds of incidences of autistic premonitions, telepathy, communication with angels, apparitions, orbs, and—yes, nightmares. Some of these youngsters are ghost seers, like Josh who, at one point, couldn't get through a night without waking up screaming, rushing down the hallway, and on occasion, grabbing attendants or staff members around the throat. And when Josh related the actual names of the phantoms who invaded his sleep, his supportive staff did not scoff; they investigated. And indeed, those very names were unearthed in the records of a nearby (nineteenth-century) cemetery. Soon the haunting began to spread as these "entities set up in the house," and now even staff persons began experiencing some of the effects of a Presence: PK, phantom giggles, mirror apparitions, flashing lights, ghost cold, photographic "extras." Stillman comments, Josh's "sensitivity was being used as a 'way in' for the Others . . . [he] was a conduit or conductor that they rode in on" (W. Stillman 2006, 186).

Josh's "intake" from the old graveyard merits a brief note on cemeteries: Spiritualists in the know will warn all sensitives against going through graveyards; nonspiritualists, though, do not think twice about *recommending* them! One psychologist dangerously advises—If you are having nightmares about phantoms in a cemetery, just "approach a cemetery in waking life and . . . walk farther . . . into it over a period of days or weeks. . . . If the dreamer encounters no spectral figure, he or she should be able to 'deep six' this nightmare" (Van de Castle 1994, 351). Given the facts of negative mediumship, this is definitely bad advice for a vulnerable psychic-sensitive!

Cemeteries, as we saw in chapter 4, are not the best hangout for open psyches. One great poet found this out the hard way: Edgar Allan Poe, at age fifteen, took to visiting the cemetery nightly to weep over the fresh grave of a beautiful older woman he had adored. But then he began to sleep badly, troubled by frightening nightmares.* The dreams were always the same: he was lost in a blackness with menacing creatures moving ever closer until he could hear them breathing—no doubt the grim result of his unwise attachment to the graveyard. All about him, in the dreams, was the atmosphere of the dead and of damp, moldy graves. He told a friend that it was the most horrible thing you can imagine. When alone at night, he felt an ice-cold hand laid upon his face; or he awakened and saw an evil face gazing into his own.

> *Undeveloped mediums are the sport of lower spirits.*
>
> Vincent Crapanzano,
> *Case Studies in Spirit Possession*

---

*Other literary greats seem to have put their nightmares to work: Robert Louis Stevenson based *Dr. Jekyll and Mr. Hyde* on a nightmare, ditto Mary Shelley's *Frankenstein* and Bram Stoker's *Dracula*.

Nightmares and hauntings may have a shared history; they may be two sides of the same coin. Consider the compelling story of Jan Bartell, a psychic of the second type: her nightmares were exacerbated by her own *undeveloped* psychism. A negative medium, Jan had the "gift" but denied it, preferring a "common sense" approach. Yet from the looks of her full-length, *posthumous,* autobiography, *Spindrift,* it may have killed her! An actress, Jan had taken a Victorian townhouse apartment (next door to Mark Twain's old digs) in Greenwich Village, New York. Here, her sleep was disturbed by dreams of her own funeral and of wraiths that materialized out of the walls, sticking her with sharp glass and smothering her with sickly clouds "rank with decay" (echoes of Poe's "moldy graves" or the ghostly stench at Bill A.'s place). Jan's landlord admitted they had actually found a body in the walls, during renovations—"apparently a murder victim."

On some nights, unearthly rappings kept Jan awake. There was "ghost cold" in the apartment, apported grapes, "fussy movements" of undetermined origin, vibrating moans that changed into the sound of "horrible strangulated gurglings"; there were footsteps, perfume (a lady ghost), orbs, odd noises, an ear-splitting crash (though nothing broke), a phantom woman in white, a spirit-cat. Her own cat would freeze, straining "to follow the progress of something"; then, a small table moved on its own about 18 inches across the room.

Desperate for relief, the still-skeptical Jan went to a psychic, as a last resort. The woman told her not only was there a presence—"some earthbound spirit"—in her apartment, but that she, Jan, was "a sensitive . . . [both] clairvoyant and clairaudient. . . . You, Mrs. Bartell, are a medium!" Jan was shocked. "So what kind of medium does that make me?" she asked sarcastically. "An undeveloped one," the woman told her. "Obviously, your psychic faculties are operating without any conscious sense of direction. But conscious or not, they are operating."*

Some lingering negative force was using Jan. The editor's postscript

---

*Among nightmare subjects, Dr. Hartmann (1984, 140, 151, 166) found that about half report some paranormal experience; many are chronic daydreamers (ASCs) or suicidal.

to her book reads: "Jan Bryant Bartell finished the writing of *Spindrift* in March of 1973. After delays in the typing—*as one typist after another fell ill* [emphasis added]—she delivered the completed manuscript to the publisher on May 14. . . . On June 18, Jan died at home. . . . The coroner's report listed the cause of death as a heart attack"* (Bartell 1974, 28–29, 54, 158, 175, 101, 163, 178, 237).

More recently, the ghostly nightmare was reported by the popular medium James van Praagh. When he was a youth in a Catholic boarding school, his nightmares (seeing a boy being hanged in the presence of a priest) were not his alone: "Soon other kids had similar weird dreams about . . . a priest, a man, a noose, and a small child." The objectivity of the grisly dream was eventually proven when a town historian came forth with the history of the old building that housed the boys. Back in the early 1800s, the demented father of a sick and *possessed* boy, finding no relief from a priest's exorcisms, plotted to "get rid of the devil by killing his son and ending his suffering." And this he did, by hanging the child. Although it was well known that the Catholic school was haunted, nevertheless "it was a sin for Catholics to believe in such things." Whenever there were supernatural rattlings or worse, the priests blamed it on "some mice. . . . Go back to bed," they told the boys, "everything is all right." But the nightmares persisted and so did James's conviction: "Deep down, I knew that there was a ghost (or ghosts) haunting this place" (Van Praagh 2008, 134–37).

Catholics are not the only ones to malign such beliefs as sinful or delusional. Richard Ramirez's vivid nightmares were written off as "just a product of his wild imagination" (Carlo 1996, 202). Ramirez, you may remember, was LA's notorious Night Stalker, a sadistic serial killer. His

---

*A year later (1975), another haunting-with-nightmares—this one on the other coast—was equally well documented and detailed in Pat Montandon's very interesting book, *The Intruders*. Nightmares were only part of a great gestalt of strange phenomena at Pat's old manse: ghost cold, the dog freaking out, phantom footfalls, touches and pushes, dizziness, weird "accidents," disembodied music, sour smells, an inexplicable fire, self-opening (and slamming) windows and doors. It was a versatile presence but not a friendly one (Montandon 1975, 171–72).

nightmares, in which he was pursued by "horrible monsters . . . frightened him to the core." There is every reason to believe that Richard's disturbing dreams were the first sign of malicious entities that would eventually get the upper hand. This young man (who often slept in a *cemetery* to avoid his awful home life) became a textbook pawn of unseen forces, a classic case of demonic possession. The negative overshadowing of Richard Ramirez manifested in many ways: coprolalia, hyperpraxia, hyperactivity, staring spells, migraines and blackouts, suicide attempts, dual personality, epileptoid seizures, sexual impotence, and Satanist affiliations (Carlo 1996, 200, 98, 142, 206, 323, 285, 91, 154, 10).

Other high-profile killers fall into the same category. David Berkowitz (Son of Sam) and Arthur Shawcross both had screaming nightmares. So did Gary Gilmore, whose bad dream was always the same: he was beheaded. There must be a reason, after all, why more than two-thirds of American (and Russian) serial killers are subject to intense nightmares. The predatory work of these men is essentially impersonal, random, motiveless, pointless—"stranger killing" as it is called—committed, often enough, in a kind of trance. That state of consciousness—germane to their psychological profile—is the most vitally important yet least understood aspect of serial murder, or pattern killings as it is also dubbed. Abnormally and pathologically dissociated, serial killers are remarkably similar. With Ken Bianchi, LA's Hillside Strangler (whose story is well told in Darcy O'Brien's book *Two of a Kind: The Hillside Stranglers*) the overshadowing by an alien Somebody was so evident that two of Ken's doctors, Watkins and Ellison, diagnosed MPD. As previously discussed, Ken's murderous other / alter was someone named Steve. It was the foul-mouthed Steve who was the source of the night terrors*

---

*Research has uncovered *altered states of consciousness* (ASCs) at the root of night terrors. These nocturnal panic attacks do not occur in normal REM (rapid eye movement) sleep. Night terrors occur *before* REM sleep sets in, usually in the first hour or so of sleep. Overwhelmed by the intruder from the next dimension of life, the sleeper "jumps out of bed . . . as if fleeing from an assailant" (Noll 1990, 184–85). Sleepwalking, night terrors, and astral dreams (unlike ordinary subjective dreams) all have a life of their own, signaling the excarnate world just beyond the grasp of Ego and Conscious Mind.

that put such a fear in Ken that he would "wake up screaming."

When Ken dreamed of Steve, he, Steve, was a dead ringer for himself! In clairvoyant and dream states, the attaching spirit may impersonate the host or appear *disguised* as his victim / host—a copycat. Ken, in the dream, opened a door, and "there was my twin, me." Ken hollered at the phantom—Get out of my life! They scuffled (as in similar reports of "fighting the demon"). Toward the end of the dream, Ken reached to grab Steve but he just disappeared. Then Ken felt a cool breeze (ghost cold) and woke up. Using hypnosis, Dr. Watkins got Steve to take the spot; he then grilled him—Are you the same thing as Ken? "I'm not him," came the answer; indeed the voice was different. Steve claimed that he made Ken think "all these really morbid thoughts . . . and made sure he didn't really know what was going on" (O'Brien 1985, 141, 182).

There are striking parallels with the case of the Shoemaker—the homicidal Joe Kallinger, who would awake from his nightmares of a "big hairy man . . . screaming and thrashing." Amazing are the similarities between the Hillside Strangler and the Shoemaker, a sensitive but deranged killer. Both of them normally "nice guys." Both adopted. Both dual. Both punished in childhood by a sadistic parent who put the boy's hands over the gas burner! Both made nonentities by their overbearing parents. Both "ordered" (psychically) to kill. Both with undetected damage to the brain. Both with memory gaps (lost time), twitches, and a "twin spirit." And both with nightmares.

Let's switch for a moment to lady murderers—Lisa W., who shot her husband to death; and Ameenah A. who pushed two of her children out of their tenth-story window. Both of these disturbed women suffered from night terrors. The night before Lisa W. killed her spouse, she felt "strange, as if all of her were not quite together." Self disintegrating, Spirit approaching. The next day, "as if possessed by demons," she fired on her husband as he walked in the door. She had never used a firearm before and in fact was a proper lady who literally "sang in the church choir." Total amnesia immediately followed the shooting; she was at a loss to explain how she "could ever have done such a terrible thing" (Blinder 1985, 126–28).

Likewise, in the "tragic and bizarre" case of Ameenah A.: As her mind came unglued, "she began having nightmares and hearing voices . . . [that] gave her specific instructions." She didn't know if she was dreaming, but she began hearing "special messages sent to her on the radio": a "mentor" was speaking to her from the Void. When she was later told what she had done to her children, she was so wild with guilt and remorse, she tried to kill herself (Kirwin 1997, 54–58).

One story of a woman's brother's death hits close to home. My son and his wife, P, who was pregnant with my grandson, were still living in Spain when I began hearing of P's *pesadillas* (nightmares). She had been having them for six years, almost nightly, since the (accidental) shooting-death of her brother J. Each nightmare was a little different, but in all of them, someone she loved was threatened, hurt, or killed. I began to realize this nightly trauma can't be good for my future grandbaby. I also sensed that P's *guilt* (it was she who had invited her brother to Spain from South America) was part of the problem as was the shock factor—he'd been shot in the face and she first saw the story on TV news before ever being notified by police. So I began discussing these things with her by email, working on the guilt angle of the problem.

But the pesadillas would not quit.

Finally I suggested Mas Night, a faithist rite of spirit clearing, one that is specifically aimed at helping the unquiet dead to "move on." P jumped on the idea—and the preparations began at once. Since the ceremony is traditionally performed on the new moon, we had a few weeks to get ready. I sent P the ritual order, the "script," and she slaved over it, getting it translated to Spanish and distributing copies to her family. She followed all other instructions for arranging, cleaning, decorating the house, and setting up a temporary altar, including the relevant herbs and colors to use, and so on.

Then I asked for help, meaning participation from other faithists. All were informed of the circumstances relating to P's nightmares: all understood the who, what, how, and why of the problem. And so it came to pass that simultaneously—in four countries: America, Spain, Italy, and Ecuador—the rite was conducted on March 7, 2008. Faithists in California joined us, as well as P's mother and brother in different parts of Ecuador, thus linking the simultaneous prayers of people in a total of seven different locations. The California faithists are an especially clairvoyant bunch, and from them we got feedback reports on the spirit of J who was first "seen" in a great black cloud, then observed in street clothes, and finally in the aspect of a light being.

Afterward, we all shared our experience a bit, but the best part was hearing from P. The nightmares were gone! It worked! Whatever it was that did the trick, I still believe the *combined* efforts and prayers of a dozen people, on three continents, was the real clincher. Nothing, *nothing,* holds a candle to the darkness-shattering power of collective inspiration. It was one of the most wonderful experiences of my life.

7
COUNTLESS MENTAL VAGARIES

Humanity is surrounded by the thought forces of millions of discarnate beings who have not yet arrived at a full realization of life's higher purposes. A recognition of this fact accounts for a great portion of unbidden thoughts, emotions . . . unreasonable impulses, irrational outbursts of temper, uncontrolled infatuations and countless other mental vagaries.

CARL WICKLAND, *THIRTY YEARS AMONG THE DEAD*

Although Dr. Wickland's eye-opening discoveries go back a hundred years (more on Wickland in chapter 11), the forces of scientific materialism—Sci Mat for short—have held the stage, leaving us with a lame and shallow science of mind. While Sci Mat prides itself on data that is strictly empirical, rational, and objective, the human psyche, perforce, remains a subjective, even mysterious, thing. In the words of Dr. Keith Ablow, "the field of psychiatry . . . in its zeal to mimic objective science, has all but ignored the crucial issues inherent in . . . patients' lives. It has lost sight of the soul, while looking in microscopic detail at the brain" (Ablow 1994, 57).

159

The soul,

Forever and forever—longer than soil is brown and
solid—longer than water ebbs and flows

. . . .

I will not make a poem nor the least part of a
poem but has reference to the soul,

. . . .

Was somebody asking to see the soul?

. . . .

How can the real body ever die and be buried?

WALT WHITMAN,
FROM "STARTING FROM PAUMANOK"

The Sci Mat craze, I think, is maxing out, our current love affair with the Almighty Brain is the final act; for no physical thing, no organ—however wondrous and complex—can hold the secrets of consciousness, which has made but a temporary home in the brain. Brain research, though, struts its stuff, and we remain in thrall to a series of pseudo-breakthroughs. Beware of the hype:

- OCD: "Strange compulsions [may be] governed by control centers in the brain" (Rapoport 1989, 71)
- Schizophrenia: "Experts now agree that vulnerability to schizo-phrenia results largely from abnormal brain structure or bio-chemistry" (Duke and Hochman 1992, 47)
- Sleep disorders: "Night terrors can be considered a minor abnormal-ity in the brain's sleep-awake mechanisms" (Hartmann 1984, 232)
- Hysteria: Symptoms can presumably be caused by lesions on the nervous system
- Tourette's syndrome: ". . . seems to be a neurological disease involving a chemical abnormality in the brain" (Martin 1976, 11)
- Bipolar: "Manic-depressive illness . . . is primarily a medical condition . . . not a personal weakness. . . . Once they learn that this is a chemical disease . . . they experience a great sense of relief" (Duke and Hochman 1992, xxiii–xxiv, 144, 53)

These false assurances shifting the blame to "abnormal body chemistry" (certainly a boon to Big Pharma) are nonetheless shoddy science: Are we quite certain the "chemical imbalance" in question is a *cause* of the disorder rather than an *effect?* Sure, human nature would like nothing better than a pill that alleviates our dis-ease; but that still leaves "countless mental vagaries" that respond only marginally—if at all—to chemical intervention.

Classification of course is an inherent part of any science; but our vaunted categories, and our very definitions, will not get us far. I am talking about today's standard diagnostic categories for mental problems. In general, anything that is not outright psychosis is called a disorder—a mood disorder or a personality disorder or a character disorder. Giving it a name, though, does not mean we have found it out; the name, most would probably admit, is merely a label of convenience. Yet even here, there is a subtext: until the modern era when psychiatry took hold, aberrant behavior was ascribed to spirits. To change the name from spirit possession to mental illness does not change the facts. Indeed, by doing so we forfeit the last secret key to Mind. The exclusion of Psyche's paranormal adventures has hobbled the Science of Man, which now comes up blank and impotent in the face of countless psychopathologies.

Take MPD, for example. For a long time MPD was quietly listed in DSM (*Diagnostic and Statistical Manual of Mental Disorders*) under "hysterical neurosis" or "borderline personality disorder." This was one disorder that did not respond well to chemical treatment; indeed, "treatment for most multiples . . . was a guess-and-go situation" (Chase 1987, 100). The experts "admitted they just weren't sure what was going on. . . . [The doctor's comments] were as wishy-washy as everybody else's" (Castle and Bechtel 1989, 71, 216). Stumped by this mysterious disorder, much of the profession simply wished it away: "There is no such thing as multiple personality . . . more likely what you saw is a resistance to treatment," Dr. Mayer was told by his supervisor. As Mayer recalls, "I had spent eight years training at the American Institute for Psychotherapy and Psychoanalysis, and not once had the subject of multiple personality come up." The number of reported cases of MPD "seemed absurdly low" (only two hundred cases documented since the early 1800s)—even though the disorder has a "long, well-documented history" *under different names* (Mayer 1989, 23, 25, 29). As the husband of one multiple put it, "Unless the treatment facility specializes in MPD, he may hear yet another psychiatrist tell him, 'Well, your wife has Atypical Depression with Psychotic Features. We'll keep her here for a while and try some different medications'" (Cohen et al. 1991, 210).

Multiples like Billy Milligan were crying out: "The shrinks don't know what to do because they can't figure out what is wrong. . . . My doctors have made it clear they do not believe in multiple personality." Instead, they diagnosed him with "hysterical neurosis involving many passive-aggressive features" (Keyes 1981, 21, 397, 178). But Billy had twenty-four honest-to-goodness alters; he was clearly multiple. Yes, there *were* passive-aggressive features; MPs, in fact, often present with a range of upsets, like Beverly R. who reports, "I have been incorrectly diagnosed as having depression . . . psychosis, neurosis . . . and the list goes on. . . . Manic-depressive was probably the most popular. All of the incorrect diagnoses are actually symptoms of MPD" (Cohen et al. 1991, 54).

Speaking of manic-depressive, this "mood disorder" overlaps so extensively with other maladies that we have to wonder how serviceable our neat little categories are in the first place. Also known as bipolar disorder, manic depression varies from case to case, and is not infrequently associated with phobias, paranoia, panic attacks, ADD, NPD (narcissistic personality disorder), MPD, OCD, anorexia, and schizophrenia. Our categories, in short, are fairly ineffective if they cannot account for all the other "mental vagaries" they entail.

Something is definitely missing. So let us make bold to step into the paranormal arena.

> *The repression of psychic gifts is conducive to any kind of psychiatric disorder.*
>
> ARTHUR GUIRDHAM,
> THE PSYCHIC DIMENSIONS OF MENTAL HEALTH

Stumbling in darkness, Sci Mat has—for all the wrong reasons—boycotted the paranormal, which is tantamount to boycotting the soul. Yet, when the human soul gets caught in the vortex of dissociative gravity, that new dimension may pull us down. It doesn't matter what you call it: the tunnel, the Outer Darkness, the Shades, the astral, a separate reality, Locale II—whatever you call it, it is essentially the same thing: the unseen, nonphysical side of life—with a Force of its own.

And it is in this dimension that the *inexplicables* of human psychology take shape. It is in this dimension that we are open, *too open,* to the disembodied souls wandering about in the shadows. It is in this precarious dimension that the alters drawn to multiples wait their turn to come out and "take the spot," as MPD lingo puts it. It is in this dimension that bipolar people pick up "phantom illnesses" and "unexplainable physical symptoms" (Duke and Hochman 1992, 243, 31). No wonder bipolars overlap with multiples and even with the possessed; the pattern of overshadowing is hardly different. It is not unusual for the manic-depressive to show overt signs of entity possession; such signs include

- Coprolalia: "She [bipolar] was calling John [husband] every name you could think of" (Duke and Hochman 1992, xii).
- Different persona: Said the wife of a bipolar, "That's another person in his skin, not the one I married" (Duke and Hochman 1992, 230).
- Rapid cycling: "Rapid cyclers . . . are like yo-yos and feel as though they are being helplessly manipulated by some force outside themselves" (Duke and Hochman 1992, 35). Rapid cycling is one way of describing the bipolar's mood swings and incessant change of plans, attitudes, or even appearance.
- Logorrhea (aka motor mouth): "He talked a mile a minute" (Duke and Hochman 1992, 229).

Logorrhea

Logorrhea is a technical term that designates compulsive talking aka verbal diarrhea, pink tornado, motor mouth, and so on. It may also involve run-on sentences, careless syntax, neologisms, as well as excessively fast or loud speaking.

> *Anyone who . . . talks loudly and laughs too long may*
> *be possessed.*
>
> MARTIN EBON, EXORCISM

The psychopath named Adolf Hitler "was a compulsive and aggressive talker . . . whose speeches . . . [were] like a volcano erupting . . . a hurricane of words" (Waite 1977, 176). In Senegal, when possession-seizures ended in a fall, the abnormal mutism of the subject gave way to its opposite—logorrhea. Elsewhere, an *undeveloped* medium was nicknamed "Magpie" because "she talked so much" (Crapanzano and Garrison 1977, 95, 57).

One hears of the long-winded monologues and exuberant loquacity of numerous psychopaths, hyperactives (ADHD), obsessives (OCD), narcissists (NPD), multiples, and the possessed: In an Australian case of spirit possession, the entity "makes me talk all day . . . talk, talk, talk" (Sagan 1997, 12). And, thanks to the popularity of true crime books, the record is now full of cases involving the excessive garrulity of the criminally obsessed. Here is a quick rundown:

- Eric Napoletano: "talked nonstop," just like his mother who "never shut up" (Pienciak 1996, 382, 273)
- Eric Chapman: talked "too fast and too much" (Markman and Bosco 1989, 303)
- John Wayne Gacy: "talked a blue streak"; "babbled incessantly" (Morrison 2004, 97)
- Ken Bianchi: "too talkative"
- Fred Coe: "He talked nonstop for hours" (Olsen, 1993, 185)
- Lilly Schmidt: She "talked continuously"; would give a "soliloquy" lasting three and a half hours (Kirwin 1997, 150)
- Joel Rifkin: His was "a relentless stream . . . a verbal floodtide" (Kirwin 1997, 49)

- Diane Downs: She never came up for breath; her swarm of words was like "verbal vomit"
- Timothy McVeigh: He was voted Most Talkative in school
- Cathy Wood: "She just started talking . . . and it didn't stop" (Cauffiel 1992, 438)
- Clifford Olson: "a blabbermouth . . . he talked fast, staccato" (Hare 1993, 133)

With the publication of the manic-depressive film star Patty Duke's confessional biography, *A Brilliant Madness* (coauthored with Gloria Hochman), we see just how close bipolar symptoms come to a spiritual—not a medical—condition. Add to this Miss Duke's coprolalia and logorrhea ("She'd call friends . . . and talk nonstop"), her rapid cycling ("I rode a wild roller coaster"), her Otherness ("There is something . . . that takes over"), her telepathic episodes, phobias, tantrums, and panic attacks (at the *cemetery!*). The gifted actress may have carried an alter or two (MPD) and may have been clairaudient ("Voices talked to me through my car radio"). The overshadowing of Patty Duke (not so unusual among highly creative artists) could be summed up in her own words: "The manias and the depressions seemed to have a life of their own" (Duke and Hochman 1992, 10, 27, 29, 111–12, 1–3, 14–18).

Duke, as it happens, had also gone through an anorexic period—dropping to 73 pounds. Calling this an eating disorder does not even begin to define these baffling cases of personal (bodily) depletion. In Miss Duke's case, anorexia, depression, insomnia, and suicide (attempts) went hand in hand. What do all these afflictions add up to? Anorexia alone has, significantly, been linked to hauntings and overshadowing. Dr. Fiore's overshadowed patient Barbara, for example, barely ate; she was so skinny, her ribs stood out. She admitted feeling "spirits around me at night. . . . I've wondered if it was the boy who used to live in our home. He was killed in a surfing accident just before we moved in . . . I can almost feel him in there" (Fiore 1987, 84). Similarly, in a British case, a man suffering from exhaustion and extreme weight loss knew there was "a male spirit in the house which in fact [he] had seen on more than one occasion. The spirit had started to become attached to him . . . and was certainly draining [him]" (S. Allen 2007, 137). In the full-scale haunting of Pat Montandon's San Francisco mansion—involving every shocking aspect of the supernatural and then some—Pat's very person was overshadowed: unaccountable fatigue, severe dizziness, and anorexia (they called her Twiggy).

There is an unusually high incidence of anorexia among multiples who, as we will soon see, are creatures of overshadowing par excellence. To name a few, the famous Eve was thin "to the point of emaciation" (Lancaster 1958, 55). The equally famous Sybil, five feet, five inches tall, weighed in at 79 pounds. Yet another well-known multiple, Dr. Breuer's Anna O., would only eat on his insistence.* In fact, stomachaches and eating disorders are fairly typical of multiples.

All my essence has gone to the others.
JENNY, AS QUOTED IN JUDITH SPENCER,
SUFFER THE CHILD

This statement by Jenny, a tortured (literally) supermultiple with more than 400 alters, suggests that something was "eating" at her, or more specifically, that her alters ("the others") were consuming her. This would appear to be the case in that drained and rail-thin Briton, cited above, who finally went to see a nutritionist and was told that he had a tapeworm. Yet, after Sue Allen did a successful distant healing on this man, the nutritionist retested him. The tapeworm was gone. Had it been a spiritual tapeworm?

It is tempting to argue that Carol T., another multiple, was actually burning calories in the upkeep of her alters. She tired so easily, explain-

---

*Sometimes the patient has mysteriously lost her appetite. This happened, for example, to an overshadowed Malaysian girl. "Her food and drink were tasteless, and she could neither relax by day nor sleep at night. She resisted the food that was urged on her" (Crapanzano and Garrison 1977, 308).

ing this as a result of her "energy flow being routed to all the others, thus depleting my own energy store." Even when the "other personalities are not 'out,' it still takes a certain amount of energy for their 'maintenance'" (Cohen et al. 1991, 70).

A slightly more sinister motive was revealed in the case of a Mrs. Burton who, being a natural clairvoyant, was bothered by spirits. She consulted Dr. Wickland who teased out the attached spirit. It declared, "She eats too much and gets too strong, then I have no power over her body. . . . I want [her] to eat less" (Wickland 1974, 51)—a simple case of a spirit trying to weaken and emaciate its host in order to gain the upper hand.

In the tragic case of Anneliese, the German girl who died possessed, exhausted, and emaciated, her neck muscles got so tense she could not even swallow solid food. "Pressure on the stomach" made eating almost impossible. Father Alt, one of the priests who tried to exorcise Anneliese, was himself attacked (this is not unusual). First he developed an iron deficiency, then a drop in manganese and potassium nitrate. His kidneys also began to dysfunction. "In other words, I was leached out" (Goodman 1981, 225, 218). That was in Germany. But it doesn't matter which part of the world you are in when it comes to demonic infestation: the results are strikingly alike everywhere, and the "leaching" is not uncommon. Here are a few more examples from different lands:

- Africa: The victim "lost his appetite and almost completely ceased to eat" (Oesterrich 1935, 139)
- Senegal: "The possession syndrome . . . is characterized by depression . . . anorexia, and loss of weight" (Crapanzano and Garrison 1977, 94)
- Egypt: "The symptoms that the possessed experienced . . . included stomach pain, loss of appetite . . . and epilepsy" (Crapanzano and Garrison 1977, 179)
- Sri Lanka: Among women, conditions linked to spirit possession include hypochondriasis, hysteria, and anorexia (Crapanzano and Garrison 1977, 243)

- Italy: The possessed woman (who was finally cleared in the thirteenth exorcism) has "been reduced almost to a corpse" (Christiani 1961, 140)
- France: Assailed by homicidal urges, headaches, dizziness, and loss of weight, the woman told the doctor, "I am not mad, but I feel there is some force inside me." She could not eat, "was slowly wasting away" (Christiani 1961, 147, 151, 155)
- Britain: The woman who murdered four little children (for no apparent reason) had been a little "chunky," but by the time of her trial "had become anorexic . . . weigh[ing] less than half of what she once had. . . . She was herself in danger of death" (Ressler 1997, 54–55)

Some victims of "spiritual anorexia" become so emaciated they have to be fed intravenously. Gratefully, hypnosis sometimes makes a difference: In a nineteenth-century case, one "voice" heard by the victim claimed to be "an unhappy dead man. . . . By a hypnotic treatment, one of the demons had been expelled. . . . She [the victim] was thin and little more than a skeleton" (Oesterrich 1935, 14–15). Others, like Dr. M. Scott Peck's patient Beccah, resist exorcism and remain "dramatically underweight . . . gaunt," suicidal, and depressed (Peck 2005, 134, 151).

The leaching fatigue felt by many anorexics is not unlike a parasitic effect. The comparison seems all the more relevant in light of Robert Monroe's personal experience in Locale II. Entities that grabbed on to him during his amazing OBE experiments "attached themselves like the parasitic 'sucker' fish. . . . They weren't vicious, just troublesome. . . . They came clustering around, attracted by me. . . . It was as if I were bait" (Monroe 1971, 141). What Monroe dubbed as parasites are actually called vampire spirits in the Oahspe bible: "Spirits who inhabit mortals in order to live on the substance mortals eat and drink, oft absorbing [their] strength and life, shall be known as . . . vampires" (Oahspe, Book of Bon 14:10). Nestling in the aura of the living, vampire spirits are capable of absorbing the vitality of their hosts, sucking their "blood and flesh till the brain and heart are wild and mad!" (Oahspe, Book of Wars, 54:18); they cause their victims "to emaciate and to . . . become insane" (Oahspe, God's Book of Eskra 7:10). Such nasty entities, according to *Spiritalis* (Question #64) (an Oahspe prequel), are "evil spirits . . . grasping for spirit food and strength . . . [these] vampires love to draw substance from the fount where your own spirit feeds." Are they the same entities described by young Sally in Judith Rapoport's book (1989, 155) on OCD? The sixth-grader lost ten pounds; "an evil force is inside her." The child had begun to exhibit signs of obsession just before her confirmation.

> Soon after identifying the Presence, most clients tend to perceive it as being a parasite. . . . They often related the Presence to symptoms of emptiness.
>
> SAM SAGAN

Anorexia "exacerbates the continuous feeling of emptiness" so often expressed by obsessives. Almost every analysis of OCD stresses this hollow feeling, this sense of emptiness; patients are quoted as saying, "I am nothing," "I feel like nobody," "I felt invisible." Dr. Steven Levenkron, in *Obsessive-Compulsive Disorders,* offers in-depth portrayals of numerous OC girls whose downward spiral entails anorexia nervosa: Nina, Katherine, Lara, Alice, Diane, and others. This "vacant person" seen by Levenkron does not really know why she repeats her bizarre rituals, only that she is driven by "feelings of intense dread." She has somehow come to believe that her compulsive actions afford her "her whole security system" (Levenkron 1991, 59, 36, 62, 110).

It is a nameless dread. "Inexplicable dread" is the phrase used by a woman stricken with anorexia—along with migraines, insomnia, racing thoughts, and seizures (Cahalan 2012, 22). Yet the very young and guileless might give it a name—as did the six-year-old girl with a touching-and-counting compulsion who, during an attack, would run to her mother saying, "Mommy, Mommy, my other mind is back!" Thus does Dr. Guirdham (1982, 59) say the obsessional child is essentially the psychic child, whose open aura has attracted an unseen presence, another "self." For when persona or ego disintegrates, nothing is left to assert against spiritual parasites. The OC rituals themselves are a last desperate attempt at armor, one's last redoubt against intrusion, to stay in control and somehow rout the trespasser.

> *Obsessional rituals begin as protective reflexes against evil.*
>
> ARTHUR GUIRDHAM,
>
> *THE PSYCHIC DIMENSIONS OF MENTAL HEALTH*

There are times when the patient himself furnishes the clearest analysis: "I was a very scared little boy . . . I had a sense I was being manipulated." This OC's strategy then was to "counter bad with good. Offset . . . I am on my own against terrible forces. . . . The rituals must be strong. . . . If you're weak, the forces of evil will triumph. Resist. Fight" (Rapoport 1989, 55). Set up something, something meticulous, mechanical, or exhaustive, to counteract the encroachment. Say, constant washing. Or counting. Repetitive motion, all-out exercise. Rooted in time, the *sequential* process (of exercising, walking, running, and of all OC rituals) is seen as a defense, a tactic, against the *timeless* grip of the dreaded altered state. The first hint of nameless dread, the first inkling of arousal into ASC, prompts the repetitive, linear activity—*anything* to avoid being sucked into the timeless vortex. It is a dodge, a trick, a ruse. With the possessed boy Jamie, who feared the all-too-familiar impingement signaled by chest pains and earaches, a solution was recommended by the priest. He taught the boy a diversionary tactic: lengthy repetitions of the name of J-E-S-U-S. Over and over again, in this manner: through the alphabet, he was to recite A, B, C . . . and so on up till J; then A, B, C . . . and on to E; then A, B, C . . . and on to S; and so on. It was a "means of blocking [the possessing] influence" (Martin 1976, 253–54).

While spirit possession is almost universally scorned by the psychiatric profession, the wording of OCD specialists actually comes awfully close to descriptions of malign invasion. Dr. Rapoport, for one, defines OCD as always involving the "persistent intrusive idea, thought or impulse," while the ritual itself or the thought "is seen as alien." Rapoport further notes that "the word *obsession* comes from the Latin *obsidere,* to besiege, and indeed these patients are besieged, truly possessed. . . . These people had a 'foreign body' in their otherwise quite sensible minds" (Rapoport 1989, 238, 80). Taking all of this one small step further, Dr. Edith Fiore includes compulsive behavior in her checklist for spirit possession, as does Dr. Guirdham who unapologetically concludes that "compulsive action merges with possession" (Guirdham 1982, 52).

The problem with the standard behavioral model is its mindless, unswerving loyalty to Sci Mat. Anything that cannot be laid to rest in the tangible bed of facts, observable, replicable facts, is loosely assigned to the "inner" life. Yet the story of OCD—especially when told by the sufferers themselves—is all about the alien, the perception of unseen forces which are *outside* the mind. No, our walkers, runners, exercisers, spinners, washers, repeaters, and the like, are not running away from self but from something that *threatens to overtake* self, to possess self. To besiege self.

Nor is it a coincidence that, as Rapoport observes, the "disease [OCD] affects some of the most *sensitive* [emphasis added] people I have met." Autistic children are also highly sensitive, often amazingly psychic, or "open." Their rigid regimes and repetitive motions— spinning, flicking, rocking, twirling, their tics and twitches, also seem defensive.* Victor is an autist studied by Bill Stillman in *Heart Savants;* much of his behavior, Stillman thought, suggested "an authentic battle for control with an opposing presence."

"Plagued by presences . . . [Victor] became host to several personalities." One priest involved in his case "expressed concern over Vic's apparent loss of free will. . . . 'Is this a case of possession?' he had asked." Surely Victor's "difficult-to-manage multiple personality type behaviors" were a sign of overshadowing. And indeed, with the loss of free will, anything is possible: MPD, OCD, spirit possession—all branches of the same tree, or should I say, all brother trees in the same forest. We

---

*This whirling, at fantastic speeds, is sometimes found in spirit possession and poltergeistery. The spinning, somehow a throwing-off-centrifugal motion, is found in some multiple cases as well (see Castle and Bechtel 1989, 323; M. Smith and Pazder 1980, 32, 37).

must remain generalists, keeping the overview, the forest, in mind. To miss the forest for the trees would be the same as getting lost in our particularistic diagnostic categories, missing the Big Picture, the flight of the soul, the soul touched by the darkness.

Without the forest in view, our neat little categories only create confusion—by overlapping so much. Victor's OCD overlaps with MPD. We have yet to grasp the grand principle that underlies all this spillover. Autists, after all, tend to present with an array of disorders: MPD, OCD, anxiety, depression, post-traumatic stress disorder, even bipolarism. What is the radical, the root, that connects them all? It all goes back to the prototype of the autist—that "exquisitely sensitive" human being.

The autist has the psychic door open. Stuff flows in—willy-nilly. "Gifts of the spirit," on the one hand, foster tenderhearted souls, "knowingness . . . [and] innate gentleness." The open door, on the other hand, can mean exposure, overexposure; hence a terrible vulnerability to sensory extremes like hyperesthesia or ghost seeing. Along the paranormal spectrum are a wealth of talents seen in the autist. Foreknowledge (precognition) is second nature; clairvoyance is just as common, as are telepathy and mind reading, communing with angels, "capacity to perceive all things seen and unseen" (W. Stillman 2006, 6).

On the downside are serious difficulties, like mutism and suicidal urges—and self-harm, like Victor and other autists who sometimes "committed acts of self-injury." The OCD specialist Dr. Steven Levenkron speaks of Lauren's "self-mutilating behavior." With over a dozen scars on each arm, Lauren explains her reason for cutting herself: it's a *distraction strategy*.

"What makes you cut yourself?" the doctor asked.

"Most of the time, all the other stuff—you know, the rituals and the exercises—they use up enough energy so that this doesn't have to happen . . ."

"But what do you get from cutting yourself?"

"Pain."

"What does the pain do for you?"

"It brings me back."

"It brings you back from what—or where?"

. . . "It brings you back from being away from yourself . . . [when I] feel like I'm going to lose myself. There's no other way I can explain it. I feel myself drifting away from myself, and the pain brings me back" (Levenkron 1991, 50).

I became more aware of cutting when I found out that two of my neighbors, both young men, were cutters. How rare could this be? I wondered. When I hit the books, the first thing I noticed about cutting and self-mutilation is that it knows no bounds, no territory: cutters inhabit almost every psychiatric domain—OCD, MPD, possession, depression,* bipolarism, ASC, Satanism, and even Christian sects that go in for self-flagellation and mortification of the flesh. So here again is a world of *overlap* begging for a comprehensive view.

It was a bit of a shock, though, when Major David Morehouse began cutting himself. In his stunning and highly recommended book *Psychic Warrior,* this decorated officer tells his own story with great candor: how his helmet was hit by a bullet, how the resulting ASCs made him a perfect candidate for the government's secret experiments in remote viewing and psychic ESPionage. But with his "mind's eye open," the haunting images were unstoppable and the OBEs uncontrollable. I got the superb phrases "in the ether" and "touching the darkness" from David's brilliant testimony.

There were nightmares and depression. Worst of all were David's fears of harming himself or others. His hands trembled even thinking about the awful vision he had of killing his entire family. And then there was the cutting. He pleaded with the Army psychiatrist, "Why would I cut myself?" Was it the Dark Ones in the ether? The doctor hedged: "You mustn't let yourself believe that something came out of the darkness and lacerated you; that just can't happen, . . . I believe that the images that come freely to you . . . are messages or symbols from deep in your limbic system" (Morehouse 1998, 511, 272–74).

---

*Like the news story about a fourteen-year-old suicide who had been on depression medication: the Ohio ninth grader was a cutter.

And so it's back to the Almighty Brain for the answers, at least according to David's doctor and all her comrades in orthodox psychiatry. The cutters themselves, though, know different. The supermultiple Jenny, for instance, knows it is the dark ones, starting with her alter Wahnola, "who did things to Jenny, burned her and cut her. But people thought Jenny did it to herself" (Spencer 1989, 218). Cutting is not unusual in MPD. One of Cameron W.'s alters "found the X-Acto knife and slash, slash, slash, made three deep gashes in my right arm" (West 1999, 162). "Every time I hurt myself," averred Beverly R., another multiple, "it was always very quiet and methodical . . . I know now it was one of my inside people hurting me." Susan A. also cut herself; she comments on her changing attitude toward such "self-destructive activities" upon meeting other multiples and seeing "their self-inflicted wounds" (Cohen et al. 1991, 54, 130). Yet another multiple: The therapist asked to see her arms; they were covered with grooves. "It looked like a miniature plowfield" (Schoenewolf 1991, 22).

He would cry out and cut himself with stones

MARK 5:5

Time and place have little effect on the strange ritual of self-wounding. In Africa, a possessed man wounds himself with stones and pieces of wood; in India, the person possessed by *pisaka* "tears his flesh with his nails" (Oesterreich 1935, 173). "It is a true compulsion!" declared Anneliese Michel, the fatally possessed German girl, who inflicted wounds on herself (presumably to control her state of consciousness) (Goodman 1981, 84, 247). Or as FD put it in her anonymous testimony of the "spiritual assault" that plagued her as a naive ashram devotee, an "unseen force . . . tried to [make] me do actions against my will including hurting myself." Or, the possessed girl Marianne, in her fits, would "tear her own skin . . . or batter her head against the wall" (Martin 1976, 59). Or, Beccah, Dr. Peck's anorexic, suicidal, and possessed patient, who would slash her arms with "Nazi knives" (Peck 2005, 147).

A Swiss Army knife was the slasher of choice for a teenage vampire gang in Florida, though some used an X-Acto knife or razor blade: "Rod's arms and chest were covered with marks all up and down." The other kids "had weird cuts, too." One of the girls, Heather, in "her peculiar dream world . . . would position the edge of the blade on her inner arm . . . and slice." Had she been "taken over"? Another member, Jeanine, during one of this gang's cutting rituals, "felt like she was someone else. . . . It was as if she was on the ceiling looking down at the scene." Clearly an OBE (Jones 1999, 8, 34, 177).

When Andy H., a bipolar guy, says he *doesn't remember* cutting himself, that lost time signals self-in-abeyance. Enter the intruder. We know, too, that when a multiple's alter "takes the spot," she can harm "herself"—yet feel no pain. Miss Beauchamp's alter, for example, "had a will of her own, could hypnotize the other personalities . . . and exhibit complete tactile anaesthesia" (Fodor 1966, 280). It was the same deal with Jenny's alter Selena, who "in her anxiety, enacted self-punishment . . . by cutting or burning that she *could not feel*" (Spencer 1989, 255). Then, when Jenny "came back," the pain and humiliation was all hers.

But something is wrong with the analysis that Jenny's biographer offers. She thinks that Selena's cutting and burning "gave some relief . . . from the anxious, terrible feelings." How so? The concept hardly makes sense. Why would such abuse relieve anxiety? The rare *male* multiple (most are female) Henry Hawksworth, was burned on his arms by his alter Johnny. The question *Why* was posed through an automatic-writing technique that the doctor and patient had developed. The answer came that the burns were meant "to provide a constant reminder of his [Johnny's] existence. . . . The burns were visible signs of his presence and his power" (Hawksworth 1977, 29, 106). Maybe it *is* the dark ones, after all. Maybe Ena Twigg was right in her analysis of one particularly nasty haunting: "The spirit had been so determined to make someone *pay attention* [emphasis added] that he had overshadowed the entire family. . . . After I talked with the spirit, the haunting stopped and never occurred again" (Twigg and Brod 1973, 109).

Henry Hawksworth disliked his alter Johnny: "Johnny is not me, yet he wears my body and ruins my world" (Hawksworth 1977, 242). A haunting is one thing, but the invasion of your very own body and mind is another. Johnny, as Henry insisted, was not part of him, he was a separate identity. Now, the psychiatric profession may have (finally!) recognized MPD, but they still don't understand it. Mistakenly, they assume the alters are broken-off *parts of self,* "shattered pieces of the patient" (Noll 1990, 35). Sci Mat, of course, requires it, or, more to the point, no other "scientific" explanation is in sight . . . so, hey, let's just call it other personalities that have "split off" and submerged in one's unconscious.

Yet the sufferers themselves know otherwise: "They're not personalities, doctor, they're people"—quoth Billy Milligan, the multiple with twenty-four alters. Poor Billy. Most of his doctors wanted to *fuse* Billy's alters, merge them together presumably for "the healing process" to take place, "to make him whole again." This part of the therapist's agenda is called fusion (integration). A magnificent hybrid. But the patient took a different view: "Why do you have to fuse 'em with me? Why can't you get rid of 'em?" Billy implored his doctor (Keyes 1981, 360, 68, 80).

The pathos of his protest is echoed in the desperate words of other multiples:

- Cam West: "The person looking in the mirror isn't me. . . . Somebody else's voice [is] coming out of my face" (West 1999, 51).
- Sybil: "Integration? That's a great mirage" (Schreiber, 1973, 343).
- Carole T.: "We hate the word integrated . . . I must say, the cure is worse than the disease"* (Cohen et al. 1991, 170–71).

Yet the multiples' hue and cry is ignored. The multiple, say the experts, "simply splits off parts of herself. . . . Somehow these parts become autonomous, taking on lives and names and even personalities of their own. . . . The key to the healing of a multiple personality is fusion. . . . Feelings [must be] melded into one unified whole" (Noll 1990, 26, 30).

---

*"Aftereffects of a formal integration . . . [include] headaches, eye aches, lack of coordination and various other somatic complaints" (Cohen et al. 1991, 178).

Truddi Chase's therapist wore himself out trying to convince her that her various "extras" (there were ninety-two alters) were merely "different emotions within you." She fought back, "No . . . I tell you, they were people! . . . Would you want to be mushed up with your next door neighbor?" "Two, four, six, eight, We don't wanna integrate," came the chant of Truddi's Troops. "They were individuals, no two alike" (Chase 1987, 92, 388, 359). Even the *alters* don't want to be fused. This was clear in the Beauchamp case: the doctor "attempted to weld the four personalities . . . into one. Sally [the chief alter] was bitterly resistant"; she was "not a cleavage of the medium's self . . . [but] had all the appearance of an invading, outside entity" (Fodor 1966, 280), just as she herself claimed: "she was a spirit and not Miss B. at all" (Crabtree 1985, 57).

My friend and colleague, Steve Blake, has sagely observed, "The influence of spirits is . . . paranormal in origin but identical in appearance to what psychiatrists have traditionally termed split consciousness, secondary personalities, multiple personalities . . . though such epithets merely serve to cloak the underlying phenomena" (Blake 2014, 195). Steve then goes on to cite the trenchant words of James Hyslop, one of the great pioneers of parapsychology. It was a hundred years ago that Hyslop called MPD "the doctor's Irish stew. He does not know what it is. In antiquity it was 'demonic obsession.' . . . Today we call it such things 'split consciousness' and think we have solved the problem, when, in fact, we have only thrown dust in people's eyes. . . . What is split consciousness? We can split wood, iron, pumpkins, political parties; but split consciousness, however convenient a term . . . is a term for our ignorance" (Hyslop 1918, 289–90).

Fig. 7.1.
James Hyslop

The divine presence invades the man, it is not created by him.

Tongan shaman,
as quoted in Oesterreich,
Obsession and Possession

As long as the behavioral sciences are beholden to mechanical and so-called rational standards, pseudo-solutions will remain in force. For the reader who has a personal stake in these matters, I would like to red flag the favorite buzzwords used by professionals to *explain away* the existence of alters. These are *create, cope,* and *defense mechanism*—all of which are used to uphold the illusion, the sham, that multiplicity comes from within. To put you on alert, here are some examples of the therapist's soothing flummery (buzzword italicized):

- "A multiple *creates* other personalities to escape from his or her personal childhood Auschwitz. . . . The system becomes over-loaded with trauma and pain and *creates* another personality to share the burden" (Mayer 1989, 47, 30).
- "*Creating* an entirely new self . . . [provides] a wall to block off the [bad] experience from the rest of the self" (according to Dr. Wilbur in Castle and Bechtel 1989, xiv).
- "Multiple personality becomes a very functional means to survive . . . *creating* others to cope with the trauma" (Chase 1987, xi).
- "Jenny would require many more selves to *cope* with her life" (Spencer 1989, 38).
- "Multiple personality is one way the mind has of *coping* with problems it can't handle in any other way. [He] was incapable of being angry so he had *created* Johnny, who was all anger" (Hawksworth 1977, 226).
- "Subjected to unbearable abuse, the child 'splits off' . . . from the self that is having the experience—in effect, using amnesia . . . as one of the most basic *defense mechanisms*" (Castle and Bechtel 1989, xiv).

Even Dr. Crabtree, despite his insights into multiplicity, still presents it as a "*defense* [emphasis added] against emotional strain"; he assumes that all these extras come from "the *creative* [emphasis added] power of man's inner being" (Crabtree 1985, 49, 59). I must say, the psychologists have it bass ackwards. It is certainly not the alter personality that is the defense mechanism. On the contrary, it is all the fighting to *throw off* the intruding alter that is self-defensive, howbeit ineffective: we have seen it all—the seizures, the warning headaches, the twitches, the head banging, the compulsive running and exercising, even the cutting.

And there is a reason why behavioral scientists have opted for the coping mechanism. It all goes back to the outdated theory of Darwinian natural selection.* The social scientist has been trained to look for and find the *adaptive* value of various behaviors. (Some of these "evolutionary" thinkers even see *depression* as adaptive!) Influenced by Darwinism, theorists feel they have explained a phenomenon if they have identified its adaptive value, its function in the system as a whole, meaning how it is useful in keeping the ship (of society, of the group, of the individual) afloat. It follows on the wrong assumption that if a particular behavior has *survived,* it must be a good strategy, it must be adaptive, it must somehow be useful. Much of cultural anthropology proceeds on this basis. Psychology, too. Hence the extra personalities of the multiple *must* be performing some vital function. Why else would they exist? They must be either defending, protecting, or helping the host *cope* with her difficulties.

Criminal pathologists repeat the bogus solution: speaking of an alter claimed by serial killer John Wayne Gacy, forensic psychologist Helen Morrison (2004, 110) insists that Gacy "created [the alter] from somewhere deep inside of his being." At trial, she called it a "primitive psychotic defense mechanism." But let me ask you: If these alters are adaptive parts of self, why do they so often attempt to sabotage therapy? And if this is a survival mechanism, why are so many of the alters

---

*See my anti-Darwin book, *The Mysterious Origins of Hybrid Man.*

destructive, suicidal, dysfunctional, helpless? Dr. Mayer (1989, 30, 287) claims the alters are an "asset" and a "benefit." In fact, these supposedly beneficial alters are frequently the ones who commit antisocial and criminal acts. How can this possibly be adaptive?

The MPD casebook may even see "a homicidal personality emerge and take control of the body—an extremely dangerous situation" (Noll 1990, 38). No one is going to call this adaptive or any kind of coping mechanism. Yet violent or APD alters are not at all uncommon. No, they are not "created"; they are real, though disembodied, souls who have opportunistically found a suitable host for themselves. They are the "dark ones" behind raging obsessions and senseless crimes. Yet law enforcement's hands are tied: they simply cannot allow a diagnosis of MPD—for it would then open the way for "mitigating circumstances," thus precluding the fullest extent of lawful prosecution. Sadly, it is a paradox, because there is no question that these "psychos," unless cured, must be permanently taken out of circulation.

Courts and litigation aside, most of the compulsive killers I have studied are touched by the darkness, the nightside of psyche, the malignant Voice that goads them on to commit appalling crimes. Of these, many have shown signs of dual personality: John Wayne Gacy, Chikatilo, Dean Corll, Joe Kallinger, Marie Noe, Richard Ramirez, Gary Ridgway, Arthur Shawcross, Norman Simons, Danny Starrett, Peter Sutcliffe, Ken Bianchi. But it is always a debate: Though Ken Bianchi, was almost certainly multiple, detectives thought the "alter bit" was a ruse, a scam, a get-out-of-jail card invented by the killer who feigns mental illness—what convicts call the "bug stunt."

Ken's chief alter, as we've seen, was named Steve. There was also someone named Billy, a frightened nine year old. Ken's case was packed with typical MPD scenarios like lost time: at school, he was "frequently accused of doing things he said he never did." Ken was himself a sweet guy, not aggressive. His associates were "certain he was incapable of violence." His girlfriend "knew he couldn't take a life." Ken himself, in earnest, said, "I can't envision myself killing somebody." But there were so many "blank spots in my life. Places where I just should remem-

ber what's going on and can't. . . . There is something wrong with me."
Thanks to "gaps in his memory . . . he often found himself walking
along . . . not remembering [getting] to that location"—typical MPD.
(Ken could have picked up additional spirits when he worked two years
as an ambulance technician; see appendix B.)

Apart from the patently nonadaptive alters of the criminal psychopath, there is yet another factor that argues against the idea of alters
as a useful / adaptive invention *created* by the patient's unconscious to
cope with their misery. We are talking about the phenomenal *number*
of alters in the case of supermultiples. Truddi Chase had so many, she
called them the Troops: "The headache was vicious last night. There
were voices talking all at once" (Chase 1987, 261). Do you think scores,
or even hundreds, of competing personalities are adaptive? The "babble
of voices," thought one exorcist, more resemble "the tormented murmurs
and helpless protests of a mob in agony." Father David began to hear
"literally a babel of sounds . . . [many] voices . . . thousands of them. And
more thousands . . . a whole army of voices" (Martin 1976, 155–56, 245).

My name is Legion
MARK 5:9

If extra personalities are any sort of coping mechanism, it makes no sense
why *so many?* Wouldn't one or two solid alter egos do the trick? Cam
West described the noise level in his mind—the "incessant, cacophonous
racket in my head . . . like lunch time at Zabar's" (West 1999, 142–43,
228). Janet F. had "thirty-three voices, all screaming at once." And as
Barbara G. put it, "the noise is deafening" (Cohen et al. 1991, 121, 124).

Kit Castle also spoke of this multitude inside her: "They were
all talking and laughing and questioning and crying and chattering
at once. It sounded like there were hundreds of them" (Castle and
Bechtel 1989, 223). Supermultiple Jenny was driven mad by "all the
screaming souls." As mentioned, more than four hundred personalities
were discovered, in the course of Jenny's therapy: how can this possibly
be adaptive (Spencer 1989, 275, xv)?

And as one spirit returned and fastened itself on a mortal, so did another and another, till hundreds and thousands of spirits dwelt in one corporeal body, often driving away the natural spirit.

OAHSPE, BOOK OF APH 5:10

Psychically sensitive Emanuel Swedenborg (*Arcana Celestia* paragraph 59) was greatly annoyed by intrusive spirits that crowded around him, sometimes numbering in the thousands. Dr. Fiore (1987, 114) explains how such a multitude is possible: "Once they are possessed, their auras are weakened. . . . They are now open prey for still others desiring physical bodies. The more spirits that come on board, the lower the vibrations of the possessee's aura." Some of her patients were possessed by fifty or more entities.

And none of this is adaptive, creative, useful, or self-defensive in any way, shape, or form. It is total infestation.

Finally, the separate, independent identity of alters has been made abundantly clear by observing their stark differences in body language, handwriting, illnesses, posture, facial expressions, mannerisms, ages, sexes, ethnic origins, IQs, brain waves, pulse rate, and even shifting eye color! One critical difference is beyond dispute: different languages. It is manifestly impossible for the host or "core" personality to create (from the unconscious) an alter who fluently speaks a foreign language wholly unknown to him. Among Billy Milligan's twenty-four alters, for example, one is Australian, one speaks Arabic, and one is Serbo-Croatian. The latter, named Ragen, speaks the Yugoslavian language fluently and English with a heavy accent. Billy, an Ohio boy, speaks only English. The paranormal phenomenon of speaking in an unfamiliar language is known as *xenoglossy*. Not surprisingly, it is frequently reported among mediums, and is also well documented in cases of spirit possession.

A multiple personality condition is the same as being spirit-possessed. . . . When a person exhibits duality of personality, the extra personality is the spirit of a person who has died.

EUGENE MAUREY, *EXORCISM*

Multiples, in a word, are mediums, *involuntarily* channeling the departed; but they are negative mediums, with no control over—and sometimes no awareness of—their visitors from Elsewhere. As one multiple put it, "I am terrified that my people will come out inappropriately. I do not have control over them" (Beverly, in Cohen et al. 1991, 54). The case histories of multiples read like a catalog of psychic phenomena, replete with mind reading, PK, poltergeistery, OBE, levitation, and clairvoyance as well as other manifestations that are usually associated with psychic sensitives: the cold wind, hyperpraxia, xenoglossy. Why do we get multiples and hysterics speaking in foreign languages unknown to them? Why do we get the cold wind with multiples and hysterics (see Castle and Bechtel 1989, 125, 128; Chase 1987, 282; T. Allen 1994, 211) when that icy chill is normally linked to séances and haunted houses? It's time to connect the dots.

> *Some who have been put away in institutions are actually strong psychic persons who have been intruded upon by unwanted spirits and have no idea how to cope with the situation.*
>
> MARTIN EBON, *EXORCISM*

If houses can be haunted, so can people. Schizophrenics are probably the most haunted people on earth. In full-blown schizophrenia, the core (native) personality is virtually submerged and the usurping entity is itself thoroughly psychotic. Despite the anguish of all the mental vagaries discussed in this chapter—OCD, MPD, bipolarism, anorexia, autism—the sufferer may still be passably sane, functioning to various degrees in society, some even excelling brilliantly in their professions. The schizophrenic, on the other hand, cannot hold a job or even a lucid conversation. With the schizophrenic, we are no longer dealing with mood disorders but with outright psychosis. To spiritualists like myself, this also means outright possession. Indeed, "the symptoms of possession are similar, if not identical, to schizophrenia" (Maurey 1988, 88). Such symptomology usually includes some of the following: thought disorder (scrambled cognition), hallucinations (voices, often), loss of contact with reality ("out of it"), paranoia, outbursts, spasmodic gestures (tics, jerks, grimaces), outrageous notions (like the end of the world, signals from outer space, and the like).

Since spiritualists regard the schizophrenic as in the clutches of a depraved, insane excarnate, we are among the few who recommend a non-pharmacological treatment. "Patients," according to one optimistic practitioner, "can easily be relieved of possessing entities through exorcism by a competent spiritualist. . . . One half of the patients in our mental institutions suffering from schizophrenia can be cured" (Thigpen and Cleckley 1957, 14). (More on cures in chapter 11.) Occasionally we hear of an unexpected cure. A "hopeless schizophrenic" was in a car wreck, badly shaken, and "within minutes, she was completely sane—for the first time in years." Dr. Fiore reasons "she had been possessed . . . and later the spirit was forcibly catapulted out of her jarred body" (Fiore 1987, 12).

If a patient said to your average psychiatrist that he was the victim of demonic possession, he would probably be diagnosed as paranoid schizophrenic. Ironic, huh? Maybe it is time to rethink our approach, our customary categories, pigeonholes, lingo, argot. We have, I think, been spinning our wheels long enough. Round and round we go, with little agreement and less understanding. For some reason, these thoughts remind me of the time Ena Twigg (England's foremost medium of the mid-twentieth century) was interviewed by someone named Mankowicz (Twigg and Brod 1973, 60):

"MANKOWICZ: Mrs. Twigg, would you say there is any possibility that these visions and voices have the same kind of relationship to you (as a medium) as they would to a schizophrenic like Joan of Arc, say?

TWIGG: Oh, would you say that Joan of Arc was a schizophrenic?

MANKOWICZ: Without a doubt, I would.

TWIGG: Well, we can all have our opinion, can't we?"

Why not try to look at the substance of a thing rather than the easy label to stick on it? What is stopping us, really, from seeking the root causes, rather than settling for dead-end verbiage piled high and deep? Let's move on, then; chapter 8 plunges into the concept of overshadowing per se—its nuts and bolts, its how, who, when, why, and wherefore.

8
THE OVERSHADOWING

You can know things that can't ever be proven. And that
knowledge often has a certainty to it that the evidential sort
never does. There are these unproven things about which I
have a quasi-religious certainty, things I would act on more
readily than anything I could support with mere evidence.

J. MARK BERTRAND, *BACK ON MURDER*

When science and spirit work together, openly and appreciatively, for
a common good—balance, harmony, and progress are achievable goals.
But try to subsist on either one alone—science or spirit—and our
efforts eventually founder. Neither one *alone* can competently map out
or improve the human condition. They are natural partners in the mastery of life, two sides of the same coin. The enlightened man dabbles in
both; he is an inveterate generalist.

But given the failure of organized religion to bring peace in the
world, science has (temporarily) gained the upper hand. Many of our lead-
ers today make a "god of science." In fact, we have reached a point where
the secular approach is politically correct, while various systems of belief,
of faith, are not; we are advised to just keep them to ourselves. All this
has put Sci Mat at the top of the game, the alpha dog. And this is good to
the extent that the objectivity, the neutrality, of science is an international
language capable of fostering global understanding and cooperation.

But science has gone to our head, and when it becomes a denier of spirit—contemptuous of intuition, foresight, dreams, angels, second sight and ESP—distortion of truth inevitably sets in.* A good example: the human *mind* cannot be reduced to the human *brain*. Yet this is precisely the sort of reductionism that Sci Mat has thrived on. And the public eats it up. The Almighty Brain trumps all.

Besides the Almighty Brain, Sci Mat has come up with another darling to stun us with its dazzling breakthroughs: DNA genetics. Theorists today are less embarrassed discussing the possibility of an evil gene than evil spirits. Nevertheless "the genetic argument cannot explain the low homicide rate of Australia (a country even younger than the United States) whose early settlers were, in many cases, deported to the [nether] continent as transgressors against the laws of their day" (Lunde 1976, 17). Still, the game is afoot and the goal is to find "genetic determinants" for almost any unusual behavior, supposedly demystifying even our most bizarre behavior. Take sleepwalking, for example. *Time* magazine (May 18, 2015, 27) proudly announced, "DISCOVERED: That sleepwalking may be a genetic trait. New research found that among children whose parents both have a history of sleepwalking, more than 60% will develop the behavior." Pandering to human vanity, such "discoveries" seem cheering, when we can blame our quirks and our faults on some gene. O what a relief it is—to find out we are not accountable after all, being the helpless victims of heredity! Thank God we are not responsible!

But we do not inherit most of our behavior. We learn it. When we encounter some disposition (like sleepwalking) that runs in families, it is most likely nurture—not nature—that makes it so. For example, one psychologist noted that "many multiples have children who also turn out to be multiple" (Noll 1990, 33); he quotes Dr. Kluft's sardonic remark that "child abuse is the gift that keeps on giving," meaning that abused children, when grown, tend to abuse their own children. And this is how the gift is "inherited" (98 percent of multiples were victims of abuse).

Dr. Peck informs us that the mother of his patient Beccah was also

---

*I have written about this in *Delusions in Science and Spirituality* (2015), attempting to show how the exclusion of the Unseen has resulted in such popular but fallacious theories as Big Bang, Evolution, Freudianism, and even global warming.

possessed (Peck 2005, 179). Does this prove the daughter inherited it? Of course not. Many of Dr. Rapoport's OCD patients "have family members with typical OCD" (Rapoport 1989, 152). Does this mean it's genetic? Not necessarily. Even when there is plenty of insanity in the family, it does not mean genes. It means nurture. Yet Sci Mat keeps pulling us back to the guilty gene. "Manic depression . . . is familial, probably genetic" (Duke and Hochman 1992, 97). But what about the banshee spirit? In Ireland it is usually a family (not an individual) that has a banshee attached to it.

Missionaries in Japan, too, reported on a certain family that was possessed for a hundred years. Does the answer lie in genetics or in the spirits that attend the family group? Dr. Wickland recounts, "From one patient, Mrs. A., thirteen different spirits were dislodged . . . and of these, seven were recognized by the patient's mother as relatives or friends well known to her during their earth lives" (Wickland 1974, 37). In the ancient world, it was customary for the children of the magician/shaman to carry on his work. The magicians "had an abundance of familiars," and when these old men died, "the familiars would go to their sons or daughters" (Oahspe, Book of Osiris 10:10). This (spiritual, not genetic) transfer of talents or powers is recognized in all tribal cultures with totemic beliefs. This is how tribal magic works: "Members of the same totemic group have spiritual contact with each other through the totem" (Ebon 1967, 237: Rose 1957). Outside of Australia, however, the "spiritual contact" may not be so beneficial. In Sri Lanka, for one, rites of exorcism are performed by the *Kapuralaya* priesthood to remove a *preta* who is "any [deceased] person excessively attached to the things of the world," usually a near-kinsman with "excessive love of the living." Pretas are known to be miserable, greedy spirits. One man's father became a preta "because he loved him too much" (Crapanzano and Garrison 1977, 249–53). Cloying. Pressing. Impinging. Clinging.

The Ceylonese preta is more or less the same creature as the *haint**

---

*In 1998, there was lots of PK in a fine house in Manchester, Connecticut. Was it a haunting? a possession? a poltergeist? Why, it seemed like all three: eight-year-old Michael turned white and screamed, a shrill keening. He said a man came to his room of Western society, the ghost suffering from excessive attachment to the living—often overprotective parents who stick around even after their demise to "help" their offspring. As Dr. Fiore has it, there is always trouble with these "familiars" who may impose their own fears or demands. (Sometimes they are deceased spouses who "deliberately create havoc" with their remarried spouse.) Fiore further elucidates: "Many of my patients have found that their parents were with them since the parents' deaths. . . . They were often the hardest to persuade to leave. They felt they knew what was best for their children and didn't want to hear what I, a stranger, had to say about it!" (Fiore 1987, 33, 115).

> *Some departed ancestors . . . attempt to mold the lives of those who are akin. . . . The more clannish the family group, the more likely is this to be true. . . . The obsessor claims the right by ties of blood [and] has no desire to do anything but to keep the mortal in line with family ideals.*
> TITUS BULL, QUOTED IN FODOR 1966, 267

Circulating in the same kin group, especially in close-knit families, familiar spirits may give us visions, talk to us in our sleep, or even pretend to be great masters, "taking upon themselves any name pleasant to the ear" (Oahspe, Book of Aph 12:5). Being recently deceased, they are residents of the lowest (bound) heavens, with little to stop them from indulging in their obsessions. Cases in point: Olivia became OC only after her grandmother died. Katherine became OC/anorexic after her father (who had been hypercritical) suicided. Daniel became OC soon after he sat in the synagogue at his grandfather's funeral. Judging from the literature, quite a few autistic boys are overshadowed by their deceased grandfather.

(cont.) and touched his shoulder. There had been other sightings in that household—ghosts, glowing balls of light, furniture levitating, a red-eyed apparition. It seems that the grandfather had died before Michael was born. But one day Michael saw his photo and said, "that's the man who keeps coming into my room at night" (Floyd 2002, 41).

Spirits usually superpose the psyche of a human who has a similar character structure.

HANS NAEGELI-OSJORD, *POSSESSION AND EXORCISM*

Often enough it is a common bond in tastes and interests that draws an excarnate to his counterpart among the living: "To the musician, angel musicians, to the philosopher, angel philosophers, to the historian, angel historians" (Oahspe, God's Book of Eskra 4:20). There are times when the mortal visionary becomes aware of these like-minded beings who, as George Russell espoused in *The Candle of Vision,* are "brought into psychic contact with us by some affinity of sentiment or soul."

Overshadowed Artists

The great composer Johannes Brahms, for one, thought that most of his inspiration came from on high, that he was in effect a medium for deceased musicians. But only rarely are such overshadowed artists or writers inspired by angel hosts that come in great legions, phalanxes from the higher organic heavens.* Typically, it is merely a newly dead person in the *lower* heavens who returns to the earth plane *individually* to find and inspire a mortal protégé. Suchlike are essentially earth-bound entities, obsessors, "ever molding themselves to mortals of similar tastes and indulgences" (Oahspe, Book of Judgment 6:10). One of the most famous cases of this kind involved a "weekend artist" and jeweler named Frederic Thompson who began painting "for" the recently deceased noted landscape artist R. Swain Gifford. While spiritual intervention revealed that Gifford-X "was elated over his power to return and finish his work through Thompson," the latter actually

---

*There is a big difference between being controlled by a single entity and being "influenced by a congress of spirits, a phalanx, in the highest stage of purification and knowledge"—as was the amanuensis of Oahspe, John B. Newbrough. In fact, when Newbrough queried his controls about Shakespeare, the answer came, "He was attended by a vast multitude of spirits, and they virtually and really played and spoke their parts, entering within his own spirit" (Newbrough 1874, #60).

"deteriorated under the ever-increasing compulsion. He believed he was going insane." The voice would urge Thompson on; then he would black out. Gifford-X would order, "Do not forget me." Thompson, in the end, became a fairly successful full-time painter, but at the cost of considerable "personality disintegration" (Guiley 2000, 381).

The ethnographer W. H. Rivers (1968, 321) observed among the Tikopians (Melanesia) a form of possession by "*atua* or ghosts of their ancestors. . . . A chief is only possessed by the ghost of a chief, a commoner only by the ghost of a commoner." The adage "Like unto like" epitomizes all these transactions; for, the earthbound, after death, remain "in their former places: the merchant in his counting houses, the banker in his bank . . . the pope in his place . . . the farmer in his" (Oahspe, Book of Judgment 23:22). "A feather can not go against the wind; neither can the spirit-out-of-the-body come to him who will not receive it" (Newbrough 1874, x).

The Freudian, of course, sees the "dark force" strictly belonging to the patient's inner self. Freud wrote in 1923 that olden "cases of demoniacal possession correspond to the neurosis of the present day. . . . What in [earlier] days were thought to be evil spirits, to us are base evil wishes . . . impulses which have been rejected and repressed. . . . We attribute their origin to the inner life of the patient" (Freud 1923). But we cannot stop there. The great exorcist Eugene Maurey was able to profile the intruders: "With an evaluation of the invading entities, their personality characteristics can be detailed fairly accurately. The subject will exhibit a *similar personality profile* [emphasis added]." Maurey went on to observe that "those who can be aroused emotionally, who are strong willed and act on impulse . . . or complain and express negative feelings" are prime targets (Maurey 1988, 120, 48, 88).

"They feed on my negativity," said a woman with entities (Sagan 1997, 151). Expanding that laundry list of magnets is the finding that "with the skeptic, the lazy, the rich and the lustful, the ashars [good angels] have little power of protection" (Oahspe, Book of Wars 20:14). Those who have worked closely with the obsessed would add to that checklist of vulnerabilities:* nervous depletion and chronic fears, defeatism, melancholy, guilt, self-loathing, depression, shame, and vice; persons who are excitable, power hungry, vengeful, quarrelsome, and corrupt are also at risk.

> *The more corrupt a man, the easier he is to control.*
> MIKE WARNKE, *THE SATAN SELLERS*

> *If a man [excarnate] had been a heavy drinker, he may hang out in the bars and try to take over a personality.*
> JOHN FULLER, *THE GHOST OF 29 MEGACYCLES*

Dr. Fiore elaborates: "One of the strongest ties that bound spirits to the physical world was addiction—to alcohol, drugs . . . I have treated many of these addicted patients. Spirit-addicts tended to cluster around living addicts" (Fiore 1987, 35). The drinker has been the easiest to track. Popular sensitive and ghost seer James Van Praagh (2008, 142) couldn't make it out of the nightclub fast enough: "Although seeing people was difficult, seeing ghosts was not. The place was filled with them. . . . Some sat alongside people at the bar, enjoying the pleasures of vodka martinis and tequila shots . . . [I] saw a long line of people waiting to get in. Several ghosts tagged along. . . . The whole atmosphere was a scary movie in the making." Such ghosts, when seen on the astral plane, appear to be "creatures of low type which feast on the alcoholic fumes exuding from the drunkard's body" (Powell 2007, 103). Conversely, inebriation helps "open the door"—as in the case of the spirit who admitted "it had been easy for her to get into him . . . because his own spirit was loosely anchored in his body, due to the influence of a few drinks" (Ebon 1974, 43).

---

*There is something of a vicious cycle here: the mentally deranged person is all the more susceptible to invading spirit, as are the victimized and the weak as well as people drawn to high-risk work (law enforcement, military, paramedic, rescue operations). Another kind of vicious cycle sees the OC or manic personality become a workaholic—to the point of exhaustion, which condition is itself amenable to spirit entry. Pearl Curran, for example, became the host for Patience Worth-X who was able to "slip into her only because she was very tired" (Scott and Norman 1985, 303).

I hasten to add that there may be situational factors beyond a person's control, factors that can just as easily attract a predatory spirit. It probably comes as no surprise that isolation is one of those factors. This situation crosses all cultural boundaries. In Marquesan society (in the Pacific) *vehina hae* are fearful spirits of the night. The Islanders said that these returning spirits only manifest themselves to isolated individuals; so when one had to go out of his hut after sunset, he always had a friend accompany him. Sri Lankans hold an almost identical belief: here, the woman called Somavati became the victim of a spirit attack after making the mistake of walking alone at a time (after 6 p.m.) "when evil spirits are out." "Alone," in Sinhalese belief, "is a dangerous state; it makes a person vulnerable to demonic attack. Such an attack during a period of aloneness . . . is known as *tanikam dosa* "troubles of aloneness (caused by demons)" (Crapanzano and Garrison 1977, 250).

Although "demons" are unacceptable to the arch-rational mind-set of the West, some practitioners simply ignore the fiat. Dr. M. Scott Peck, for one, was in the tiny minority of psychiatrists that acknowledges possession and performs exorcisms on their patients. Significantly, Peck discovered acute isolation in the background of his most difficult cases: Jersey and Beccah. When Beccah's possessing spirit spoke through her mouth, it declared, "I attacked her when she was five because she was always alone." Consulting his colleagues on similar cases, the brave doctor found that "each of their case histories described the patients as being lonely to a greater degree than one might expect. . . . I have begun to suspect that loneliness may be a precondition for possession" (Peck 2005, 179, 245).

Although failing to explore its implications, conventional psychiatry is aware of this pattern, especially in MPD cases. The famous Sybil was effectively isolated from normal child life by all the prohibitions and dogma of her family's fundamentalist faith. Too, Dr. Mayer found that one of his multiple patients first took on an alter "when she was left alone in the house, locked in a closet" (Mayer 1989, 187). Acute loneliness figures in numerous MPD cases, and in many instances, we see that the isolation is actually enforced; "abusive fathers," observes Mayer, "work diligently to keep their families isolated . . . to keep the secret intact" (Mayer 1989, 210). Billy Milligan's first "inner friend" appeared before him when he was not quite four years old and lonely. It was the same night that his father attempted suicide. After that, whenever he was lonely "he would just close his eyes. When he opened them, he would be in a different place" (Keyes 1981, 147, 157).

Solitary existence may be shaped by negligent, absentee parents, as was the case with Rod Ferrell, the animal-torturing teen vampire / killer who more or less *brought himself up*. Stark isolation can be a breeding ground for obsessions. In Dr. Rapoport's high school survey (1989, 113), most OC teenagers fell into this pattern. "As we hit true cases, we heard stories of lonely and odd childhoods." When Beth came to Dr. Levenkron with a full-blown case of OCD, therapy revealed that her father had deserted his family, the mother was a working alcoholic, and all her siblings were older and already moved out. Beth became a latchkey kid, "nearly always home alone." And it was a neighbor who molested this "easy prey" at age nine.

Not even chronic illness or frequent surgeries or permanent disability can match the psychic destructiveness of isolation, especially in the formative years. Indeed, it is one of the most common elements in the breakdown of self, discovered across the board—in obsession, possession, MPD, and psychopathy. Picture the desperately lonely child who creates imaginary playmates—like the "other personalities now living in her body" that Lauren "had made up and given names when she was a frightened, lonely child" (Mayer 1989, 111). Or Arthur Shawcross who "never had friends," but created imaginary ones. "I wanted someone to play with so bad." He talked with his conjured companions and heard their "tinny" voices. Artie's schoolmates called him "Oddie." "My child life was all being alone"—Arthur Shawcross, serial killer.

An imaginary playmate can grow into an alternate personality.

RICHARD NOLL, *BIZARRE DISEASES OF THE MIND*

The Shoemaker, another deranged killer, "longed for a friend but never had one" (Schreiber 1984, 278); he too took on imaginary playmates to fill the void of his lonely childhood. As this fantasy life spins out of control, the wish for imaginary friends becomes a standing invitation to wandering spirits. And the dubious spirit companion is welcomed with open arms. It is like Fred Archer said in his survey of possession: the most stubborn cases betray isolation; "many persons subjected to obsession, especially those leading lonely lives, come almost to love their chains" (Archer 1967, 103). Occupied now with this secret world, the antisocial personality begins to take shape. Criminal psychopathology, thanks to our fascination with murder and mayhem, is well documented, and here we find time and again the notorious "loner."

> *The relationship of these murderers to other persons was shallow. They had been essentially lonely men.*
>
> MANFRED GUTTMACHER,
> *THE MIND OF THE MURDERER*

Isolation figures frequently in the backstories of heinous crimes. Chikatilo, Ted Bundy, Zodiac, Andrew Cunahan (spree killer), and Jerry Brudos were all creatures of solitude. One FBI statistic tells us that 71 percent of serial killers felt isolated in childhood. It almost makes you want to get up and do something about all the separateness, even the "individuality," we have built into our modern lifestyle. The homicidal lone wolf, in any case, is a stock character in our rogues' gallery. Here is a quick survey:

- David Berkowitz (Son of Sam): "I was always a loner . . . [which] led to my downfall" (Klausner 1981, 101)
- George Trepal (the Mensa Murderer): "constant feelings of isolation"
- Eric Chapman (grandmatricide): "was a very isolated young man" (Markman and Bosco 1989, 303)
- Richard Ramirez: "had no friends." He was "the consummate loner . . . never revealed his heart to anyone" (Carlo 1996, 199, 324)
- Arthur Jackson: "was just a total loner . . . isolated from the rest of humanity"

- John Hinckley Jr. (would-be assassin of President Reagan): "had no friends and few acquaintances" (Caplan 1987, 59)
- Leon Czolgosz (the man who assassinated President William McKinley): "was a quiet, solitary child. . . . He never had a close friend" (Donovan 1962, 73)
- Eric Napoletano (serial killer): "You could say he was a lonely kid," reported his mother. "But he always got a lot of toys" (Pienciak 1996, 52)
- Arlyne G. (matricide): "As a child I was very lonely" (Markman and Bosco 1989, 320)
- Paul (Alaska's "environmental savior" and mass shooter): "was always alone" (Blinder 1985, 74)
- John Wayne Gacy: as a child, was "a loner, sickly and weak" (T. Cahill 1987, 15)
- Peter Sutcliffe: was a mama's boy; "he remained friendless"; neighbors would later comment, "He were a loner, y'see . . . always very remote" (Burn 1985, 17, 27, 41)
- Bobby Joe Long (compulsive rapist turned serial killer): "I was always alone as a kid" (Morrison 2004, 149)
- Danny Starrett: prowled for girls in his car; "When I was alone in a car," Danny explained, "when I was alone, period, I was vulnerable. As long as I was around other people I was safe. . . . Whenever I was alone, bad things were bound to happen" (Naifeh and Smith 1995, 156, 160)

The isolated soul is vulnerable. Then again, vulnerability may also arise out of a single devastating experience. A crisis, shock, surgery, or unconsciousness are all known to presage the first bout of serious overshadowing. Injury, grave illness, pure terror, and unconsciousness all represent the lowest possible state of human vitality in which the mind is utterly defenseless and unable to resist the intrusion of a strong spirit. Patty Duke remembers her first manic episode occurring at eighteen, after she was rushed to the hospital for emergency surgery on a ruptured appendix. Recovering back home, "I literally went crazy. I was

hallucinating and raving and ranting and not sleeping and not eating"
(Duke and Hochman 1992, 7–8).

The helplessness and sudden loss of composure (*compos mentis*) and
self-command present prime opportunities for prowling spirits in search
of a vacant "home." Like Patty, the young woman named Annette suffered from a perforated appendix; it was then complicated by pulmonary
embolism, collapsed lung, heart failure, and coma.* Resuscitated, she
woke up a different person, querulous, abusive, and contemptuous, and
within hours developed acute suicidal depression. Dr. Guirdham, who
had been treating Annette, was floored: "The effect . . . was shattering.
It was as though she had changed identity. . . . She was in the depths of
as intense a depression as I have ever encountered. . . . It was as if she
had lost her psyche. . . . I had never seen so vertiginous a plunge. . . . In
my view, this was a case of possession.† . . . The abusive interlude which
she displayed burst like a rocket to the astonishment of her nurses and
doctors. This was one form of possession. The sudden plunge into sheer
hell [deepest depression] was an example of a more malign invasion. . . .
She said that something certainly not herself was speaking and acting
for her" (Guirdham 1982, 44–45).

In a similar scenario, the obsessed boy Zach had suffered seven
operations for congenital intestinal problems. Likewise did Dr. Fiore's
patient Howard "pick up an earthbound entity" at age four, during his
tonsillectomy. Fiore states that a great many of her patients were possessed when very young, "especially following hospitalizations for such
surgeries as tonsillectomies or during severe illnesses. Picking up a spirit
at that tender age and growing up with it 'on board' made it nearly
impossible for [them] to discern the boundaries of their own personalities from those of their possessors" (Fiore 1987, 3). Fiore, insightfully,

---

*The comatose state need not produce derangement. John Myers, the great medium,
acquired second sight at age five after emerging from a coma, just as England's Dr. John
Lilly met his "guardians" while in the comatose state. Whether we attract benevolent
guardians or hell-bent *obsessors* will depend on our overall character and fortitude.
†In the next chapter, under "rapid cycling," we will have a better look at the nature of
this vertiginous plunge into the possessed state.

compares this encroachment to the immune system: the "aura is to the emotional-spiritual dimension of a person as the immune system is to the physical body. Just as a weakened immune system leaves the individual susceptible to diseases . . . so a diminished aura creates a vulnerability to spirit intrusion."

Every case is different. There are many circumstances that can jar loose or interfere with the natural composure of mind: grave illness, intolerable strain, total exhaustion, blackout, accident or injury, indeed trauma of any kind. In Egypt, for example, "the origin of possession in a traumatic event" was generally supposed (Crapanzano and Garrison 1977, 185). Or fever—the deranged killer Dean Corll's troubles may have begun at age seven with rheumatic fever, involving a heart murmur and followed by blackouts. Trouble also began early for Marie Coe, the Philadelphia woman who would later smother eight of her babies to death. "Mad of a fever," as the old expression goes. Stricken with scarlet fever at age four, Marie had lapsed into a coma and almost died. She was only brought around by a blood transfusion. Soon after, her family noticed "a marked change in her personality . . . quiet as the grave and withdrawn, as if in her own world . . . mentally slow. . . . She was never the same again." Marie's comment much later: "I guess it took a toll on my . . . um, noodle." There may be a bit more to her story: After the scarlet fever, she had been given a cocktail of experimental drugs by her doctors, causing "irreparable brain damage" (Glatt 2002, 10–14, 19).

Shock and terror also play their part. "The impingement by spirit entities," Dr. Wickland stated, "the encroachment, is made possible by . . . sudden shock" (Wickland 1974, 20). It is second nature for our own spirit to withdraw from pain or horror. Every instance of the unhinged mind should be checked for early shock/trauma/abuse to find the original scene of flight; the victim, terrified and vulnerable, simply vacates the body like a house on fire—an automatic, not a planned or conscious response. Once you start looking for it, the incidents come in spades. For some, the sudden death of a near one is the trigger. One of Dr. Sagan's clients housing an entity she called "the ape," remembers when it came in: "It was . . . [when] my father died . . . I was thirteen. My brother and my uncle picked me up from school. And the ape jumped inside me in the panic that followed" (Sagan 1997, 12).

It might also be noted that the victim of untimely death may himself "bulldoze his way into" the nearest body, as Dr. Fiore discovered, using a technique of hypnotic recall: her patient Tony was regressed to the time he had witnessed a fatal accident in which the victim, a young girl, "joined him," as he comforted the dying girl. Tony told Fiore, "She doesn't want to leave me." In the same way, another spirit "entered my [Fiore's] patient, a male nurse, while he was administering mouth-to-mouth resuscitation, as the spirit's body died from a drug overdose" (Fiore 1987, 50, 114). In a similar scenario, a terribly disturbed girl (satanic victim) named Jadie seemed to be inhabited by Tashee, another satanic victim, who had died. Jadie explained, "When Tashee died, her ghost got inside me" (Hayden 1991, 262).

If the host is healthy and strong, attempt at impingement may amount to no more than a momentary jolt. One of the FBI's premier profilers, Robert Ressler (who, by the way, coined the term *serial killer*) experienced this firsthand on the night of May 9–10, 1994, when mad killer John Wayne Gacy was executed by lethal injection. Ressler knew Gacy well, from prison interviews and correspondence. The two had actually been raised in the same neighborhood in Illinois. On that fateful night, Agent Ressler recounts, "I awoke with a start . . . hyperventilating. . . . My chest was heaving. I was having a weird anxiety reaction . . . I wondered if I was having a heart attack." He then turned on the TV and caught the news: "'At such and such a time, John Wayne Gacy was executed,' and the time announced was, to the minute, the moment that I had woken up in that weird fright. Whether or not John Wayne Gacy had passed through my room on his way to hell, just to scare the serial-killer hunter who had grown up only four blocks from him . . . I don't know, but it was an uncanny experience" (Ressler 1997, 92–93).

MPD, probably the most uncanny of today's mental disorders, begins in traumatic childhood abuse, almost always sexual molestation. The shock of it, as we have seen, sets the stage for secondary personality: enter the alter who nestles protractedly in the child's atmosphere. The most forceful or able or ardent of these "lodgers" is likely to become the dominant alter, who then directs traffic as the number of alters mounts. The little victim has no idea what is going on and, what's more, is too young to do anything about it. Truddi Chase, for example, was only two years old when she was first raped; once her being (vacated by fear and shock) was thrown open to homeless spirits, a multitude found lodging therein: her Troops, all ninety-two of them. Often enough, the alter personalities are "born" as a result of a specific traumatic incident. We see this in Billy Milligan's story: asked when "your people first came into existence," Billy recalled that most of them came when "Daddy Chalmer" (his stepfather) first assaulted him, at age eight.

Billy, Truddi, Eve, Sybil, Kit, Jennifer, Toby, Alex, and a thousand other multiples who had been commandeered by vagabond spirits were, in the first place, helpless children, abused sexually or even tortured. (Among multiples, the only exceptions I have found to actual sexual assault were victims of brutalization, usually in satanic cults.) And there is little that distinguishes them from the frankly possessed. One specialist, commenting on *spirit possession,* said "he did not know how his patients became possessed, although he almost invariably finds a history of sexual abuse in early childhood" (T. Allen 1994, 241). In the case of a "demonized woman," it was found that her stepfather had repeatedly molested her sexually. Dr. M. Scott Peck's patient Jersey (possessed) was molested by her father shortly after she underwent extremely painful appendicitis surgery—double whammy! A missionary among Baronga tribesmen in southeast Africa observed that most instances of spirit possession "have begun by a distinct crisis in which the patient was unconscious" (Oesterreich 1935, 139).

Preconditions are legion. "A succession of serious physical illnesses can help precipitate an attack of possession" (Guirdham 1982, 53). Or possession may follow a frightful accident. A female patient treated by Dr. Fiore for spirit possession was amazed by some of her own behavior: "That's just not me. . . . I've never been the same since the accident. My husband says I'm like two different people" (Fiore 1987, 38). Accident (especially when combined with terror) can unhinge psyche, as in the freakish case of sixty-four-year-old Ira Attebury who for no apparent reason shot up a San Antonio, Texas, parade (with "enough ammunition to start a war") and then took his own life. Sure, Ira was a loner, gun collector, and paranoid, but what could explain this "senseless, shocking" mass attack that left two dead and fifty wounded? His brother helped fill in some details: Ira, it seems, had been involved in an accident in which two women were killed. They ran a red light and his truck plowed into their car; but he himself was pinned in—and afraid it would burst into flames. "Things have been different since that wreck. . . . He imagined things that weren't quite true" (Douglas and Olshaker 1999, 228–30). Afterward, profilers pondered, "Could the accident have caused some physiological change?" But does a change have to be physiological to be significant? Doesn't psyche count? Doesn't the mind count? Why is it so hard to grasp the "possibility that human minds could be invaded or at least influenced . . . by nonphysical intelligences from out there somewhere" (Hunt and McMahon 1988, 17)?

> *The brain is indeed a machine that a ghost can operate.*
> DAVE HUNT AND T. A. McMAHON,
> *THE NEW SPIRITUALITY*

When psyche has been shattered by shock, its "skin" ruptured, "the surface of the aura is loose and . . . it will easily take in any thought forms that make strike on it. . . . Because of this . . . such people [can] pick up, like human fly-papers, any forms that may be about" (Butler 1978, 226–27). Communicators from the Other Side have tried to explain how they themselves impinge through thought waves. "We impress it [the mind] with our message," declared one automatic script; then "the inner mind receives our message . . . [It] is like soft wax, it perceives our thoughts" (Fodor 1966, 22).

In Sri Lanka, where the Kapurala priest acts as exorcist for possessed persons, there is a clear and sharp distinction between the good gods on the one hand, and spirits of a low order on the other: *avesa* is the term used to describe those possessed by evil spirits, while *arude* is for those possessed by a wise divinity. Like the Sinhalese, we must recognize the difference between higher inspiration and the darker forms of overshadowing.

Much of what we have discussed in this chapter, and in this book, has aimed the searchlight on the less savory aspects of discarnate influence, akin to the avesa or the "unclean spirits" spoken of in the Holy Bible. Yet those scriptures also speak of "gifts of the spirit." Just so, the second sight enjoyed by the sound-minded and honorable medium has long been known as "the gift." Overshadowing, in other words, has two sides: the dark and the light. The exemplary medium, skilled and virtuous in the application of her gift, is a light-worker. "Many psychics are ultrastable people and endowed with too much resilience to attract the attention of hostile entities" (Guirdham 1982, 53).

The same may be said of some of our most distinguished creative and inventive luminaries. Otherworldly communicators have attested that many of the world's great artistic achievements and momentous inventions were impressed on mortal minds from their world. A single literary example: Isabel Allende, who said, "ghosts came to my aid"; the Seeing runs in her family. She got the ending of her first novel from her deceased grandfather in a dream. The Allende family is of Basque lineage—very psychic, like the country Irish. Even Isabel's famous uncle, Salvador Allende, the assassinated president of Chile, was an intuitive man whose hunches seldom missed.

For the poet-artist William Blake, it was his "celestial friends" who provided him with inspiration; his "Milton" and "Jerusalem" were written from their immediate dictation. I believe, too, that a person engaged in humanitarian work will attract a great number of good spirits. Yet in all truth, every one of us is endowed with the still, small voice.

And it hath been shown thee that not only the seer, prophet, and miracle-worker, but that all people are subject to the influence of the spirits of the dead, even though unconscious to themselves.

OAHSPE, BOOK OF DISCIPLINE 3:10

9

ρOSSESSION

I am looking for people who would believe me.

ANNELIESE MICHEL, POSSESSED

"Father Arnold, it is really difficult to imagine what [it] is like. How is it possible that they can force a person like that? You have no power of your own at all. I don't understand at all how something like that is possible."

ANNELIESE MICHEL,

AS QUOTED IN FELICITAS GOODMAN,

THE EXORCISM OF ANNELIESE MICHEL

Most of the books written today about mind/consciousness/psyche can be read, put down, and easily forgotten. One great exception is *The Exorcism of Anneliese Michel* written by the anthropologist Felicitas Goodman. It was the "true story" upon which the 2009 American film *The Exorcism of Emily Rose* was based. Anneliese's story is all the more compelling in being the first modern case of *death* by spirit possession.* Yes, Anneliese, a lovely and intelligent college girl (majoring in education and theology) in Germany, lost her life battling demonic possession.

That was in the early 1970s. Neither the psychiatrists' drugs nor

---

*We sometimes hear of vodoun deaths in Haiti and sorcery (imp) deaths in Polynesia.

the priests' incantations could save her. A strict Catholic, Anneliese set her problems in motion by her own zealous but "naive piety." Willing to make a penance of herself, she believed the only salvation was to pray for others incessantly. She later explained herself to Father Renz: "Oh Father, I never thought it would be as cruel as this. I always thought that I would want to suffer for others so they would not have to go to hell . . . but then things got really awful" (Goodman 1981, 150; all page references in this section about Anneliese are to the 1981 Goodman book). The world, she thought, could be saved by prayer and by contrition, starting with herself: "I am a sinner" (1981, 173). But then, a Voice began telling her she was damned. She was playing right into the hands of demonic forces. One time when she was in her depths, Father Rodewyk visited her; he asked, "What is your name?" And the answer came, "Judas," spoken by the girl in "an altered, much lower voice."* (Judas the Betrayer was her main demon.) But soon she "came to," whereon she and Father Rodewyk had an "entirely reasonable conversation." However, "the cramps [seizure] started again" quite suddenly. Then she slapped him in the face. Father Rodewyk, before leaving, told the family, "We are dealing with a case of possession" (1981, 85).

The first fratzen (demonic faces) appeared in 1970. Betrayed by her religious ecstasies, Anneliese would sit with her rosary and sublime thoughts, when "suddenly, like sheet lightning on the distant horizon, she saw a huge, cruelly grimacing face . . . [that] left her with a chill of nameless fear"† (1981, 21). There would also be the devotee's stigmata— small wounds mysteriously opening on her feet, like the wounds of the Lord on the cross. Too, as she approached the Virgin's shrine, "the soil burned like fire" and she could not even look at the medals and pictures of saints, so intensely did they shine (1981, 34).

---

*During possession the voice may be "completely unlike that of the natural voice of the speaker" (Goodman 1988, 96).

†The vision/visage may spread to the victim; one visiting friend was right in the middle of a normal conversation with Anneliese when "her face contracted into a real Fratze, a hideous, grimacing countenance . . . [it] was so demonic" (1981, 72).

We have seen this painful acuity of the senses before, this hyperesthesia that marks the altered state. Goodman reports that Anneliese's nervous system was by nature exquisitely sensitive, excitable. "The hypersensitive," she reasons, may then be subject to "a lingering captivity," any arousal unnaturally prolonged (1981, 206). The arousal, in Anneliese's case, may have begun in earliest childhood. She was the sickliest of all her sisters, having survived scarlet fever at the age of five. High fevers in childhood, as mentioned earlier, have long been known to presage psychism, opening the door. Then, at age eleven, Anneliese had a bad fall—on her forehead (appendix C). And then, at sixteen, came the first blackout; that night, in bed, she was pinned down by "a giant force." A year later came another blackout, then (temporary) paralysis.* More illnesses followed and, in their aftermath, she became more anxious and withdrawn, at the same time that her interest in religion increased.

We have variously called the door that shields us from psyche's outer realm the dam, the barrier, the threshold, just as Anneliese's biographer calls it "the threshold that separates this world from the other"; once you cross that threshold into "a different reality," it is all the more difficult "to return to 'business as usual'" (1981, 99, 206). The altered state, for Anneliese, brought problems that the reader of this book is already familiar with—anorexia, for example. Father Renz thought the demons were preventing her from eating anything good. "I was not permitted to eat." Two months before her death, she began to refuse food. The pathologist said she died of starvation. The last two months of her life she was also unable to sleep, catching maybe an hour or two of slumber here and there. Also, one year before she died, she began to have difficulty walking, reminding us of the awkward gait sometimes observed among the obsessed. Obsession, as we have also seen in these chapters, may entail an unnamed dread, an apprehension with no face or definition, arising, no doubt, from the presence of the "uninvited guest."

---

*In Morocco victims of the *jnun* may experience "complete paralysis of the limbs and face" (Crapanzano and Garrison 1977, 44).

For Anneliese, this took the form of anxiety, depression, and despair—without her knowing the reason for these emotions. All she knew was a "feeling of abject terror" (1981, 151).

The OC "commands," nonetheless, were clear enough. "I got the command to strip. What in the world is that supposed to mean? I don't hear it. I simply realize that I have to do it. It is a true compulsion" (1981, 151). Goodman notes, "Neither was she able to change the way she was behaving. 'My will is not my own,' she would say over and over again. 'Someone else is manipulating me.' It was that way in the bus . . . Father Alt tells what happened: 'On the way home Anneliese behaved in a most unseemly way toward Frau Hein. She spoke with a voice like a man's . . . she simply was not Anneliese anymore. . . . These vocalizations . . . talking very loudly . . . [were] frightening and chaotic . . . [and] much faster than hers'" (1981, 35, 248), recalling others touched by the darkness who talk/laugh "too loud or too long." It was, again, "with a completely altered voice" (1981, 73) that she ordered her boyfriend, Peter, out when he came to visit her.

It was a mixed bag of dissociative and ghostly manifestations. Anneliese was clairvoyant in her last year of life. "She became telepathic, knowing, for instance, who was praying for her in some other town and at what time. She began divining . . . [and] the dead visited her" (1981, 206). All the while, the ghost cold and molestations would come over her unpredictably. Father Alt would suddenly see "her face change; her eyes darkened, and she became absent" (reminding us of the eye darkening/dilating previously discussed). The attack, Anneliese said, felt like "being hurled into a dark pit. . . . My real self sits in a hole inside of myself and has nothing to say about anything . . . as if someone else were giving the orders" (1981, 21).

In her fits, she would grunt for hours on end or scream incessantly, loudly and coarsely; this would be followed by trembling and twitching that were then replaced by stiff contortions, even catatonic rigidity—inert for days. Like other victims of possession, her stiffness brought uncanny heaviness; the men found it almost impossible to lift the delicate girl. When she felt an agitated state coming on, she actually asked her family to tie her up to prevent self-injury: self-biting, head banging, smothering, and the like. But she would also lash out at others, striking blows and kicking, not unlike the spirits in chaos as described in Oahspe—"battling against all who came along . . . screaming . . . striking out . . . in an unending nightmare of madness" (Oahspe, Book of Wars 54:17). There was also the classic stench of evil hauntings, "like rotten eggs, like dung," a repulsive burning smell. And the air turned cold. In the midst of it, Father Alt felt "as if a negative force was surrounding me . . . [the stench] was literally infernal" (1981, 55, 46).

When assaulted by her unknown oppressors, Anneliese felt "a crushing sensation." The priests even witnessed quarrels among her demons, as to "who should get Anneliese," sounding all the day like disputes between MPD alters, known to carry on their own conversations and debates. One of Anneliese's unseen oppressors would say,

"Come on, let's go."

"No."

"Then you leave."

"No . . . Shit, I'm not leaving" (1981, 98).

Her repertoire included two more of the foremost signs of possession: hyperpraxia and coprolalia. "Along with her excitation came muscle power that was close to superhuman. Peter [her boyfriend] saw her take an apple and effortlessly squeeze it with one hand so that the fragments exploded throughout the room. Fast as lightning she grabbed Roswitha [her sister] and threw her on the floor as if she were a rag doll" (1981, 82). As for coprolalia, "furious profanity" came spilling out of the devout girl. "From her mouth demons rave and curse."

When the doctors' drugs did not help her, Anneliese, her family, and the priests decided on exorcism. After her death, the law, viciously, went after them for negligent homicide. (The American movie focuses on that aspect of the case: the trial.) Anneliese's seizures had been diagnosed as epilepsy by her doctors and so she was given the anticonvulsant Dilantin. But convulsions can have various causes, which is to say, not all seizurelike reactions represent a *physical* ailment. Goodman, in fact, calls Anneliese's disturbance a "shamanistic illness" (1981, 240), the seizures appearing to be a side effect of *trance*. And this is where the mighty controversy arose, polarizing the whole affair into a wicked debate between the pro-drug (medical / psychiatric / Big Pharma) faction and the paranormalists, who simply inferred an unknown but intelligent force at work.

I believe Goodman got it right when she argued that Anneliese was not epileptic. Haven't we already seen enough cases of misdiagnosis—among multiples, psychopaths, mediums, schizophrenics, hysterics, and the possessed? Their "seizures" signal a violent jolt into the altered state; we know this because that state often involves other dissociative reactions: hyperpraxia, coprolalia, blackouts, suicidal ideation. In fact, I do not regard these "seizures" as too different from the temporary spasm/jerking we all experience occasionally between the sleeping and waking state, something like the startle response. Anneliese was actually a "clinically healthy person . . . [prone to] switching into a different state of consciousness" (1981, 209). Her convulsions bespoke what has been called the RASC, religious altered state of consciousness—popularly known as trance. The medications given her "did nothing to blot out . . . the terrifying ghostly countenances. . . . She insisted that they could not heal [her]. . . . She therefore began demanding religious support" (by summer 1973) (1981, 242).

Mood stabilizers and certain seizure medications are sometimes given to multiples but can result in further complications such as *worse* dissociative episodes, hallucinations, even double vision and incontinence. Why? Goodman, I think, got to the root of it; drugs like Dilantin can have an unseen but powerful effect on the brain, which, now relaxed, inadvertently opens the door to the dwellers on the threshold. The anticonvulsant, as Goodman put it, "interfered with what her brain was designed to accomplish," namely, *to keep psyche in check*. The drug then "predisposed her toward opening up that pathway. . . . For Anneliese it was a disaster" (1981, 240–41). The absences (blackouts) only increased as did her flat affect, insomnia, headaches, stiff limbs, depression, fratzen, and stenches.

The drug won out and the demons came back.

FELICITAS GOODMAN,

THE EXORCISM OF ANNELIESE MICHEL

Only a few years after Anneliese's almost sainted death, the DSM, *Diagnostic & Statistical Manual of Mental Disorders III,* the psychiatric bible, began flirting with labels like "trance/possession disorder," under the weight of a growing number of possession-like cases in the United States and Canada. Previously banished to the Siberia of scholarship, the subject of possession has been long taboo in this smug age of science.

Though twentieth-century psychiatry put off (for the longest time) dealing with these mysteries, it became impossible to avoid by the mid-eighties at which time DSM III was forced to consider trance/possession disorder. Put on the table, it came up again in 1995, scotching the tabooed word *possession,* and sanitizing the syndrome (in DSM IV) as "dissociated trance disorder," in which one's identity is replaced by a new one attributed to a spirit. Still, this Other World has not yet been canonized by the scientific community.

Wade Davis, another anthropologist, stated the problem well when he said, "for the nonbeliever, there is something profoundly disturbing about spirit possession. Its power is raw . . . devastating in a way to those of us who do not know our gods" (Davis 1985, 214). Soul-capture (*coup n'ame*) is one of the many concepts explored in Wade's brilliant study of Haitian vodoun, where *loa* is the good spirit and *baka* the evil one. It is no coincidence that much of our finest documentation of spirit possession has come from anthropology. Step out of Western society and possession rites are the rule, not the exception. In Morocco, the possessing spirit is called *maquis.* In Ceylon, it is *preta.* In India, *bhut.* In Persia, it is *druj.* In Brazil, *exu* and *orixa.* In China, *shieng.* In Japan, *kami.* In Sudan, it is *zar,* while among the Zulu, it is *umoya.* In classic Judaism, it is *dybbuk*—a disembodied soul wandering about. In Ethiopia, it is the *wuqabi* spirit, thought to inhabit the ether over the whole empire. In other parts of Africa, it is the *jinn* (variations: *jnun, all-ejeni, ya-ijeni, enanyi-njenyi*) who can seize and possess mortals. In Melanesia, it is *tamate* or *atua* (ghosts of one's ancestors) that can enter a man, causing him to shake and quiver all over. Erika Bourguignon compiled studies of possession-trance and found it to be widespread throughout the non-Western world; in her sample of 488 societies from all parts of the world, some type of possession belief was found in 360 societies (74 percent) (Bourguignon 1967, 1973).

The trance state, as we saw with Anneliese Michel and others, brings remarkable ASCs, including clairvoyance, and so we are not surprised to learn that possession and psi go hand in glove.

> *All individuals suffering from possession in its different forms are psychic. They show clearly in their history a capacity for precognition, clairvoyance [and] telepathy.*
>
> ARTHUR GUIRDHAM,
> THE PSYCHIC DIMENSIONS OF MENTAL HEALTH

In China, the victim of possession is called *hiangto,* which actually means "psychic-medium." Likewise, the possessed in India is called *pishachucopudruvu* or *shivashakti,* which, again, points to psychic powers. Those powers, in some parts of the world, are welcomed and exploited with alacrity. In Tikopia (Melanesia) for example, the man possessed by atua "begins to shout and when the shouting is heard by the people, all run to hear what the atua has to say. . . . Then the people sit down in the house and ask questions" (Rivers 1968, 321).

Indeed, the basic components, actually criteria, of possession, as outlined in the Catholic *Rituale Romanum,* are all psi factors: xenoglossy, telepathy, precognition, hyperpraxia, coprolalia, "switching," automatisms, amnesia, ghost cold, unpleasant odors, and fratzen. Illinois' "Watseka Wonder" was a classic case of possession: In 1865, one Mary Roff died and promptly took over the body of Lurancy Vennum, who was just an infant. Lurancy proceeded to have Mary's illnesses and also exhibited supernormal faculties: gave proofs of clairvoyance, made accurate predictions, and had OBEs in trance, afterward describing in detail her astral journeys. As Catholic analysts have occasionally observed, the Prince of Darkness, "without our knowing how he gets control of the body, takes up residence in . . . the nervous system [and] deprives the soul of its normal mastery over limbs and body; he distorts the face into a strange demonic cast [fratzen] which expresses his fury and frustration. . . . He often uses language of an extreme coarseness [coprolalia], even if his victim should happen to be a gentle, well-bred person. . . . [The victim] cannot control the completely alien contortions, gesticulations and words . . . and thus cannot recall it later. Quite frequently the possessing spirit moves up and down the victim's body . . . [or] makes one limb as rigid as an iron bar" (Christiani 1961, 70–71).

All this, of course, is a description of full-blown possession, the seizure itself always involving some loss of consciousness. Yet it is the more ordinary encroachment, the *threat* of attachment, that interests me, for it is much more common, though far less obvious. As such, the overshadowing may be kept secret or hidden from view, particularly when the person himself does not know what is wrong with him and cannot identify that nameless dread. All he knows is that he is in hell. Best termed *psychic nagging,* this apprehension suggests the presence of a negative entity. Here I list some of the most frequently noted effects and dispositions linked to that overshadowing; malign invasion, methinks, is indicated if four or more of these attributes apply:

- Strange laugh or guffaws, often the rat-tat-tat machine-gun laugh
- Inexplicable pains or physical upsets, quite often *in the stomach*
- Uncontrollable temper, striking out; as Anneliese explained, "I cannot control myself. I want Peter or the girls around, but all of a sudden I throw things at them" (Goodman 1981, 72)
- Trancelike staring, fixity, or stubborn withdrawal, accompanied by flat affect or confusion; "out of touch"
- Sadness, rejection, depression, negativity—for which no reason can be given
- Outbursts, viciousness, betrayals, rampages that seem out of character; chronic changing of plans
- A sense of Other; Tony, for example, "felt an alien presence reprogramming his mind" (Sarchie and Collier 2001, 131)

- Frequent mishaps or accidents, as well as deliberate self-harm
- Rapid mood change

Rapid cycling: There's a lady in my garden club who never looks the same twice. I mean, every time she shows up, I whisper to my plot partner, "Is that *Dolly?* Yes, apparently so. I know it's not much to go on, but I think she has "lodgers." Sometimes even a single indicator is striking enough to put you on alert. But usually there is more; one of Dolly's personas, for instance, is quite provocative (which is *very* typical of multiples): she'll be wearing a low-cut blouse and bending over her plants in such a way as to tantalizingly expose her fulsome chestware. Another pose, bent in the dirt, reveals several inches of "plumber's crack."

I was starting to connect these dots when I read about the "ever-changing appearance" of a certain narcissistic psychopath (Olsen 1983, 72) and yet another whose demeanor could shift so much, even momentarily, that, as one acquaintance put it, "he doubted that anyone would recognize the man" (Adams et al. 1998, 244).

When change of persona or behavior is notably abrupt it is called rapid cycling. Strongly diagnostic of ASC but generally overlooked, the "quick change artist" may be under the sway of spiritual parasites, like the Japanese man (possessed) who exhibited "at top speed . . . a long succession of faces [that] came and went, one flickering after the other" (Martin 1976, 5). Psychiatrists, who for the most part reject the idea of spirit possession, would probably label that man a schizophrenic, or perhaps an extreme *cyclothyme,* the term denoting manic-depressives known for quick switches. They "zigzag between highs and lows rapidly. . . . They might bounce from euphoria to despair and back again within hours . . . like a race car gone berserk." Some bipolars "can go from high to low in about two seconds" (Duke and Hochman 1992, 35, 178). But there is something more than manic-depression going on here.

As Dr. Guirdham insightfully points out, although "a textbook diagnosis would be . . . manic-depressive psychosis . . . the split-second factor . . . [indicates] malign invasion." The glib textbook conclusion does not explain the "knife-edge speed [of] these appalling symptoms. . . . An ordinary manic-depressive [shift] requires at least months to build up. . . . This was a case of possession" (Guirdham 1982, 44–45). If it were simply bipolarism, there should be a buildup. But there is no buildup in rapid cycling.

Nor are cyclothymes as easy to medicate as ordinary bipolars. "This condition," admits Gloria Hochman, "is the most difficult to treat." The patient is "resistant to medication. One drug after another has been tried, and has failed" (Duke and Hochman 1992, 36–37). Surely the ineffectiveness of drugs (as in Anneliese's story) betrays the multiple's untreatable somatics, which seem to come and go as unpredictably as do their alters. But we know this: when the switching is rapid, the headaches are worse (Spencer 1989, 201). With the multiple Alex, there was "a rapid fluctuation between love and hate. One minute he would be asking for a hug and the next he would be calling me names" (C. Smith 1998, 116). And with Truddi's Troops constantly vying for "the spot," she was simply "unaware of things discussed even moments before" (Chase 1987, 147). It was the same with Sybil when she would return from the Void "all at once"; she didn't know where she was or what had happened (Schreiber 1973, 92).

And when Cam West, who had twenty-four alters, walked into a convenience store with a sudden thirst for a soft drink, "I couldn't remember what I'd come in for." He was, at the time, on his way to a multiple's support group meeting. When he finally got there, someone named Sarah was speaking; then, "a heartbeat later, Sarah's face went blank," and the next thing you knew, an alter named Margie took the spot. After Margie spoke for a minute or two, "then, click, the channel changed and she was gone and Sarah was back." Cam, who went on to write a Ph.D. thesis on MPD and a book (*First Person Plural*), recalled that his "switching was rapid and out of control . . . [like] free-falling into the angry engine of madness." His insights help us understand the ever-changing (and therefore hard-to-medicate) somatics of the multiple personality, his own "alters coming out in rapid succession, each with his or her own pain" (West 1999, 144, 158, 152, 162).

Rapid cycling is so typical of overshadowing that we encounter it in everything from MPD to bipolarism to frank possession. And if we explore the domain of the psychopath, the echo is resounding. Once again, the dissociative deviant (criminal) mind leads the way in sheer volume of documented cases. Let us summarize:

- John Wayne Gacy "contradicted himself from one sentence to the next" (Morrison 2004, 110). On a few occasions, right in the middle of the crime (vicious assault) there was a sudden "softening" and he let his victim go, apologizing profusely. (Besides Gacy, other offenders are known to have stopped midcrime and freed their terrified victims.)
- Arthur Shawcross could go "from quiet to violent in a split second"; conversely, "the raging bull turns into a choir boy" (Olsen 1992, 60, 408).
- Dean Corll was given to "startling changes of mood."
- Marie Noe, when asked an innocuous question, "became animated as if a switch had suddenly been turned on in her head" (Glatt 2002, 132).
- John Kappler, in a stressful situation (as recounted by his son), would change his "demeanor dramatically . . . I saw him start to shake and shake. . . . He leaped up and attacked me . . . I had to really fight him off. I put a boot heel in his solar plexus but he kept coming [hyperpraxia]. . . . He made a lot of vulgar references [coprolalia]. . . . Father would fall in and out of himself. He'd be dad and then all of a sudden he'd be this dirty, snively roach" (Ablow 1994, 16).
- Diane Downs was known for her mercurial emotional swings.
- Paul Keller, on the slightest provocation, would fly into a rage, with verbal abuse directed at anyone who happened to be near. "Then, just as quickly, he could shift emotional gears and become utterly charming" (Douglas and Olshaker 1999, 60).
- R. L. Yates's wife would see him go into a room and come out "a totally whole different person" (Barer 2002, 245).

- Peter Sutcliffe "would lurch from taciturnity to overexcitement" (Burn 1985, 62).
- Arthur Jackson could be lucid one moment and bizarre the next.
- "Gladys" would "bounce back and forth between . . . despair . . . and grandiose self-confidence" (Blinder 1985, 91).
- Ted Bundy, Joel Rifkin, Fred Coe, and quite a few other notorious maniacs have been labeled "chameleons" for their ever-changing appearance and moods.

Richard Macek's "outburst came completely out of the blue," wrote forensic psychiatrist Helen Morrison after an interview in which he, a supposedly "affable prisoner," made a sudden threatening gesture. "We were . . . stunned," Morrison recalls, chalking the incident up to "a mere aberration" (Morrison 2004, 25). Her naive assessment only betrays the ignorance (or collusion) of court psychiatrists (hired guns), trotted out by prosecutors to prove the deliberate viciousness of the accused. The question of responsibility (versus not guilty by reason of insanity) is a can of wriggling worms we will not open. Nevertheless we cannot help but notice Morrison's inappropriate surprise and her failure to spot the rapid cycling of her subject. Avoiding it, of course, means steering clear of questions of self-control: Was the criminal really in control of himself, of his actions? Maybe not. Maybe we need to make a deeper study of psyche's autonomous forays into Terra Incognita.

Something of fearful power exists in a dimension beyond
the material realm.

DAVE HUNT AND T. A. McMAHON,
THE NEW SPIRITUALITY

No doubt, it is absolutely necessary that law enforcement keep these very dangerous people off the streets; to that extent, one can entirely sympathize with their refusal to entertain mitigating circumstances such as involuntary violence, spirit possession, or anything else that could get them (legally) off the hook. However, in the wider field of human psychology, there is no justification for the experts' failure to keep up with parapsychology. The only explanation for their caution would be career impediment: No major league publisher, no funding source, or institute of higher learning is ready to put their weight behind the Unseen. The conservative agenda rules. Materialism rules. Skepticism rules. When it comes to the human mind, we are a century behind all our vaunted advances in technology and physical science.

But the Sci Mat paradigm will fail us, and the first sign of collapse will be in the mental health arena. It's already upon us. A little chastening would go a long way, were we to humble ourselves to the time-tested thinking of traditional cultures. A single example from Malaysia: "In Kelantanese thought, there is no separation of mind and body. All illnesses, psychic and physical, are caused by some spiritual weakness . . . [that] permits malign spiritual forces, capable of causing a variety of symptoms, to invade the person" (Crapanzano and Garrison 1977, 299).

Recently, in the fascinating case of an American journalist's complete breakdown, the discovery of and treatment for autoimmune encephalitis (inflammation of the brain) got all the credit for her eventual recovery. The whole ordeal, told by the journalist herself, Susannah Cahalan in *Brain on Fire*,* was a paean to the Almighty Brain, with little insight into the Mind—despite the fact that her affliction had all the earmarks of a psychic attack:† "inexplicable dread" (2012, 22), migraines and trouble sleeping (2012, 31), racing thoughts and logorrhea (2012, 55, 35), rapid cycling and lost time (2012, 12, 33, 41), brownouts and trance (2012, 47), seizures and catatonia (2012, 40), OBEs and hyperesthesia (2012, 36, 42, 20–21, 28), grimacing and inappropriate laugh (2012, 107, 29), "erratic behavior," tantrums, panic attacks, and paranoia (2012, 64, 36, 222). As happens all the time with MPD, her

---

*As of summer 2015, shooting began for a film based on the book.
†The French psychic-medium Minou Drouet began her career of literary channeling with a serious bout of encephalitis, "brain fever." She vouched that "the poems came to her from a mysterious realm called 'the Otherwhere'" (Spraggett 1967, 130).

doctors kept changing her diagnosis. Another victim of encephalitis, a young girl in Tennessee, behaved so strangely and lashed out so violently, that she was variously thought to be suffering from schizophrenia, autism, and cerebral palsy (Cahalan 2012, 222).

Medical opinion, of course, traced all this strange behavior to Cahalan's (anti-NMDA-receptor autoimmune) encephalitis. Well and good; she made a fine recovery under excellent medical care. Yet her emotional state—intolerable stress—just prior to the disease's onset was never considered a trigger. When FBI agent John Douglas was himself stricken with viral encephalitis ("his brain . . . fried to a crisp"), the doctors told him the illness had been "brought on or complicated by stress" (Douglas and Olshaker 1995, 7–8). At work, Douglas's unit, led by the pioneers of criminal-mind hunting, was highly charged, tense, under unspeakable pressure. As his colleague, the equally dedicated and brilliant profiler Robert Ressler, recounts (1992, 59), "Nearly everyone in our unit fell victim to . . . stress. One woman profiler bailed out . . . because the work was giving her nightmares. . . . Several of our people developed bleeding ulcers and three had anxiety attacks. . . . Four of us . . . had periods of rapid and unexplained weight loss . . . but not purely physical reasons for [it] were discovered. It was all stress-related."

In Susannah's case, everything about the lifestyle of the young New York reporter was taking its toll. It was, she said, "so many things. The job. I'm terrible at it. Stephen [her boyfriend] doesn't love me. Everything is falling apart. Nothing makes sense." Sobbing uncontrollably, she admitted also to a certain "pressure of fear," adding, "There's something else. But I don't know what it is" (Cahalan 2012, 37).

Something else: The ineffable "jitters," the "acting out of character" and feeling "not like myself . . . like you're not in this world" (Cahalan 2012, 36, 18, 33). The hints here and there of bipolarism (Cahalan 2012, 48), of delusions, mania, even schizophrenia: "I can hear their thoughts" (Cahalan 2012, 84). Too, her dramatic weight loss (anorexia), a symptom, as we have seen, of leeching, which can result from "contact with occult rituals" (Sarchie and Collier 2001, 62).

> *All they [demoniacs] need is an entranceway into their*
> *prospective victim provided by . . . witchcraft or by a curse.*
> FELICITAS GOODMAN, *HOW ABOUT DEMONS?*

Indeed, Susannah had a frightening OBE ("I can see myself from above") after contact with a Wiccan, who later apologized but sort of downplayed the experience: "It's probably just residue from the astral travel you experienced during the reading we did yesterday" (Cahalan 2012, 36). On a strictly intuitive basis, I sense a hidden factor of jealousy in this psychic attack of Susannah's.* First off, she is very beautiful, enough to arouse any woman's envy. On top of that, journalism is a very competitive and aggressive profession, cutthroat even. Not for the fainthearted. The backstory, in this case, may involve (unmentioned) rivalry. I am simply speculating here, but what if someone put the hex on her (even unintentionally)? The whammy would be all the more effective if the target was somehow vulnerable. And Susannah was vulnerable.

Let me explain. Susannah's troubles began in an incomprehensible fit of jealousy.

> *Almost everyone who has . . . uncontrolled attachments for*
> *people, quick love affairs, jealousy, infatuations . . . may be*
> *possessed.*
> MARTIN EBON, *EXORCISM*

Susannah had this irresistible urge to snoop on her boyfriend. She found herself "pulling open [his] drawers and rifling through his

---

*In this connection, it is intriguing that in the case of Anneliese Michel—whose earliest diagnosis was "a cerebral disease of the convulsive type" (Goodman 1988, 115)—a friend had commented, "'She was not born yet when she was cursed.' A woman had done it out of *envy* [emphasis added]. She was 'a neighbor of her mother's in Leiblfing'" (Goodman 1981, 98). This reminded me of another tragic case we have mentioned: Mrs. X, a once-contented housewife who, most unexpectedly, had killed herself. "We lived together happily . . . and because of this there were many jealous thoughts centered upon us. . . . Somebody started to upset us." In no time at all, "I remember feeling very strange, as if somebody had taken complete hold of me." Unexpectedly, she hanged herself (Wickland 1974, 133).

clothes, flinging them on the floor, until I found the jackpot . . . letters and pictures, most of them from exes." Then, "I caught sight of myself in the mirror . . . clutching Stephen's private love letters. . . . A stranger stared back from my reflection; my hair was wild and my face distorted and unfamiliar . . . I had lost two hours. It felt like five minutes." Then, a migraine and nausea came on. And her hand went numb. "I went through all of his stuff. It was like I was possessed" (Cahalan 2012, 12–13).

Because we don't understand mediumship and don't understand overshadowing, we don't understand possession. And because we don't understand the nonphysical world, we grope for answers in the world of matter.

The form thou dotest on is dust.

E. BULWER-LYTTON

And when we are in the dark, the demonic finds that much more to work with. Low-grade spirits will not cease to prey upon us mortals until we let in the Light—which itself furnishes a gentle mantle of protection. But with no knowledge of postmortem existence, we continue to swim in the Sea of Oblivion, the toy of dark forces and spirits in chaos—the undead. The longer we play dumb to the incorporeal powers, the deeper they can hack into our lives.

The temple of science is ready for parascience. Are you?

10

THE REINCARNATION HOAX

Nowadays a lot of people will say they are not really religious, but spiritual. What does that mean? Do they know what spiritualism involves? Indeed, the whole idea, the popular notion, of spirituality is so open-ended as to invite every and any sort of charlatan and wannabe on to the platform to gain an audience and talk twaddle.

Sure, the NDEr, the clairvoyant, the visionary, the dreamer, even the tripper may have had a glimpse of the preternatural, but so what? He has only dipped a toenail into the cosmic ocean. And even if he has gone for a swim, his companions and guides are, perforce, the newly dead who "not yet knowing of the higher heavens, will teach falsely of . . . [the] everlasting kingdoms" (Oahspe, Book of Aph 5:7).

What, you may ask, is meant by the "everlasting kingdoms"? Let's pursue this, for it is at the heart of our quest for the meaning of heaven, of the hereafter, of eternity. What happens to us when we die? The end of mortal life, as spiritology teaches, coincides with the beginning of our immortal existence. Only a tiny, infinitesimal portion of our life is spent in the flesh. Learn this and you have already mounted the ladder of light.

We climb from world to world in the continuing Road of Life.

HOPI MYSTERY PLAY

Life is everlasting.

HOPI ELDER DAN KATCHONGVA

Part of the befuddlement that is so widespread today hinges on our conception, or should I say misconception, of *immortality*. With Sci Mat at the reins, the term has come to imply eternal life *in the flesh,* which is to say, living forever *in a physical body*. Utterly lost is the concept of the Ongoing, the living scheme beyond the body, beyond earth life, beyond the mortal coil. How is it that we have lost sight of our birthright into the heaven worlds? We will answer that question in this chapter by taking on the spurious doctrine of reincarnation and all its seductive but misleading trappings.

> Behold, the Father's places rise higher and higher! Not downward to the earth, or to reincarnation, the invented tale of drujas, but upward to Wisdom, Goodness, Love, and Happiness! . . . Yea, I raise the dead, the souls of the dead, into worlds shining, brilliant, full of loveliness! I do not take them backward to toil and sorrow; but upward, onward, to heavens of delight, that never perish.
>
> OAHSPE, BOOK OF WARS 55:11
>
> AND BON'S BOOK OF PRAISE 37:3

In many ways, the New Age, with its passing nostrums, has done more to distort the truth than to reveal it. Not the least of these follies is the naive and uncritical exaltation of ancient systems of belief. Who says the so-called sages of Old Egypt or India or China comprise an unfaltering guide to philosophy? Often enough, beneath their decorous doctrines lies some form of idolatry or the machinations of a powerful, corrupt priesthood. This, I believe, was the case in ancient Egypt, where the teaching of reincarnation first took hold. Case in point: I was recently introduced to a self-declared pundit who says he learned about the human soul (the "Higher Self"), and reincarnation from a being who came to him clairvoyantly. This mysterious being identified himself as the Egyptian god Thoth. I was instantly reminded of Thothma, which was the god name of Hojax, the Egyptian king and builder of the Great Pyramid. Yes, Hojax/Thothma was a great adept; he could hear the spirits and talk with them, he could cast himself in the death trance and go spiritually to the lower heavens and return at will.

Seeing the powers of Hojax, Osiris the False proceeded to use him for his own ends. Osiris was a most powerful angel, but a tyrant. He called to Hojax and said—Thou art Thothma, the god, and you shall be god of the earth! And whoso goeth forth warring for thee shall succeed brilliantly—And it came to pass that Osiris' proxies inspired war and slavery, for Osiris had instructed King Hojax to build the pyramid and, in order to erect it, the people were put into bondage. What's more, Osiris taught that everlasting life was proven *in the flesh* by reincarnation. And this was the beginning of the earthbound doctrine of reincarnation.

After Thothma, for hundreds and hundreds of years the Egyptians were the most learned people in the world, especially in astronomy and adeptship. But woe came unto them; the land became flooded with millions of drujas who inspired the people of Egypt to return after death and dwell with mortals.

The drujas flatter thee, telling thee thou wert this or that great man in a former reincarnation.

OAHSPE, BOOK OF THE ARC OF BON 28:16

These drujan spirits professed that they themselves had lived on Earth, as great philosophers and men of renown. All a lie, but what they did was watch about when children were born, and obsess them, driving hence the natural spirit and growing up in the body of the newborn. "Thus there were habited with mortals . . . seven hundred million such engrafters . . . who for the most part held the spirits of their victims in abeyance all their natural lives" (Oahspe, Book of Lika 14:9 and 14:18). Of them, Moses said, "they thus invited into Egypt spirits of the lower heaven . . . and when young babes were born they were obsessed, and these evil spirits in justification of their sins taught reincarnation" (Oahspe, Book of Saphah: Osiris 116).

Gus Cahill (1965, 194) elaborated on this phase of Egyptian life: "the drujas, the angels of darkness . . . gained great power over the land, dwelling in mortal guise, rotting the moral foundation of the people. Because of the delusion of reincarnation, the spirits of the dead had no desire for any higher heaven but to return to the earth and there regain the physical life. . . . Sometimes dozens or even a hundred such souls of darkness would live and die in the same physical shell. . . . So the people of Egypt suffered mental diseases, and their bodies became corrupt because of the foulness of the drujas with whom they lived, and the people became idlers and vagrants."

Immortality in the *flesh,* then, is not a new but a very old idea. Wherever it is found, it thrives on the same philosophy: the opinion that there is no higher heaven, no other place to go—no other field of action—than right here on earth. "They know no other life but to continue engrafting themselves on mortals. . . . They could not be persuaded that Etherea [cosmos] was filled with habitable worlds" (Oahspe, Book of Bon 14:12–13). And so, for the Egyptians (and others), embalming and mummifying became de rigueur, in order to prepare for regaining their natural bodies and dwelling again on the earth. The (now extinct) Guanche people of the Canary Islands seem to have imbibed these pathological ideas from the Egyptians. These islanders customarily preserved the remains of their dead, fearing that the disintegration of the body would preclude their immortality, hence the embalmed mummies found there, though in very poor condition. "It is astonishing that none of them weigh more than six or seven pounds" (Lissner 1962, 188–89). Even more astonishing that people would believe a dried out, ghastly, shrunken corpse could be brought back to life!

But common sense or sound reasoning have been known to play a minor role in popular beliefs, especially when the credo offers some kind of feel-good consolation. To find a captive audience, deceiving spirits need only play to human vanity, ignorance—or fear. Like Scheherezade (who told dazzling fables only to keep herself alive), the spirits of reincarnation chase away the specter of death (everyman's bugbear) with the promise of renewable life on earth.

Even very smart people get sucked in. The oldest con in the world, reincarnation is curiously contagious. As England's professional magician, the distinguished James Webster, put it, "This grotesque philosophy has . . . hit the streets of every major European city. . . . The illusion is as perfect as that of a clever stage magician who has his audience in his hands, spellbound." For many, this is the coin, the currency, in which the doctrine of past lives is sold: fascination per se, pandering to a frankly narcissistic craving.

Ask any psychiatrist: One of the hallmarks of narcissism is intolerance of *boredom* (addictive search for novelty): the narcissist gravitates to rousing, thrilling schemes, flights of fancy, or almost any antidote to prosaic, humdrum existence. Even if she is merely amused by it, that is sufficient reason to embrace it, to entertain it. The more sensational the better, answering to the flamboyance so typical of NPD. Society itself, especially in America, is awash in this syndrome, the media more geared toward the shocking or scandalous report than to solid news. The attention-getting ploy, the hype, is as American as apple pie. Style trumps substance, easily engaging the narcissist—who specializes in fraudulence, deception, manipulation, grandiosity, exhibitionism. No theory is too startling; the more mind-boggling the better. Common sense is such a bore; we would rather be amazed.

But this is Ego speaking, not our better judgment. This is narcissism writ large: awesome wins the day; while sober, humble, and guileless fact fades to dark. Fertile soil for the advancement of falsehoods of every stripe . . .

In the Age of Thor, some 15,000 years ago, "mortals who were obsessed believed themselves to be the reincarnation of Thor or Apollo. . . . And so great became the superstition of the nations . . . that in the fall of a leaf, they found proof of the second coming. . . . All corporeal worlds pass through the age of too much belief . . . then into [utter] unbelief . . . [and then again] he goeth to the other extreme, believing all things, and not using his judgment" (Oahspe, Book of Thor 6:2–4).

Reincarnation, unabashedly, revolves around self—or should I say *selves*—sequentially, of course; it feeds the narcissist's premier sense of

Fig. 10.1. Saddam Hussein, obsessed with the idea of rebuilding Babylon, believed himself to be the reincarnation of King Nebuchadnezzar II; he invested more than $500 million in developing his pet project and had a seal struck depicting an image of himself side by side with the ancient tyrant.

self, vanity per se. Here is a doctrine (a religion, for some) that assures the perennial return of your favorite personage—me! Diagnostic of NPD are fantasies of greatness or honor or being special; some folks may not achieve it, but ah, they *were* somebody important in a past life. Take Eric C., for example, a narcissistic paranoid killer (offed his grandmother) who thought he could "save the world." Found not guilty by reason of insanity, Eric was actively psychotic and had been "told" that, before he was born, he was Jesus Christ. Further details suggest that Eric was in the grip of demonic possession: logorrhea, self-mutilation, violent shaking fits, migraines, attempted suicide.

Priscilla Ford, who killed six people, bystanders, when she deliberately rammed her car into a crowded sidewalk, shared with Eric C. the distinction of having once been Jesus Christ. She had also been Adam; and in her current incarnation was an "instrument of God" (Markman and Bosco 1989, 340–41). Richard Chase, the notorious Vampire of Sacramento (six kills), thought he lived before and had ridden with Jesse

James. Another killer in our rogues' gallery, the Shoemaker, thought he had been a butterfly in a previous life. Rod F., Florida's teenage vampire killer, bright but deranged, encouraged his followers to recall "their past lives together in France." He bragged about being able to "channel the spirits of . . . Shakespeare and Plato . . . [and] revive ancient prophets, bringing them back from the dead." Rod's girlfriend thought "that she and Rod had lived before, together as vampires." She said, "In your past lives, you lived the same existence with the same people. The whole point of life is to go on a quest to find those same people again" (Jones 1999, 162, 130, 267).

Then too, there was the testimony of Herb Mullin (who killed a total of thirteen people as a necessary sacrifice to "save the environment.") His parents' reincarnation beliefs, Herb said later, had warped his development. They thought that curbing their son's enjoyment of life "would improve his birth-position in the very next life" (Lunde 1976, 66).

This last brings us to the subject of karma. Perhaps you are familiar with the notion of karma, which the reincarnationists have co-opted to buttress their contention that our deeds from past lives carry over, often in the way of payback. Under this scheme of karmic debt, our current suffering or failures can be blamed on the transgressions or sins we committed in a previous incarnation. But here again, the narcissist's bias lies concealed: Consider only the NPD strategy (under "sense of entitlement") that typically places blame *elsewhere,* leaving our own reputation intact. Lightening the load of personal accountability, the past-life focus conveniently turns away from here-and-now issues.

> *Reincarnation has robbed man of his personal responsibility*
> *. . . reducing him to a state of spiritual impotence.*
> JUSTIN TITUS, *ETERNAL PROGRESSION*

Of course the moral escape hatch is attractive to the self-centered soul. In this landscape, social conscience or duty need not trouble us. In the trenchant words of James Webster, "Reincarnation paralyses the initiative of millions. Those imprisoned by it rarely strive for social improvements or justice, for that would then deprive people of their karma—a merciless law of consequences." The narcissist, like his first cousin the sociopath, both with deficient conscience, impresses us as someone bereft of natural emotions such as compassion or remorse, the shortfall known in psychiatry as "no empathy" or flat affect (no show of feelings). And how well this dovetails with the reincarnationist's heartless conviction that hardship and suffering come well earned, yea deserved, by those who have yet to work out their evil karma!

This fictitious version of "God's justice" presumably satisfies our sense of fairness; how satisfying it is to know that "if a man has murdered another . . . he will be struck down by a murderer during . . . his next incarnation" (Kueshana 1970, 77). The next thing you know, these "just desserts" are part of a formula that excuses every human atrocity merely by discovering its karmic origin. In the Jewish Holocaust, for example, the victims purportedly "chose to be incarnated at this time . . . to be the victims of the Holocaust as a selfless act of sacrifice, to make us all aware that . . . there were those who would attempt to rule and control humanity . . . and that evil people existed." But, rejoins one reviewer, "Aren't we already aware of the existence of evil?" (Picknett and Prince 2001, 194). But no, every horror and calamity known to man was *meant to happen,* according to this fatalistic outlook, and that includes African slavery, genocide, natural disasters, accidents, wars, terrorism, and 9/11. All these things were, allegedly, planned and prearranged for souls to hasten their destiny.

This disgusting doctrine found many believers in ancient times, and has quite a number even to this day.
J. B. NEWBROUGH, *THE CASTAWAY*

As it was in the olden time, so will it be again. . . . Drujas will teach that the spirits of the dead go into . . . woman and are born over again in mortal form.

THUS SPAKE ZARATHUSTRA,
OAHSPE, BOOK OF FRAGAPATTI 30:20

The Brotherhood of Eloists tell us that the "Divine Spark brought us into being at conception . . . a new creation destined to [grow] throughout eternity" (the Eloist publication *Radiance,* Feb. 1990, 1).

> Every man, woman, and child born into life | will quicken with a new spirit . . . at the time of conception. Neither will | give to any spirit . . . the power to enter a womb or a fetus to be born again. . . . Beware, O man, of angels who say that a spirit re-entereth the womb and is born again in mortality . . . for these are the utterances of the angels of the first [lowest] resurrection. . . . Behold, | provide My heavenly places broad, boundless, so that the soul of man can never reach to the boundary thereof. . . . My heavens are for raising the soul upward, for ever and ever.
>
> OAHSPE, BOOK OF JEHOVIH 6:21
> AND BON'S BOOK OF PRAISE 37:2

In fact, the only way to "reincarnate" is to take over someone else's body. And that is possession, spirit possession, plain and flat. As Stephen Blake (2014, 209) put it, the obsessor "is no more an incarnation than a marionette is the incarnation of its controller." When a spirit maneuvers into someone's body and soul, it is then an obsessing spirit, known to cause suffering both to itself and its victim. Experienced mediums are all too familiar with this uninvited lodger; Grace Rosher, for one, warns of spirits who would try to use you in a wrong way. Those who know best sometimes describe these spiritual parasites, these freeloaders, as troublemakers, like Susy Smith who warned that anyone who dies rebellious is a potential source of mischief.

Joe Fisher, one-time member of a reincarnation cult but turned whistleblower, came to see these past-life "selves" as "mischievous and possibly malevolent discarnates . . . humans who no longer had physical bodies . . . neurotic entities . . . who longed to live and breathe once more" (2001, 270–71). Deeply involved for more than three years in channeling spirit guides who were espousing reincarnation, Fisher finally pulled away when he felt himself losing control: He was an impassioned wreck. "I'd fly high—but then I'd come crashing down again. The more my centers were supposedly opening, the worse I felt. . . . The emotional swings were phenomenal [rapid cycling?] . . . I underwent raging storms of emotion—nostalgia, crying fits, great highs, depressive lows." Admitting his own gullibility, Fisher finally describes how these "impostors . . . [and] masters of deception . . . were brainwashing me. It was magnificently done" (2001, 249, 265, 224).

On November 1, 1922, which is All Soul's Day in Europe, a very famous deceased medium came through to the small Wickland Circle using the entranced Mrs. Wickland as the "live-wire." The "visitor" was Madam Blavatsky-X, one-time empress of the occult, high priestess of Theosophy, and professor of reincarnation—all of which dogmas she recanted that evening. Before taking questions from the sitters, she remarked, "Some may say this is not Madam Blavatsky, but do not doubt—it is. They may say, She would not say so and so, she would not talk so and so—but it is Madam Blavatsky." Much of her discourse seemed almost like a confession;* she owned, "I was a medium and I could have done a great work, but I became obsessed . . . I had many earthbound spirits around me."

It may have been her first "airing" since her death in 1891, though she declared in her opening words that "there is no death." She called this a truth, not a theory. She hastened to tell her story, and thus began by admitting her worldly ambition: "I wanted to be a leader in some way or another . . . I studied reincarnation and I thought there was truth and justice in the theory that we come back and learn and have more experiences. I taught it . . . but I was mistaken. Memories of 'past lives' are caused by spirits . . . representing the lives *they* lived. . . . When I came to the spirit side of life I learned that reincarnation is not true. Still, I did not want to believe that. . . . I tried and tried to come back to be somebody else, but I could not. We cannot reincarnate. We progress, we do not go back. . . . When we go to the spirit side . . . we go on to a higher life."

---

*For a complete transcript of the "Experience," see Wickland 1974, 351–57.

Fig. 10.2. The controversial "HPB"

Blavatsky-X said it all in one sentence when she identified so-called memories of past life as nothing more than thoughts or recollections *conveyed by discarnates.* It might be relevant at this juncture to mention that such transfer of thought relies on two (often unseen) factors. For one, the mortal recipient is probably psychic, which is to say, his door or *valve* (Robert Monroe's term) or whatever you may call psyche's portal, is ajar, *whether he knows it or not.* He has a high psi-Q. There are so many people in this category, most notably those who have been opened, willy-nilly, by an early trauma. If a head count of all these ambulatory mediums were somehow possible, I would guess that every third person would fit the bill.

While this factor speaks for the mortal side of the equation, the second factor involves the Other Side, specifically, the circumstances in which our excarnate, our wannabe reincarnator, met his own end. Consult the extensive literature on alleged past lives, and a singular pattern soon emerges: *most died a sudden death.** An unusual statistic, it is a giveaway, indicating the restive soul whose mortal life has been unfairly cut short; deprived of a smooth transition, the traumatized victim becomes fixated, still hovering at the edge of life, unable to move on. Some were children who died a violent death. Others died in a fire; yet others in war. Some were murdered; others perished in an accident or natural catastrophe. Reincarnationists have never been able to answer this obviously skewed statistic whose true significance only comes to light when we factor in the earthbound penchant of these unfortunate souls.

> To induce the spirits of the dead to rise up from the earth . . . to make them put away earthly desires, to become pure and wise and strong . . . what an endless labor for thy God and his exalted angels!
>
> OAHSPE, BOOK OF JUDGMENT 15:6–7

Died in a fire: The well-known psychic John Edward (2004, 73) was once impressed with the strong "feeling that I was in a burning room." The spirit, it turned out, was attached to a woman at one of his group readings; the spirit had perished in a fire. It was the mediumistic Edward who "felt the heat."

Died in war: The medium in Joe Fisher's little reincarnation klatch (mentioned above) related details of her last life as a Czechoslovakian teenager in World War II, executed and thrown into a pit. Yet the medium delivered the information, not in the first person, but in the third person, just as hosts everywhere tend to speak in this way, in the third person, about the excarnate personalities invading their space.

---

*This circumstance is treated in depth in chapter 7 of my book *Delusions in Science and Spirituality*. It is also a matter of record that persistent phantoms, when investigated by trained mediums, inevitably go back to a sudden death experience. Wilma Davidson, British psychic and spirit rescuer, once went on an organized "ghost walk" and discovered that "none of these poor departed souls seemed to have had a normal death; they either died brokenhearted, were murdered, or worse. . . . Several ghostly figures ran past us in the shadows" (Davidson 2006, 72, 61–62).

We saw this in Ted Bundy's portrayal of "the entity" responsible for the murders; just as Danny S. could not control *Him,* the perpetrator of the crimes that Danny-as-host committed.

Murdered: Suckered into the past-life interpretation by his gullible psychiatrist, Michael G. was brought into trance and picked up the tormented spirit of a murdered woman, a one-time prostitute who had been stabbed to death by her stepfather. But rather than clear his patient of the miserable/abused spirit, the therapist actually pegged her as Michael's *former self* and made him "confront" her suffering. This he did, "screaming, weeping, and protesting," as his obsessed "body arched and thrashed across . . . [the] floor" (Whitton 1986, 97–98).

Reincarnationists have also made much of our phobias, co-opting them and placing their origin in some past-life terror (ineptly overlooking their likely genesis in early life). Carol Bowman (2001, 214), for example, cites a client who is petrified of loud noises. The fear, reasons Bowman, goes back to a previous incarnation in which the client died from a loud shot. Phobias, however, frequently show up in people who are prone, in the first place, to ASCs, people with a high psi-Q, highly sensitive individuals who are acutely reactive to sounds, smells, visual stimuli, touch, and taste. Indeed, this is the same *hyperesthesia* that we see so often among those with a damaged aura.

Let's get down to nuts and bolts. Let us decide, once and for all, whether symptoms that belong to the deceased and are passed on to the living are due to reincarnation or due to overshadowing. It must be one or the other. To zero in on this question, we might tackle the business of mysterious bruises and birthmarks. These, argues the reincarnationist with supreme confidence, are the soul's own wounds carried over from one life to another. In fact, these marks or wounds are actually trotted out as *proof* of reincarnation.

Take Miss Mills, for example: When a line of blisters appeared on her back, she said this was where she'd been struck with a burning torch as she was led to the stake—in her life as a thirteenth-century Cathar heretic! Mills, it should be noted, was not the only returned victim of the Inquisition. As mentioned earlier, she and a few other women were actually persuaded of the fact by their psychiatrist who, "obsessed by it . . . [declared] that dozens of the Cathars . . . reincarnated in the twentieth century . . . to prove the reality of reincarnation." Nevertheless, the late Colin Wilson, who had the opportunity of personally interviewing the doctor, came away with the impression that "all that has happened is that a patient has become fixated on her doctor, and looks around for ways to gain his interest . . . Miss Mills is also, significantly, an unmarried lady. She gets drawn into the fantasy . . . until a whole group of her friends are convinced that they were thirteenth-century Cathars. An interesting case of group hysteria" (Wilson 1973, 128, 135).

That was in England. It was, however, here in America that the birthmark theory gained traction, thanks to the work of Dr. Ian Stevenson at the University of Virginia. On the surface, his research appears to be scrupulously scientific and objective. Yet Stevenson's claim—that he eliminated all *other* possible explanations of these bruises and birthmarks—is disingenuous and deceptive. It is, in my view, a falsification of the record, and indeed, a breach of faith with the very discipline in which he made his name: parapsychology.

Reincarnation as Body Snatching

Stevenson's many anecdotes, rather than proving reincarnation, actually document the typical stunts of entities lingering on the earth plane. Indeed, Stevenson's cases "suggestive of reincarnation" fall apart completely when taken simply as cases of *body snatching*. A Hindu man, for example, is poisoned to death; instead of waiting the theoretical ten or twenty or fifty years, he "reincarnates" immediately. Not only does the time lapse fail to fit the theory, but the fresh body is *not that of a newborn*, as theory stipulates; for the spirit of the poisoned man has overtaken a *three-and-a-half-year-old* boy who has apparently died of smallpox, leaving his body vacant. And sure enough, upon reviving, the little boy identifies entirely with the life and habits of the poison victim; the boy is no longer quite "himself," and instantly recognizes all "his" former family members when taken to them (Langley 1967, 231). The scenario, though, is seriously akin to ghostly intrusion, the mortal victim (or host) serving merely as a target of opportunity for the homeless spirit. None of this can be understood or appreciated without a grasp of overshadowing, the subtle ways in which the unquiet dead can impinge on the living.

Steve Blake, the English mathematician who took the time to write a 450-page book refuting reincarnation, states that we should not go about the debate by quibbling over beliefs or terms, "but by establishing the true nature of human spirituality" (2014, xv). How true this is! Blake's brilliant rebuttal (in chapters 2 and 8 of *Reincarnation Refuted*) of Stevenson's work covers a lot of ground, including the question of bruises and birthmarks as well as Stevenson's errors in logic and even fieldwork methodology. In Stevenson's work, says Blake, "spirit intrusion is arbitrarily called reincarnation." In the field, "he draws on local superstitions to buttress his argument. . . . When interviewing subjects, his questions are couched in the language of reincarnation. This means that he gets the results he wants. . . . The exercise becomes a self-fulfilling prophecy" (Blake 2014, 296). Stevenson's followers often tout his evidence as overwhelming. But, as another critic, Gus Cahill (1965, 127) put it, "By the researcher ignorant of the spiritual universe, unquestionable 'evidence' of reincarnation is gravely recorded and published, to the conviction of a marveling public."

Parapsychology, as I am sure you know, deals with a great range of human phenomena that simply cannot be explained by the current "scientific" yardsticks. Most popular today are NDEs and OBEs. So let us consider the bruises and scratches that may directly result from an OBE: "If," cautions Dion Fortune, "an occultist, functioning out of the body, meets with unpleasantness on the astral plane, if his subtle body is struck or shot at, the physical body will show marks. I myself have many times found curiously patterned bruises on my body after an astral skirmish" (Fortune 1981, 52).

Apparitions and hauntings, of course, are also a big part of today's parapsychological curiosities, and we do wonder how Dr. Stevenson could have overlooked the numerous cases that directly link phantoms with wounds. A few illustrations should suffice:

- A séance circle in San Francisco gets out of hand: the medium is struck and bloodied on her cheeks and hand. The house, it turns out, is haunted by the medium's own deceased mother who is "reproachful of her daughter's . . . scandalous life" (Fodor 1966, 388).
- An old jailhouse in New Orleans, where not a few had died on the gallows, is "said to be haunted by angry, vicious ghosts." One of them nearly strangles a desk sergeant, "flinging him to the floor and leaving ugly bruises on his throat" (Hurwood 1971, 5).
- In the 1960s, the Toronto *Telegram* reported weird phenomena at the Mackenzie House (belonging to the prime minister). There were unaccountable footfalls, the piano playing by itself, an "oppressive presence," and other strange apparitions—one of which attacked the caretaker's wife, leaving three red welts on the left side of her face, like finger marks (S. Smith 1970a, 40–43).
- *Prime Time Live* and CNN covered the case of eight-year-old Michael J., a Connecticut boy who saw the apparition of his grandfather with blood-stained teeth. Scratch and bite marks began to appear on Michael's body after a year's worth of phenomena besieged the household*—orbs, ghost sightings, flying silverware, and even furniture moving of its own.

The poltergeistery in Michael's case suggests that paranormal marks and bruises may devolve on the ghostly presence, not past lives. As some see it, the "biting poltergeist" has a purpose: to force humans to vacate homes that they feel belong to them. They might also cut and slash; or leave scratches and welts, as in a Rumanian case (Rogo 1979, 177–79); or assault with gashes, as in the South African case witnessed by policemen and doctors (Archer 1967, 181); or puncture, choke, and sting, as

---

*Scratches are among the most common forms of psychic marks in cases of possession.

in the meticulously documented Indiana case (Roll 2004, 51–55). As William Roll indicates, the ability of psyche to suffer a wound from "an invisible force" actually has a name, *repercussion*, and it is known to occur in religious mania, conversion hysteria, possession, poltergeistery, multiple personality disorder, hauntings, satanic rites, autism, mediumship, and criminal psychopathology.

Our skin, our envelope, is the first to bear the brunt of a close encounter with the powers of the Darkening Land. Paranormal eruptions of the skin are not all that rare. In fact, skin diseases such as psoriasis and herpes were, in former times, thought to betray spirit possession. Even modern analysts like Titus Bull thought some of his patients had been "overshadowed by entities who pressed too close . . . casting on [them] a reflection of their own memories and ills" (Fodor 1966, 40). Concerning these bodily ills, another modern psychiatrist has written, "In my experience, when a person dies with an illness, the soul will carry the energy pattern of that pathogen. If the soul attaches to a living human, that human may then manifest the illness carried by the departed soul. I have seen a number of illnesses remit after the attaching spirit leaves the body" (Dr. M. E. Gibson, in Tymn 2008, 8).

Among experienced mediums, repercussion is painfully familiar. H. F. P. Battersby (1979, 29), for one, has felt his own psyche "strike obstacles in space which block its free movement and cause a repercussion to my nervous system and a shock to my physical body." In the early days of *Light* magazine, many such experiences were reported by mediums and occultists, most of whom believed that these fresh injuries came from spirits of a low order. Some saw it as the unintentional effect of the recent dead, reproducing the symptoms of their last bodily illness in the body of the medium, causing her great discomfort. This is what happened to the well-known medium Stainton Moses after a friend of his committed suicide: Moses woke up in the middle of the night and saw his friend's spirit trying to reach him. Moses was repulsed and horrified by the vision. In the morning, he found on his forehead an oblong red mark in the exact spot where his friend had wounded himself. This is the same approach taken by Vivian Garrison who looked

*Fig. 10.3. Stainton Moses, one of England's most
distinguished seers of the late nineteenth century*

for the *espiritus obsesores* oppressing a person afflicted with "the symptoms of the disease of which they [the spirits] died" (Crapanzano and Garrison 1977, 426).

In the early days of modern spiritualism, mishaps of this sort were a common occupational hazard among mediums. W. E. Butler (1978, 186–87) explained that weakness in "the auric skin . . . well known to those who studied these matters . . . were called 'orbicular wounds.' Certain practices in connection with mediumship can cause orbicular wounds; and for this reason the older occultists were not altogether in favor of the indiscriminate development of mediumship."

"All the symptoms I felt were his," one victim spoke of his attached entity, in a Japanese case (Crapanzano and Garrison 1977, 349). Even "friendly" spirit familiars, as Eugene Maurey pointed out (1988, 131), can be dangerous, especially when they have died of an illness and can bring "that particular illness to you."

If the reincarnationists paid the least attention to the ways of overshadowing, their sham of a theory—and its bogus "evidence"—would melt away. And how do they explain MPD? Would they call the alters reincarnating souls? The irony is that most of these clinging discarnates, these spiritual parasites, "know nothing more than babes, though, for the most part, they had been full grown adults as to earth-life. Some are engrafters who dwell with one mortal during his life-time, and then engraft themselves on another mortal during his life-time, and so on, calling themselves re-incarnated" (Oahspe, Book of Judgment 4:11).

Holding the native spirit in abeyance, such excarnates may be inferred in the more severe cases of MPD where the host or core personality has actually been in abeyance since infancy. You may recall Truddi Chase, the supermultiple whose native self "went under" at age two. Her biographer confirmed that medical conditions such as allergies, rashes, tumors, and cysts develop suddenly when different alters take over. Kit Castle (with seven alters) had an array of symptoms—rash, cramps, incontinence, double vision, crippling back and neck pains; yet, no sooner were they tested than they disappeared "like a ghost." And this is typical of multiples: "mysterious symptoms seem to come and go" (Noll 1990, 37), just as readily as the alters themselves take turns "on the spot."

> *The spirit indicates its interest in possessing an individual through . . . some affliction, to get his or her attention.*
>
> VINCENT CRAPANZANO,
> *CASE STUDIES IN SPIRIT POSSESSION*
> (ACCORDING TO THE WUQABI CULT)

Both MPD and reincarnation are forms of spirit possession—though both have been otherwise labeled. Take the case of thirty-year-old Julius K. who developed a tumor on the left side of his brain. (It was surgically removed.) His grandfather had had the exact same type of tumor at the identical location. Given these circumstances, the reincarnationist might well cite the tumor as evidence of the grandfather's re-embodiment in his grandson. However, consider these facts: After the death of his grandfather, Julius (four years old), underwent a dramatic personality change that, into adulthood, involved fits of violent temper—of which he was unaware. Checking for possession, Eugene Maurey, a friend of the family, discovered the presence of a negative entity.

I'll let Maurey tell the rest of the story: "Throughout his life the young man had exhibited many of the personality characteristics of his grandfather, displaying the same unruly disposition. . . . Furthermore, his grandfather did not believe in an afterlife and would be the perfect candidate for an earthbound spirit. Without further delay, I requested the presence of the grandfather's spirit. I then explained to him what had happened to his grandson. . . . After the explanation, I lovingly performed the exorcism. Something must have happened, as there has been a steady improvement in Julius's personality since my talk with his grandfather" (Maurey 1988, 75–76).

Browsing among old ghost stories, the great psi researcher Nandor Fodor found a seventeenth-century chronicle of marks and blisters left on a girl by the apparition of a man who had "led an evil life." Indeed, when his spirit-form appeared, he revealed some of his crimes. We know, too, that some of our modern-day criminal offenders (Gacy, Shawcross, List, Macek, and so on) bear a palpable imprint of negative overshadowing: an actual mark. Psychic blisters keep turning up in the stories of psychopathic killers under control of extremely violent spirit familiars: red blisters erupting on Richard Macek's skin were "an almost supernatural event" (Morrison 2004, 28). "Nerve blisters" afflicted Arthur Shawcross. John List (familicide) tended to break out in "blotches" and big red welts. John Gacy, when young, "acquired a birthmark" that seemed to have disappeared from his mother's arm "and reappeared on John's . . . as though it was a kind of supernatural experience" (Morrison 2004, 84).

The record, in short, is full of paranormal markings, not the least of which fall to the demonic attack. The St. Louis boy, whose story was remodeled for the classic film *The Exorcist,* was painfully slashed and scratched by "something evil, something not of this world. . . . The Lutheran minister suspected diabolical possession" (T. Allen 40, 45).* Men of the cloth were not unfamiliar with the religious phenomenon known as stigmata, as it affected persons obsessed with the crucifixion— blood and wounds appearing in their palms.

Certainly the stigmata of religious ecstatics are in the same general family as the welts and bruises erupting on all the hosts described in these pages. Having suffered them herself in her occult excursions, England's Dion Fortune came to believe that "such marks must be of the same nature as the stigmata of saints and the curious physical marks and swellings sometimes seen in hysterics" (Fortune 1981, 52).

And at the bottom of it all is the mediumistic power, still so reviled, even feared, in this vaunted Age of Materialism. None of the above-mentioned eruptions or manifestations—indeed, nothing "supernatural"—could occur at all if human beings were not endowed with transcendent faculties. And the best way to gain a footing in this hinterland of the mind is to first acknowledge, then study, ASCs: altered states of consciousness.

The altered state, as we have seen, may involve *automatisms*—such as xenoglossy, where the entranced or controlled person is seen and heard speaking a foreign language with which she is otherwise totally unfamiliar. I won't bore you with the many examples that have come out of psychoanalytic literature, ghost chronicles, church histories, spirit circles, even hospital records (where the anesthetized patient comes to, speaking a language she doesn't know!). Once again the reincarnationist co-opts the phenomenon, like Ian Stevenson who collected many instances of xenoglossy and offered them as evidence of past lives (lived as a native speaker of that tongue). Stevenson, of course, totally disregarded the temporary fluency of psychic-mediums, channeling in Greek, Gaelic, Chippewa, Monomonee, Raratonga, Polish, Latin, Serbian, and Dutch—all in the

---

*Precedents, especially among Catholics, were well known from old records of exorcisms. Perhaps the most famous was the ordeal of Sister Jeanne des Anges, the Prioress of Loudun's convent, who exhibited paranormal scratches that erupted on her body; a bloody cross magically appeared on her forehead, fading only after three weeks.

context of "sittings" and communion with spirits. Stevenson's oversight is all the more glaring in light of the Catholic *Ritual Romanum,* which lists xenoglossy among the top four criteria of spirit possession.

I can't resist a single case in point: It involves a youngster who, though quite normal in every other way, never spoke a single word until age three. His mother was Canadian and so was the father, though he had been born in Hungary. Anticipating the birth of the child, the father's mother, who spoke no English, came over from Hungary to help out. Yet seeing her son so "Canadianized," she became obsessed with the fate of her grandson, actually developing "a morbid fear that . . . the same sort of thing would happen to her grandson, that he would know nothing of his forebears and lose all trace of his true homeland." She begged her son to give her enough time to teach the expected child the language and customs of the Old Country; for the sake of peace, he granted her wish. But it never came to pass, for just after the baby was born the old lady died. When the beautiful blue-eyed child turned out to be quite mute, doctors and specialists had no answer. Then, one night, his parents "found him standing up in his cot, staring fixedly at one corner of the room and talking excitedly and without any difficulty, except that the language was . . . Hungarian." After that the boy was silent again, and remained so for another year, after which he began to speak English, but with a heavy Hungarian accent (Underwood 1986, 180–81).

Well, if you want to call body/mind invasion by an earthbound spirit "reincarnation," you are free to do so, but at the risk of twisting the science of soul. Spiritology begins and ends with an understanding of our *incorporeal* self, the spirit part that, at death, flows effortlessly from Corpor to Es, from physical embodiment to the angel world. For those who cannot envision any conceivable existence *without a body,* reincarnation is the perfect solution. It maintains the materialist fallacy, all the while pretending to be a "spiritual" philosophy. Indeed, it has in many ways eclipsed and perverted modern spiritualism. As Steve Blake has so aptly observed, "In reincarnation, human consciousness is dependent on the physical body. . . . [It] has become a surrogate for survival." Blake says he wrote his book as a challenge to the theory of reincarnation, which most unfortunately, has "effectively neutralized the principal finding of psychical research, namely, that we all survive bodily death and continue to exist as discarnate spirit beings" (Blake 2014, 194).

Making us dependent on a physical body (to continue our progress and work out our karma) is incompatible with the most fundamental definition of spiritualism. It is, in James Webster's words, like riding two horses (spiritualism and materialism). Grahame Mackenzie, who

CLERK: We are completely over-booked on Napoleon, Anne of Cleaves and Joan of Arc .... How does Atilla the Hun grab you?

THIEF: Don't you arrest me! These belonged to me in my last incarnation.

Client: I feel sure I was Florence Nightingale in a past life.
Medium: Oh, but Florence communicates regularly through our home circle.

New Arrival: Please take me to meet my dear wife at last.
St. Peter: Sorry you are just too late. She has reincarnated as your grandson.

Fig. 10.4. Cartoons from James Webster's book The Case Against Reincarnation, *created and drawn by his brother Tony Sheldon.*

interviewed Webster not too long ago, advised his readers: "For a most excellent page-turner on how the illusion of reincarnation plays itself out, see James' book *The Case Against Reincarnation*." Explaining his position on Mackenzie's website, James avers, "There is not a single case of scientifically proven reincarnation; every suggested case has a rational explanation"—usually part of a mediumistic event.

This is not my first, and probably not my last, attempt to convey the phoniness of a doctrine that has us hopping from one body to another . . . throwing dust in our eyes and blinding us to the true meaning of immortality—the eternal progression through the cosmos that is every man's birthright and inheritance. Sooner or later we will all discover the truth of the matter.

11
FREEING THE GHOST

Exorcism stands in relation to ordinary psychotherapy as radical surgery does to lancing a boil.

M. SCOTT PECK, *PEOPLE OF THE LIE*

Sometimes there is a common chord in beginnings and endings. I am thinking of spirit entry and spirit *release,* which may indeed share a common stimulus: a jolt, a shock, a body blow. There must be a reason Aldous Huxley said, "In many cases old-fashioned whipping was probably just as effective as modern shock treatment." No, not a punitive whipping,* but a good thrashing just the same. Even today some Pentecostal and Holiness churches attempt to drive out the devil by hitting the sufferer on the head with a bible. Chances are, this is not too different from schizophrenic head banging, the tormented soul's tactic meant only to break the spell. It was a method that Anneliese Michel used to "shock the systems back into their proper functioning." When she "felt it [the takeover] coming, suddenly I had to knock my head against the wall" (Goodman 1981, 151).

Dr. Carl Wickland's case of a New York "boy thug" illustrates not only the traumatic onset of a criminal career, but, amazingly, also its traumatic termination. Frank James, after a fall from a motorcycle at

---

*T. K. Oesterreich (1935, 212), in one case, records an incident from 1891, in Palestine, where a sheik *whipped* the possessing spirit out of a woman.

ten years of age, changed from a cheerful lad into a surly, insolent boy, developing into a confirmed criminal. Eventually he was declared insane and sent to an asylum; he escaped, and while pursuers attempted his capture, they hit him on the head with a club. Frank then fell unconscious and was taken to a hospital. When he awoke, he was extraordinarily changed—gentle and deferential, showing no further indications of an unbalanced mind. From that time on he exhibited not the slightest impulse to commit crime of any kind.

Literally beating the spirit out of its victim was not uncommon in days past. In a Polish ghetto, the deranged spirit inhabiting a sick girl had, in life, been a drunk, beggar, and suicide (by drowning). The girl's people sent for the rabbi to release the dybbuk. The rabbi proceeded to strike the girl violently; she collapsed and at that moment the spirit left through the window. The same method was used in Syria: A child was subject to epileptic fits; when "he felt the spirit come upon him, the sheik struck the child a blow . . . so violent that it made a wound through which the spirit came forth" (Oesterreich 1935, 207, 212).

Maybe this is the genesis of the good old sobering slap. When one of Henry Hawksworth's alters got out of hand, Dr. Allison "moved swiftly from his chair and struck him lightly on the forehead, between his eyes, with the open part of his palm.* It was a technique discovered by a Swedish doctor [Wickland?] and it always forced whatever personality was in control of the body at the time to submerge" (Hawksworth 1977, 232).

On the serendipitous end of the same spectrum come a few stories of fortuitous dislodging. A woman bothered by a negative entity had run her car into a telephone pole, damaging it frightfully and herself somewhat. Yet the accident somehow shook loose her unseen tormenter; she has not heard from him since (S. Smith 1970b, 154). Best of all is the story of George, reported in an Associated Press story on

---

*Ralph Allison is one of the few American psychiatrists who began treating cases of MPD as possession by spirits. He says he actually was inspired by New Testament readings of Christ casting out demons.

February 24, 1988. The headline read BRAIN WOUND ELIMINATES MAN'S MENTAL ILLNESS. A twenty-two-year-old man, identified as George, was driven to suicide by his severe washing compulsion (OCD). He put a gun in his mouth and pulled the trigger. Not only did he survive, but he was miraculously cured. The bullet had lodged in the left frontal lobe of his brain, performing a lobotomy. "George is now at college and leading a normal life" (Rapoport 1989, 9).

Although the psychosurgical lobotomy pretty much went out of style, shock treatment remained in vogue as an answer to the "bad spirits" of depression and other ills. Since this chapter is devoted to methods of spirit clearing, let us begin with this well-known strategy for accomplishing just that: ECT, electroconvulsive therapy. "After falling out of favor for a generation, ECT has returned to favor because of the growing recognition of drugs' limitations" (Betty 2012, 31). The shock might come unbidden: In another accidental clearing, a psychotic patient came out of a car wreck "completely sane." Dr. Edith Fiore (1987, 12) then "wondered if the reason that electroshock therapy sometimes worked . . . was by the same process: the possessing spirit was shocked out of the body." Dr. Noll (1990, 143) is another who cites similar results, like the PTSD victim who had memory gaps, but after ECT "remembered his true name and the details of his life."

Nevertheless, the success rate for ECT seems rather mixed. Reports of satisfactory recovery (Maurey 1988, 32; Guirdham 1982, 45; Duke and Hochman 1992, 147–48) barely edge out those in which ECT failed to eliminate further suicide attempts (Cohen et al. 1991, 54; Wolfe 1986, 184; Duke and Hochman 1992, 37). Even when there is improvement, it may not last very long. Why is that? Although "the possessing entities are made so uncomfortable [by shock treatment] that they simply give it [the body] up," it may only be for "a short time. The entities always stay in readiness to move right back in unguarded moments" (Ebon 1974, 70).

Enter Dr. Carl Wickland, who understood the difference between success and failure in these proceedings. In fact, I suspect that Wickland was the (unsung) inventor of ECT, which began its official career in the late 1930s. A few decades earlier, Wickland, a Swedish-American, had begun using a prototype of ECT *in combination with verbal exorcism.* Here's how: He passed a small charge of electricity through the patient, thus dislodging the attached spirit and shifting it over to the medium (his wife Anna). To generate the charge of static electricity he used a Wimhurst machine. "The discarnate entity," Wickland explained, "is much more sensitive to the mild shock than the patient himself." As one such spirit declared (speaking through the medium), "I do not want those knockings any more. I will stay away" (Wickland 1974, 49). Wickland also enlisted the aid of intelligent helper-spirits, invisible coworkers he called the Mercy Band, angelic allies charged with carrying off the entity to an appropriate place on the Other Side.*

Clearing—on the Other Side.

According to the Mercy Band, there are training schools in heaven where earthbound spirits are brought for enlightenment. Many passages of the Upper Book of Oahspe describe such places of learning and rehabilitation. For example, when vagrant spirits were found returning to earth and making trouble, the angels "little by little cut off these evil spirits and took them away to [special] colonies and disciplined them" (Oahspe, Book of Fragapatti 33:18). In stubborn cases, celestial dispersers, captors, and constables are sent to make an arrest. The hospitals in heaven also minister to souls in chaos and all manner of diseased spirits, bringing them away from their corporeal haunts and restoring them.

---

*If the entity is not conducted to a place of Light, it can easily return, or as so often happens, even jump on the exorcist. Hence the caveat, "Experience hath proven that to dispossess familiar spirits in one place is but to drive them to another" (Oahspe, Book of Osiris 10:2). The work then consists of more than just getting rid of the possessor. The exorcist should direct the entity to a better place, in the spirit world. For every possessed person the exorcist helps on this earth plane, there are usually ten or more attendant spirits coaxed along to a better life in their world. "Spirit release not only heals the client, it heals the attached spirits" (Betty 2010, 4).

Fig. 11.1. Dr. and Mrs. Wickland

Using his clairvoyant wife Anna as the "psychic intermediary," Dr. Wickland spent *Thirty Years Among the Dead* (as his book is titled), endeavoring to bring them (the Dead) to a realization of "higher possibilities." Almost all reliable spirit-release work of the twentieth and twenty-first centuries is based on Wickland's pioneering work (whether credited or not). In California, the Wicklands founded the National Psychological Institute for the treatment of obsession. Rather like Africa's tribal exorcists, Wickland would first make the spirit identify itself: "Who are you, friend?" he would ask. But if the spirit reneged, claiming to be the very body of its host, Wickland would retort unflinchingly that Anna "is a psychic sensitive who allows ignorant spirits like yourself to control her body" (Wickland 1974, 44). A few more examples of Wickland's patter:

"You must realize that you have lost your physical body. . . . You are only using our friend's body."

"Now, my friend, I want you to understand your condition. You have lost your physical body and are now a spirit."

"You cannot stay here, obsessing this patient. You had better be humble and ask for help."

The Wickland method—of contacting, reasoning, persuading—continues to this day in England's rescue circles. It was after a U.S. Army base in Saudi Arabia was hit by a scud missile, that one such circle was "visited" by an Army sergeant who did not realize he had died. He was still barking orders to his men when one member of the circle cleverly suggested that he try to walk through the wall. This he did, and said, "By God, you're right!" After a while, the circle got him to look for spirit helpers on his side of life. In another session, they got an Iraqi-sounding voice plaintively crying out, "I cannot find paradise." For him, a helper arrived and he was taken in hand and led on his way. (This case was described on the Spirit Release website; unfortunately it is no longer available.)

Of course, rescue work is nothing new. "All over the Third World," comments Dr. Stafford Betty (2012, 23), "right down to the present day, spirits—both good and bad—are taken for granted as realities. . . . Exorcisms are commonplace throughout South and Southeast Asia, Central and South America, and sub-Saharan Africa; there is no place in the world where they are unknown." And spirit release has been going on for thousands of years. Here is a small sample of its international range.

TABLE 11.1. CROSS-CULTURAL METHODS OF SPIRIT REMOVAL

Where	Worker	Method
Ethiopia	possession healers	coax *wuqabi* spirits to abandon their haunts
North Africa	*shechah* (shaman)	whirling dance and other rites undertaken to expel the spirits of jinn and zar
Nigeria	medicine men	mediumistic channels used to expel "outside forces" from psychotic individuals

Where	Worker	Method
Hawaii	*kahuna*	returns a wandering spirit to its own "body"
Tahiti	healer	chants and implores: "Confess all your sins and throw off those evil monsters" (Henry 1928, 211)
Melanesia	*gismana*	extracts tamate (possessing spirits) by stroking the body, blowing on the eyes, yawning, and spitting
Old Italy	priest	lays the (incubus) ghost by anointing with a decoction of a dragon's organs in oil and wine
Turkic Central Asia	*baxsi* (exorcist)	ritual sacrifice (goat), séance, and dreamwork combine to drive away the evil spirit
China	*dang-ki*	the exorcist chants, incants, tosses rice and salt in the air, and never accepts money
Malaysia	*bomoh*	summons the troubling spirit, drives it downward, and sucks it out of the big toe
Sri Lanka	*kattadirala* (exorcist)	rite of "sacred thread" wards off spirit attack
Mexico	*macobero* (white witch)	rubs victim with special oils and summons the appropriate spirits to chase away the evil forces
Puerto Rico	witch doctor	mounts the molesting spirit, interrogates it, finds out why it is causing the difficulty, and then "educates" it (Crapanzano and Garrison 1977, 423)

This person seems quite normal. But there is a personality within her quite different from her own. . . . We have known about this phenomenon of possession from remote antiquity onwards. That is why the Church created an order of exorcists.

FATHER APPOLLINAIRE FOCACCIA,
QUOTED IN LEON CHRISTIANI,
EVIDENCE OF SATAN IN THE MODERN WORLD

Sadly, as we saw with Anneliese, not all exorcisms have the desired effect. In the case of the Jabuticabal poltergeist (Brazil), bricks were falling of their own, and the family sought the help of a priest. He performed an exorcism; "the phenomenon did not cease, but rather became worse" (Guiley 2000, 198). Nevertheless, a very similar case in Africa did meet with success: Bishop Weston of Zanzibar had been called to a clay hut where pieces of the wall were being thrown about. One chunk even hit him on the head. Whereupon, "I went into the house and began the exorcism, pronouncing the ritual prayers. The manifestations ceased at once. . . . No disturbing phenomena have reoccurred" (Fodor 1966, 294).

In spooky old England, the Anglican Canon Pearce-Higgins knew what to do when it was discovered that an ancient house—full of phantoms, moaning sounds, and stuff hurled about—was once a priory with an unsavory history. The ghost-hunting cleric went to work, finding and then convincing the long-deceased monks that they were indeed dead, hence urging them to seek the light. To help them on their way, the canon prayed, "O thou unquiet spirits, go thy way, rejoicing that the prayers of the faithful shall follow thee and that thou mayest enjoy everlasting peace." The disturbances ceased (Spraggett 1967, 159).

A kabbalistic invocation for banishing the dybbuk is a little more forceful:* "Hear me, hear me, oh thou sinful, stubborn spirit. I order

---

*The prayer was spoken in Hebrew. I have been told that the *Ana B'Koach* is another ancient Hebrew prayer with the power to reach attached entities.

thee to depart from the body and soul you usurp and to go in peace whence you came. . . . Leave, leave, I command thee . . . vacate at once this much-tormented person. . . . The Lord shall fight for you, and ye shall hold your peace" (Kuhn 1963, 28).

Whether the setting is religious, secular, or mediumistic, all such efforts in the modern world seem to be confined to very small, often very private, groups. The Work, as I find it, is scattered, individualistic, self-determined, and—apart from ghost- and orb-hunting societies (which are not primarily involved in the *removal* of discarnate personalities)—is not really organized or united into any larger body or shared philosophy. As such, you will find these initiatives under different names: exorcism, ghost laying, spirit clearing or spirit cleansing, rescue work, restoration, banishment, depo (depossession), entity release, and so on.

There is a certain weakness in this disjunction, this lack of wider consensus, but maybe that will change. For the nonce, let us keep in mind a few basic, perhaps universal, guidelines:

1. The entities need to be more than expelled; the Work, there-fore, should not be started without assistance from "helpers," the equivalent of Wickland's Mercy Band or of the medium's "controls." Note also that Dion Fortune (1981, 65) cleared one case (in a week's time) with a "treatment given to the *entity* that was causing the trouble, not merely to the patient; it was the release of the obsessor . . . and helping him heavenward that gave freedom to his victim."

2. Nor should the Work begin without the knowledge and desire of the host. (We tried this once, in a distant healing, and it backfired on us.) Nevertheless, a few British groups have become quite adept at "remote spirit rescue" aka "absent treatment," some practitioners asserting it is actually easier to work apart and that "unseen forces can indeed be manipulated from a dis-tance" (Fortune1981, 70).

3. Follow-up is important. What sort of timeframe can be expected? No telling. The medium Harriet Shelton (1957, 75) calls it "a

long, slow process of reaching and reforming the earthbound spirit who clings stubbornly to his victim." Still, there are some who say they have done a successful healing in ten minutes. Others report a course of dozens of sessions before the obsessing spirit was released. Australia's Sam Sagan (1997, 179) claims his clearing process takes no more than twenty minutes. Dr. Fiore, on the other hand, mentions one case resolved only after three years of hypnotherapy. Which, again, is certainly in contrast with one parish priest who obtained the boy's release "in only three hours" (Crabtree 1985, 95); just as Father Theophilus exorcised one woman who had shrieked, screamed, and wept for nine months in less than seven hours. Yet it took more than thirty sittings for Dr. Titus Bull to cast out the multiple obsessors afflicting one of his clients. Meanwhile, psychiatrist Ralph Allison purportedly cleared one patient in two-and-a half minutes (Mayer 1989, 162).

No doubt there are times when the affliction hinges on some sore point or perceived slight on the part of the excarnate. There was this gent, for example, who had clandestinely purchased a manuscript of formulas written by the deceased occult wizard Aleister Crowley—all the while knowing that the manuscript was actually willed to a certain museum. The man soon became very ill; doctors could do nothing for him. Finally, in desperation, he handed the manuscript over to the museum, and totally recovered his health (Glass 1969, 184–85).

It might be noted that hypnotism is another potent tool giving the operator the opportunity to talk directly with the possessing entity. Dr. Fiore's work with depossession (depo) took advantage of her skills in hypnosis, reviving the method that had been so creatively pioneered by the eighteenth- and nineteenth-century physicians Franz Mesmer and J. M. Charcot. Working mostly with "hysterics," these founders of modern hypnotherapy discovered that their hypnotized patients "seemed to manifest new lives of which the host personality was unaware" (Mayer 1989, 35).

Often neither mortal nor spirit is conscious of the presence of the other.

CARL WICKLAND, *THIRTY YEARS AMONG THE DEAD*

But not all are unaware: we remember Fiore's patient Peter who said that he sometimes felt "that another being was speaking through him." She decided to try hypnosis "to check for possessing entities." She found several, and following (though not crediting) the Wickland method, addressed them in this manner, "Why are you imposing yourself upon this man's life, causing him problems, when you know that you have gone through the change called death and should be progressing in your own spirit lives?" One of them replied, "I don't want to go." Another: "So what!" After this session she concluded, "Peter and I had our work cut out for us" (Fiore 1987, 70–71).

"Hypnosis is very helpful," attests one multiple (Cohen et al. 1991, 124). This is probably because alters who are eager to emerge come out easily when the host is entranced. For multiple Jenny, remembering her childhood was greatly facilitated by hypnotic regression. "Her memories have been recovered by . . . hypnosis. She has shown remarkable recall of details" (Spencer 1989, xix). Such recalls can bring the multiple back to the traumatic moments when the alter made his or her first appearance. It can lay bare the hitherto unseen trajectory of a lifelong pattern of overshadowing.

Fiore has also provided patients with "depossession tapes" (1987, 149) that they can take home and use when the going gets rough. Tapes, auto-suggestion, and other methods of psychic self-defense might prove a reasonable adjunct (or even alternative?) to the psychoactive drugs handed out to beleaguered patients. The occasional disclosure exposing the risks of these mind-altering pharmaceuticals is only the tip of the iceberg. A single example: when David Morehouse was given Halcion and Prozac for his "hallucinations," their "effect was devastating" (Morehouse 1998, 275).* Indeed, a few of these wonder drugs,

---

*David, if you recall, had become a perfect recruit for the Pentagon's psi spy program after a wound to the head (friendly fire) left him, in a word, psychic. That's when the

like Ritalin or Adderall, may sometimes *cause* hallucinations. We've already had a glimpse of the hazards of Dilantin (in Anneliese's case); while the use of Thorazine in MPD cases that were misdiagnosed as schizophrenia has also been disastrous (Keyes 1981, 359, 396). Neither can we expect positive results from antidepressives and antipsychotics, when the underlying problem of spirit possession remains unsuspected, undiscovered, and untreated by mental health professionals.

> *The cure is not a drug but rather a ritual manipulation.*
>
> FELICITAS GOODMAN,
> *THE EXORCISM OF ANNELIESE MICHEL*

Indeed, Anneliese's biographer, Felicitas Goodman, came to see that Anneliese's tragic death might have been averted: "The afflicted person needs to be trained to terminate the . . . trance on command, upon being given a signal. . . . [This procedure] represents the repairing of the barrier between the two types of consciousness, the ordinary and the altered one. It is the erecting of the dam that Anneliese spoke about in [her] tragic note begging for help . . . [from] Father Alt" (Goodman 1981, 234).

Over the years, practitioners have come up with a raft of formulas and suggestions for terminating the trance or otherwise thwarting the unwanted entity—from ringing bells to scattering eucalyptus leaves to waving a willow whisk. FD, the "former devotee" mentioned earlier, wrote that she found relief by putting holy water on her body and sprin-

---

(cont. from p. 253) visions began. And the nightmares. And the depression. And conversations with angels, mind reading, and time-travel. "I began seeing things in my mind . . . [even] seeing forward in time or predicting the outcome of certain events . . . images darting endlessly in and out . . . my mind's eye open all the time" (Morehouse 1998, 511). Carefully trained in remote viewing (a form of controlled OBE) for the purpose of State Intelligence, Morehouse listened to "focus tapes" with tonal frequencies designed to help "achieve an altered state." He became very good at it. But there was no way to control the side effects—"touching the darkness." He told his wife, "I'm scared . . . that bullet did something to me, something strange. I can't turn it off. I can't stop these goddamned images . . . and they're driving me out of my mind." Literally.

kling some on her bed. "I also find that making loud noises like clapping one's hands loudly and popping balloons or paper bags . . . scares it off." But all the nostrums in the world cannot compare to a thorough psychic / emotional cleansing. It begins with self.

> *We may not be able to prevent the minds of others from sending us suggestions, but we may so purify the soil of our own natures that no harmful ones can find a congenial seed-bed.*
>
> DION FORTUNE, *PSYCHIC SELF-DEFENSE*

Depend not on words or prayers, but begin to save yourself by purifying your flesh, by purifying your thoughts, and by the practice of good works done unto others. For through these only is there any [hope] for you either in this world or the next.

OAHSPE, BOOK OF JUDGMENT 14:36

This is the hard part. Purifying self. Disciplining your very thoughts. Guarding your very emotions like a sentinel conscientious on his watch. At the end of the day, we are thrown back on ourselves. We all do have the power to do this—to monitor self. Not just power, but also wisdom and love. These three—Wisdom, Love, and Power—are the givens, and they are our blessed weapons against all evil. No, there are no shortcuts to inner peace, which remains but a distant dream until the day we take up these givens and declare the Light as our dependable guide. Goodwill and careful judgment are also essential—not optional. But best of all is self-control: poise, self-discipline, and the willpower to make things right.

Abeunt studia in mores.

APHORISM:
"ZEALOUS PURSUITS BECOME HABITS"

Twice in my own life have I been taught this lesson by a friend. In the one case it was a Persian gentleman who said to me, "You would be great if you could control your fire." In the other case, it was a wise woman who told me that the little secret of life is mastering your own emotions. Ah, what a lesson! Nasty spirits are drawn to the grand roster of untamed emotions: fear, anger, worry, resentment, apathy, animosity, contempt, jealousy, selfishness, vanity, self-pity, guilt, chronic grief, sadness, wretchedness, distrust, stubbornness.

* * *

Undeveloped, undisciplined mediums are the sport of the lower spirits.

VINCENT CRAPANZANO,
CASE STUDIES IN SPIRIT POSSESSION

In England, the term *negative psychic* is used to indicate an *undeveloped* medium—open but not developed, not schooled in vetting psychic input. The concept is also found among Puerto Rican *espiritualistas,* who call the undeveloped medium *debil* (weak—and vulnerable to random spirits). What an important concept this is! In this particular system, *espiritus obsesores* give bad thoughts or tell people to do stuff they don't want to do—all possible because of the undeveloped condition; for they are meant to do good for others with their (cultivated) gifts. Failing this, their guardians "may simply turn their backs on them, leaving them vulnerable to any ignorant spirit that wants to make use of them." The cure: to develop, *estar en desarrollo,* "to be in development" (Crapanzano and Garrison 1977, 402, 426).

We've got so many passive mediums walking around, who, if they only realized their true condition, could begin to protect themselves and, with a little training, conquer their (undiagnosable) problems—everything from migraine headaches to tics, psychosomatic ills (especially stomach problems), accidents, nightmares, antisocial behavior, and even poltergeistery and hauntings. Where negative mediumship is *completely unconscious* (meaning the person is totally unaware of their "gift"), awareness alone can make the difference between healthy and pathological psychism. When natural mediumship is overlooked, denied, or repressed, don't be surprised if it becomes troublesome in the course of time. A double-edged gift, indeed—something that must be understood, nurtured, disciplined. Otherwise it is a loose cannon— likely to run its own (disaster) course. Like any power, psychism needs to be contained and wisely managed.

Absent development, the passive medium inevitably falls prey to disturbing dissociated states. The powers of psyche are so keen that they can overwhelm the normal run of consciousness: psyche then becomes *too* independent from self, *too* autonomous, *too* open, *too* unconstrained, *too* separate.

> *An undeveloped sensitive can very easily be taken unawares.*
> ENA TWIGG, *ENA TWIGG, MEDIUM*

Before a formal clearing is begun, it should be established that the sensitive is in fact targeted by negative spirits. This is where the outstanding work of Rev. Eugene Maurey comes in. Clearing at a distance, Maurey enlisted three very useful aids: comprehensive knowledge of human psyche, otherworldly "escorts" led by a figure named George (his spirit control), and a good pendulum.

Divination by pendulum has been around for thousands of years, beginning with the early Egyptians, Greeks, Chinese, and Polynesians. The object is to gather certain information from helpful spirits. Today the pendulum is used mostly by health workers/healers. Maurey's diagnosis of a person usually involved about five pendulum readings. He began with the question, "Is this person possessed?" Then, "How many entities are involved?" Then, "Do I have permission to clear this person?" Such readings can provide "all the information necessary to perform an exorcism." Maurey used a quantitative system of ratings: see his book *Exorcism,* chapters 6 and 7 for detailed instructions.

When a case came to his attention and he suspected negative overshadowing, Maurey promptly began investigation by using the pendulum, posing a few simple questions that could be answered with a yes or no swing. More often than not, he found that the obsessing personality was of the antisocial sort (APD), in contrast to the conventional personality of the unknowing host. Maurey also checked for potential allies: Does the subject have any *positive* entities on board?

In his own words, "When I first started this work, I made the mistake of speaking directly to the possessing spirits. I was not aware how evil some of them could be. One almost killed me! Since that time, I let my obliging spirit guide, George, do the work. . . . When the entity measures on the extreme negative level, take special precautions! Such entities are dangerous and the exorcist must be firm and operate through an intermediary [such as George]. . . . When you are ready for the clearing, say aloud or silently, 'I now address the entities and negative programs in and around [this person.] You are not of this world. You are on the other side of the veil called death. You will now find spirit guides standing beside you whom you [can] trust. They will . . . lead you to your next level of spiritual development' . . . Then take several deep breaths and direct the pendulum to swing in a full clockwise motion. Then say, 'Go!' Finally, relax, and watch the pendulum gradually return to the neutral position indicating all entities have left" (Maurey 1988, 120, 129).

I was most intrigued by Maurey's distant clearing of dangerous criminals. What would law enforcement say if they knew they had a silent partner / crime stopper working in his living room in his pajamas with a simple pendulum? An amateur criminologist, I was already familiar with the Coleman case. As Maurey tells it,

Authorities had identified Alton Coleman and his girlfriend, Debra Brown, as participants in a six-state crime spree, which included assault, rape, kidnapping, and murder. On checking Coleman for possession, I found he was controlled by a dangerous entity and had an additional 24 entities nearby. . . . Both [he and Brown] were then exorcised at a distance.

Two days later both Coleman and Brown were captured without out resistance. Without apparent reason, they had simply returned to their old neighborhood where they were immediately recognized and apprehended. . . . What caused the two to return to their former habitat where they were . . . easily apprehended? Was it that they were no longer controlled by vicious entities? . . . And what would happen if every parolee is exorcised when leaving prison? . . . Could their antisocial behavior be changed and their criminal activity stopped?

. . . Even when a criminal has not been identified, nor his whereabouts known, he may still be cleared. (1988, 137–38, 146)

In fact, this is what happened in the clearing of Richard Ramirez, LA's Night Stalker, the killer who was touched by the darkness: flat affect, lone wolf, sleep disorder, stalking, staring spells, fantasy life, coprolalia, suicidal thoughts, and pointless, though compulsive, killing. Maurey, as it happened, was lecturing in California (1985) when he learned that the *still unknown* Unsub, the Night Stalker, had murdered fourteen women.

"I decided to stop the killer."

After determining that two vicious entities were controlling the killer, Maurey performed a distant exorcism and cleared the intruding spirits. Within days, Richard Ramirez slipped up, and his identity became known; for he broke his own night-preying rule and tried to steal a car in broad daylight. He was immediately captured.

Maurey: "I believe that when the intelligent criminal spirits left, the killer no longer had their cunning to guide him. He then fell easy prey to his captors" (1988, 141).

Release work, in truth, is nothing new; it's probably the oldest form of psychotherapy in the world. No, it is not a step backward to engage these principles; but a step in the right direction and the next, inevitable, phase of the Consciousness Revolution. It is the Big Picture. It is proactive.

APPENDIX A

COPROLALIA

The chronic, excessively foul mouth may well be a first clue to negative overshadowing. As Rev. Maurey (1988, 148) observed, "persons who can hear the entity speak will often report how abusive the language is." Strange howls, blasphemy, and coprolalia (offensive, filthy language) were once considered a standard sign of demonic possession. For example, from Therese, the possessed woman exorcised by Father Pier-Paolo, came "the usual stream of abuse" (Christiani 1961, 139). The main criteria of possession, according to the Catholic *Rituale Romanum,* include coprolalia. A woman, Mrs. Fl., exorcised by Dr. Wickland (1974, 40), "though a refined lady of gentle disposition, became very wild and unmanageable, swearing constantly. . . . She used extraordinarily vile language."

Neither is it unusual for the manic-depressive to show signs of entity possession, coprolalia leading the way. One bipolar lady, as we've seen, fell to calling her husband "every name you could think of" (Duke and Hochman 1992, xii). The same holds true for MPD. Eve, for one, would have spells where she "spoke in a jaunty tone, often using vulgar phrases" (Thigpen and Cleckley 1957, 22). Obsessives, too, may be prone to "offensive words or phrases" (Rapoport 1989, 92).

The encroaching spirit who "perverts the tongue and distorts the lips" (Oesterreich 1935, 11), who hurls the wounding insult and disgusting four-letter words, has remained remarkably unchanged over the centuries, from earliest records to the present moment. We have

had a look at the true stories on which two of America's most popular "possession" films were based, and both involved victims exhibiting
coprolalia: Robbie (*The Exorcist*), shrieking curses and vulgar sexual-
isms, and Emily Rose (*The Exorcism of Emily Rose*), calling the priest
"carcass," "arsehole," and the like.

According to the guidelines laid out by the priestly rites of exorcism, J. K., a doctor who went murderously insane, exhibited signs of
demonic possession, including voices, unusually rapid speech, exaggerated grimacing—and coprolalia, or "screaming obscenities. . . . He made
a lot of vulgar references" (Ablow 1994, 59, 106, 16).

Vulgarity in the media (especially in Hollywood films) is no exception to the rule. Arguably, the industry itself has been infested with
spirits of a low order, the *F* word spilling off the celluloid with a vengeance. In Professor Twitchell's words (1992, 212), "Vulgarity is victo-
rious." What does that say for the mental and spiritual health of this
nation?

APPENDIX B

EXPOSURE TO DEATH

Exposure to the *dead* is one more neglected factor, especially for the predisposed person; contact with death and dying may be more risky than we realize. Dr. Edith Fiore, one of a handful of American psychiatrists who treat their deranged cases by dislodging the troublesome spirit, has incisively written about the three places with the greatest concentration of spirits: hospitals, funeral homes, and cemeteries; when drinking follows the funeral service, any spirits who followed the guests home can easily possess them (Fiore 1987, 115).

Hospitals: "Children often come down with obsessional . . . disorders after a period of hospitalization" (Levenkron 1991, 127). As Fiore explains, "Doctors, nurses, hospital personnel, paramedics . . . undertakers, and people who work in cemeteries are all targets for possession. . . . If we could see clairvoyantly, we would probably be shocked at the number of spirits that populate hospitals . . . latching onto people (Fiore 1987, 113). In a near-death condition in a hospital bed, Betty Eadie (1992, 126–27) felt the presence of "several hideous creatures of a clearly malevolent nature that were intent upon attacking her." "Hospitals," wrote psychic-medium James Van Praagh (2008, 143), "are a very big draw for ghosts. . . . Whenever I visit people in hospitals, ghosts are always milling around. Some are there to siphon off energy from people in weakened states . . . some are ghosts who are newly dead and somewhat confused as to their whereabouts."

Cemeteries: Expert at the removal of troublesome entities,

Rev. Eugene Maurey speaks from experience about cemeteries: "Hundreds reside in such places. . . . Hospitals and prisons are also prime targets for an exorcist. . . . A spirit person's [trajectory] will be governed by his beliefs. . . . A person who had no belief about after-death . . . finds he must shift for himself. . . . Unfortunately, he may remain in the hospital where he died or in the cemetery where his body was interred. He has become earthbound." And if a patient "has been given a general anesthetic for a surgical operation, he may find upon resuming consciousness, that he has one or more of [these] entities on board" (Maurey 1988, 24, 92). Interestingly, Richard Noll (1990, 37) has found that nursing is "a common occupation among female multiples."

The Ski Mask Rapist, it turned out, was a onetime hospital cardio-vascular technician.

Sensitives, especially those who are sensitive *and do not know it,* can be caught unawares. Graveyards can wreak havoc on the sensitive. The actress Patty Duke, who bravely shared her "brilliant madness" with the world, recalled that whenever she passed the local cemetery she was instantly overtaken with a panic attack. Patty was a sensitive but did not know it; she was prone to dissociative states ("something takes over"), dramatic mood swings, violent outbursts, suicidal thoughts ("demons inside me"), as well as undeveloped mediumship (hearing voices), OBEs ("left my body"), obsessions, precognitions, phobias, and manias.

Dick Sutphen, a sensitive, "became hysterical at the edge of an ancient graveyard in Arizona, and literally had to be dragged, sobbing, back to his hotel room. For hours afterward, he was delirious, talking about being killed" (Weisman 1977, 45). (The input from spirits concerned a massacre that took place four hundred years ago, when a Spanish priest had issued an order to destroy all the Indians who refused baptism.)

Mental disturbances of all kinds may have their source in the intrusions of hostile or parasitic or chaotic entities. . . . Mankind's superstitious dread of night in the graveyard is not as laughable as the cultivated would like to pretend.
AUGUSTINE CAHILL, *DARKNESS, DAWN, AND DESTINY*

So don't tarry long among the tombstones, if you think you are a sensitive. In Brazil, the spirits of suicides, called *exus*, "spend much of their time in cemeteries which are regarded as particularly dangerous places for mediums with undeveloped abilities" (Crapanzano and Garrison 1977, 337).

We have seen many abused children become psychic. Richard Ramirez is one example. Californians will remember, with a chill, the reign of the Night Stalker who took fourteen innocent lives in the 1980s, terrorizing the women of LA. There had actually been many signs of dissociation, ASC, and malignant overshadowing in this tall young Tex-Mex guy: hyperactive disorder, fantasies, early epilepsy, sleep disorder, staring spells, and blackouts. It didn't help that Richard had been forced to witness a wife-murder. Richard developed something of a dual personality as well as suicidal tendencies; he also exhibited certain cardinal signs of possession: coprolalia and hyperpraxia. While still living at home, this excellent candidate for negative overshadowing would take to sleeping in the Corodova Cemetery (El Paso) to get away from his father's rages. He'd grab his sleeping bag and run. "The boy slept in the cemetery frequently."

Did Richard pick up *exus* or demons or wandering spirits of darkness at the Cordova Cemetery? Peter Sutcliffe, his opposite number in England, almost certainly became obsessed at the Bingley Cemetery. The Yorkshire Ripper, whose identity spurred his country's largest manhunt to that date (1981), had taken a job as a gravedigger at Bingley Cemetery in his teens and later worked at the town morgue. Ultimately convicted of thirteen counts of stranger murder, he had had a close encounter at the graveyard: Peter heard a voice that led him to a particular grave; the voice now emanated from the headstone. It was just the beginning. With the passage of time, the voice began inciting him to violence, telling him that prostitutes (who would become his victims) were the cause of society's problems. From that point on Peter was "compelled to kill" (Burn 1985, 38, 242, 246).

Across the Atlantic, in New York, David Berkowitz (Son of Sam) had a fascination with cemeteries, especially after his mother's death.

"I just used to have the urge to go. Just hang around, talk. I used to visit all the graves there . . . I would, you know, talk. . . . I felt akin to them." David's rapport with the dead is curiously reminiscent of Jim Huberty's confession that he was "more comfortable with the dead than the living" (Douglas and Olshaker 1999, 231). Huberty was the man who, in 1984, shot up a McDonald's in San Isidro, California, killing twenty-one innocent persons. Jim had attended mortuary school and worked for two years at a funeral home.

In nearby Las Vegas, John Wayne Gacy, at age twenty, also found work as an ambulance driver for Palm Mortuary and was later assigned to the mortuary itself as an attendant. Here, he, morbidly, took to *sleeping* in the embalming room. "About that time," Dr. Rappaport would later note, "he was definitely borderline." Another forensic psychiatrist on the case, Dr. Freedman, pressed Gacy for further details of his job in Las Vegas. Bodies, he noted, were "all around: dead things. A silver-gray coffin with white interior, open. John got inside with the body. He wanted to feel death, in the darkness" (T. Cahill 1987, 309, 323, 44, 46).

No surprise, our rogues' gallery has a statistically significant number of "death workers." Ken Bianchi worked (two years) as an ambulance driver. Mark Hofmann's father was a mortician. Profiling Jack the Ripper as an Unsub (he was never caught), Douglas and Olshaker (2000, 69) imagined that he might have been "a mortician's helper, hospital or morgue attendant." Charles Davis (rapist and killer of five) was an ambulance driver with a unique approach to murder; he'd kill the woman and then arrange things in such a way that he himself would be assigned to pick up the body. Rod Ferrell (double homicide of girlfriend's parents), while still in high school, was recruiting friends and classmates into his little vampire coven, many of the rites and ceremonies performed *at the local cemetery*. Far from the (desultory) effects on a Gacy or Berkowitz or Bianchi, Rod and his followers were actively seeking "the embrace" of spirits, "readily accessible . . . [as] the coffins were above-ground" at the majestic St. Louis Cemetery (in Kentucky).

"I'm not mortal."—Rod F.

Aware of otherworldly beings but in the most sinister way, Rod wanted "to have other vampires join me so I can teach them of the world beyond." According to his twisted logic, the greatest benefits would accrue from invoking the "Horned One" and "messengers of the gods of prey." How successful he was! The coven indeed "began to make contacts in the spirit world," and Rod, entranced, spoke of "angels falling from the sky . . . and different killings." Members began experiencing markedly paranormal states, absorbing spirit powers, producing automatic writing, communing with and joining souls "that have walked the earth for thousands of years," going on OBEs, and undergoing ASCs (Jones 1999, 17, 22, 26, 56, 59).

Strange to say, Rod—product of a horrendous family life—attained a kind of, shall we say, anti-enlightenment, a kind of inverse (perverse?) wisdom. His damaged psyche could only call in malign beings. Almost poignant is the way this dark soul named the cemetery where his vampire cohorts convened; he called it—the Birthplace. Indeed, one would have to be virtually reborn to overcome the terrors of a childhood like his, filled with abuse, neglect, ignorance, hypocrisy, and shame.

APPENDIX C

TRAUMA

The trail we are following starts with a traumatic event so overwhelming as to send psyche reeling, catapulted into the Intangible, the next zone of existence referred to variously as the Threshold, the Void, the Second State, Elsewhere, and so on. Although we have legal beagles who disdain the "abuse excuse," the stark reality remains: our multiples and our most serious sociopaths were almost all victims of early trauma. The fact that many serial killers suffered severe *head trauma* has never been properly factored in.

It is, however, not brain damage per se, but precarious states of consciousness—in a word, *Psyche exteriorized.* Many of us have heard of the formula "fight or flight," which portrays the survival instinct at work when faced with a mortal threat. If the menace cannot be confronted or fought off, the only alternative is escape, flight. And it is no different for *psyche* when faced with terror, shock, or pain. The mind naturally seeks escape from life's bombshells; a sudden insult to the organism triggers the flight response—absenting from self. Isn't this what *causes* the shell of a person, this "garage without a car"? *Something* in his or her experience—something traumatic—has occasioned the disconnect, the flight from self, which in psychologese is known, blandly, as *dissociation*.

Shock, injury, grave illness, surgery (under anesthetics), pure terror, and unconsciousness all represent the lowest possible state of human vitality, and it is in this state that the mind is rendered utterly defenseless, hence *unable to resist* "the intrusion of a strong spirit personality. This is involuntary possession" (Maurey 1988, 76).

It is equally compelling to discover how many top-flight mediums began their psychic career in accidents, injury, or illness. Sylvan J. Muldoon, Vincent N. Turvey, and Oliver Fox—all well-known sensitives of the early twentieth century, "had their psychic faculties intensified by long periods of illness" (Battersby 1979, x). Sylvan Muldoon, in a sleigh accident, was thrown out on his head; he promptly left his body and saw himself lying motionless by the side of the road. Ena Twigg, suspended above her body, was likewise aware of herself lying below during a surgery (under anesthetic).

Dr. Guirdham has shown that psychism is more likely to occur "after long, debilitating illnesses such as typhoid and cholera" (1982, 53). It was known, for example, that Nettie Maynard had suffered both fragile health and protracted illnesses since childhood, having tempted death as she lay ill with typhus fever at age eight. She was, in hindsight, but one of countless mediums and seers who had survived serious childhood illness only by some miracle: D. D. Home, Lurancy Vennum, Eileen Garrett, Rev. Stainton Moses. As for the last, the great British seer William Stainton Moses—who would pass into spirit the same year as Mrs. Maynard, 1892—he was once told by his controls that "the tempering effect of a bodily illness has been in all your life an engine of great power with us."

We also learn that Mrs. Piper's psychic powers were strongest during times of poor health. During the period of an ovarian tumor, her readings were most accurate. Her spirit operator would fade away when her health returned.

Unfortunately, these seers—Piper, Muldoon, Home, Garrett, Moses, and Maynard—are in the minority, having turned their weakness (for spirit) into an asset: the gift. Most others afflicted in childhood become the hapless victims of obsession, possession, multiple-personality and other "disorders": Billy Milligan (MPD), raped by his stepfather; Sybil, the famous multiple, sexually tortured by her mother; Jersey (possessed), molested by her father, and so on. The pattern remains consistent as we shift focus to obsessive-compulsive disorder. Dr. Rapoport supplies many examples from among her OC patients: Jacob had collapsed, at age eight, of a bleeding cerebral aneurism, and fell into a coma. The obsessed boy Zach, also studied by Rapoport (1989, 45), underwent seven operations for congenital intestinal problems—which Rapoport (oddly enough) mistakenly characterizes as "unrelated to his OCD."

Although any one of these illnesses, shocks, or blows might thrust psyche toward no-man's-land, head trauma is by far the leading cause of troubles. Nothing can disrupt or disorient personality more than concussion; the head, after all, was long considered the seat of the soul. In the heyday of spirit circles, sitters were told by their controls that they, the invisible operators on the Other Side, act upon the brains of the sitters to accomplish the phenomena of the séance room.

One psi researcher put it plainly, in a chapter title: "How to Become Psychic—By Falling on Your Head"; his examples included Edgar Cayce, the famous Sleeping Prophet, who as a child was knocked out by a baseball. There was also the well-known Dutch psychic Peter Hurkos who fell off a forty-foot ladder, suffering damage to the brain stem; he woke up in the hospital a mind reader. After the accident, Peter's parents said he was now "someone else." In a similar case, "CE" was possessed by a dead Austrian artist; he, CE, had earlier been hospitalized with a serious head injury.

One of the earliest and best-documented cases of "secondary personality" was that of Doris Fischer. Doris, in fact, was multiple (MPD). The first alter had come on board when Doris was only three: her drunken father had thrown her down so violently that her head was injured. Another personality emerged when she was eighteen after she suffered an injury to her head and back.

Head trauma and crime: Case histories are brimming with inappropriate, bizarre, or violent behaviors that were forerun by head trauma. Yet the authorities, meaning jurisprudence, are not eager for these facts to emerge, fearing that "extenuating circumstances" behind criminal acts would weaken the hand of prosecution. But the fact remains, some of the most vicious—and inexplicable—crimes have been committed by individuals with a history of grievous head injury. Of course, law enforcement and their "hired guns" (paid psychiatrists) have found a way around this: a causal relationship (between the trauma and deviant behavior) has never been proven. True enough . . . but the raw statistics of the matter could hardly be coincidental (see facing page table C.1).

Among criminal offenders, a propensity for altered states *due to head trauma* still goes unrecognized. And this for legal, not psychiatric, reasons, namely, to avoid risking a stronger defense that could put a truly dangerous individual back on the streets. Nevertheless, our growing corpus of criminal biographies shows an inordinate amount of head trauma. No, this is not any sort of "abuse excuse," nor rationalization, and certainly not a means to get dangerous offenders off the hook. But only to comprehend the underpinnings of inexplicable, senseless, random acts of violence.

There is so much that remains to be explored—if the law weren't so shy of finding mitigating circumstances—sometimes as obscure as scuba diving: Zodiac (serial killer) had brain damage, tissue damage from lack of oxygen at birth *and/or* from scuba diving "too long." Dean Corll (serial killer) also took up skin diving but he had to quit when he nearly fainted (he had also suffered from rheumatic fever and heart murmur). Chris Longo (familicide) was also a scuba diver. Yet the question remains: Was it brain damage per se that set off homicidal behavior? Or—did that compromised mind *become susceptible to controlling spirits?* I think so—especially in light of the fact that these victims of concussion or of brain damage go on to exhibit a great range of *paranormal behavior,* manifestations in the domain of psi. A mere sampling is shown in table C.1.

TABLE C.I. PARANORMAL BEHAVIOR
AFTER HEAD INJURY

Name	Offense	Trauma	Paranormal Behavior
Ottis Toole	serial murder; accomplice of Henry Lee Lucas in "recreational killing"	hit hard in head with rock	seizures, commune with dead mother, voices urge suicide
Henry Lee Lucas	matricide and serial killer, rape, mutilation	assaulted (head) with board by mother— unconscious 3 days	dizzy spells; blackouts; "float in air"; "at mercy of various forces"
Dennis Sweeney	killed N.Y. Rep. Allard Lowenstein in 1980 . . .	. . . one year after head injury (pump-jack accident)	voices tormenting him
Todd Hall	arson (resulting in 8 deaths)	lobotomized at 14 after skateboard accident; in coma 6 weeks	fugue: doesn't think he "did it"; blackout
Richard Chase	Vampire Killer of Sacramento (6 victims)	beaten by a gang, head pains	spoke with invisible people; "zombie"; motivated by subhuman forces (Markman and Bosco 1989, 192)
John Wayne Gacy	killer of 33	multiple head traumas	fainting, blackout, automatisms, alter personality, paranormal strength
Arthur Shawcross	serial killer (11 victims)	multiple traumas to head, unconsciousness	OBEs, voices, precognition, paranormal strength, hyperesthesia, alter(?), fugue

TABLE C.I. PARANORMAL BEHAVIOR
AFTER HEAD INJURY (continued)

Name	Offense	Trauma	Paranormal Behavior
Danny Starrett	serial rapist	several head injuries, blackouts	*him*; "I feel a presence . . . another to obey"; lost time; automatic drawing
Gary Heidnik	bondage killer	serious head injury in grade school	dizziness; hallucination; "divine messages"
Joe Kallinger	killer	beaten on head with a hammer	night terrors, ESP, clairvoyant
Ken Bianchi	Hillside Strangler	falls on head	sees alter and demons, lost time
Peter Sutcliffe	Yorkshire Ripper	severe blows to head in accidents	hallucinations, trances, mind reading, hearing voice of God
Richard Ramirez	Night Stalker	2 childhood accidents: concussion and unconsciousness	visions, apparitions, dual personality
Bobby Joe Long	rapist; serial killer	twice hit by car	OBEs, visions
Richard Speck	killed 8 nurses	many head injuries	blackouts, lost time, dissociative episodes

BIBLIOGRAPHY

Ablow, Keith. 1994. *The Strange Case of Dr. Kappler.* New York: The Free Press.
———. 2005. *Inside the Mind of Scott Peterson.* New York: St. Martin's Press.
Adams, Terry, Mary Brooks-Mueller, and Scott Shaw. 1998. *Eye of the Beast.* New York: St. Martin's Paperbacks.
Allen, Sue. 2007. *Spirit Release.* Winchester, U.K.: O Books.
Allen, Thomas B. 1994. *Possessed.* New York: Bantam Books.
Allende, Isabelle. 1993. *Paula.* New York: Harper Collins.
Angel, Criss. 2015. "Question Everything." *Time,* Sept. 21, 75.
Archer, Fred. 1967. *Exploring the Psychic World.* New York: Wm. Morrow.
Baldwin, James. 1985. *The Evidence of Things Not Seen.* New York: Henry Holt.
Barer, Burl. 2002. *Body Count.* New York: Pinnacle Books.
Bartell, Jan. 1974. *Spindrift.* New York: Hawthorn Books.
Battersby, H. F. Prevorst. 1979. *Man Outside Himself.* N.J.: Citadel Press.
Betty, Stafford. 2010. "Spirit Release." *Searchlight,* Dec., 4.
———. 2012. "The Growing Evidence for Demonic Possession." *Journal of Spirituality and Paranormal Studies,* Jan., 23–40.
Blake, Stephen. 2014. *Reincarnation Refuted.* Surrey, U.K.: Grosvenor House.
Blinder, Martin. 1985. *Lovers, Killers, Husbands, Wives.* New York: St. Martin's Press.
Bourguignon, Erika. 1967. "World Distribution and Patterns of Possession States." In *Trance and Possession States,* ed. R. Prince. Montreal: J. M. Bucke Foundation.
———. 1973. "Introduction: A Framework for the Comparative Study of Altered States of Consciousness." In *Religion, Altered States of Consciousness, and Social Change.* Columbus: Ohio State University Press.

———. 1976. *Possession.* San Francisco: Chandler and Sharp.

Bowman, Carol. 2001. *Return from Heaven.* New York: HarperCollins.

Bulkeley, Kelly. 1995. *Spiritual Dreaming.* New York: Paulist Press.

———. 2008. *Dreaming in the World's Religions.* New York: NYU Press.

Burn, Gordon. 1985. *Somebody's Husband, Somebody's Son.* New York: Viking.

Burnham, Sophy. 1990. *A Book of Angels.* New York: Ballantine Books.

Butler, W. E. 1978. *How to Read the Aura.* New York: Destiny Books.

Cahalan, Susannah. 2012. *Brain on Fire.* New York: Free Press.

Cahill, Augustine. 1965. *Darkness, Dawn, and Destiny.* London: Regency Press.

Cahill, Tim. 1987. *Buried Dreams.* New York: Bantam Books.

Caplan, Lincoln. 1987. *The Insanity Defense.* New York: Laurel Book.

Carlo, Philip. 1996. *The Night Stalker.* New York: Pinnacle Book.

Castle, Kit, and Stefan Bechtel. 1989. *Katherine, It's Time.* New York: Avon Books.

Cauffiel, Lowell. 1992. *Forever and Five Days.* New York: Zebra Books.

Cavett, Dick. 2014. "Boxing the Black Dog." *Time,* Oct. 25, 54.

Chase, Truddi. 1987. *When Rabbit Howls.* New York: E. P. Dutton.

Christiani, Leon. 1961. *Evidence of Satan in the Modern World.* New York: Avon.

Clarke, David. 2004. *The Angel of Mons.* West Sussex, U.K.: Wiley & Sons.

Coddington, Robert H. 1997. *Earthbound: Conversations with Ghosts.* New York: Pinnacle Books.

Cohen, Barry, Esther Giller, and Lynn W. 1991. *Multiple Personality Disorder from the Inside Out.* Baltimore: Sidran Press.

Coniff, Richard. 2014. "Fearless." *Smithsonian,* May, 14.

Conradi, Peter. 1992. *The Red Ripper.* New York: Dell Book.

Costello, Peter. 1994. *The Real World of Sherlock Holmes.* New York: Carroll & Graf Publishers.

Cox, Mike. 1991. *The Confessions of Henry Lee Lucas.* New York: Pocket Star Books.

Crabtree, Adam. 1985. *Multiple Man.* New York: Praeger Books.

Crapanzano, Vincent, and Vivian Garrison, eds. 1977. *Case Studies in Spirit Possession.* New York: John Wiley & Sons.

Cummins, Geraldine. 1965. *Swan on a Black Sea.* London: Routledge & Kegan Paul.

Davidson, Wilma. 2006. *Spirit Rescue.* Woodbury, Minn.: Llewellyn Publications.

Davis, Wade. 1985. *The Serpent and the Rainbow.* New York: Warner Books.

Depue, Roger. 2005. *Between Good and Evil.* New York: Warner Books.

Dobie, Kathy. 2008. "Denial in the Corps." *The Nation,* Feb. 18, 11–18.

Dokoupil, Tony. 2012. "Mortal Injury." *Newsweek,* Dec. 10, 42–44.

Donovan, Robert. 1962. *The Assassins.* New York: Popular Library.

Douglas, John, and Mark Olshaker. 1995. *Mindhunter.* New York: Pocket Books.

———. 1998. *Obsession.* New York: Pocket Books.

———. 1999. The Anatomy of Motive. New York: Scribners.

———. 2000. *The Cases That Haunt Us.* New York: Pocket Books.

Doyle, Arthur Conan. 1901. "Strange Studies from Life." *Strand Magazine* 21:483.

———. 1924. *Memories and Adventures.* Boston: Little, Brown.

———. 1926. *The History of Spiritualism.* 3 vols.

———. 1930. *The Edge of the Unknown.* New York: Putnam & Sons.

Duke, Patty, and Gloria Hochman. 1992. *A Brilliant Madness.* New York: Bantam Books.

Eadie, Betty. 1992. *Embraced by the Light.* Placerville, Calif.: Gold Leaf Press.

Ebon, Martin. 1967. *Beyond Space and Time.* New York: New American Library.

———. 1971. *They Knew the Unknown.* New York: World Publishing.

———. 1974. *Exorcism: Fact Not Fiction.* New York: Signet.

Editors of *Psychic* Magazine. 1972. *Psychics.* New York: Harper and Row.

Edward, John. 2004. *After Life: Answers from the Other Side.* Carlsbad, Calif.: Princess Books.

Emmons, Noel, ed. 1986. *Manson in His Own Words.* New York: Grove Press.

Eno, Paul. 2006. *Turning Home.* Woonsocket, R.I.: New River Press.

Estep, Richard, and Cami Andersen. 2016. *The Haunting of Asylum 49.* Wayne, N.J.: Career Press.

Findlay, Arthur. 1931. *On the Edge of the Etheric.* London: Psychic Press.

Finkel, Michael. 2005. *True Story.* New York: HarperCollins.

Fiore, Edith. 1987. *The Unquiet Dead.* New York: Dolphin.

Fisher, Joe. 2001. *The Siren Call of Hungry Ghosts.* New York: Paraview Press.

Floyd, E. Randall. 2002. *In the Realm of Ghosts and Hauntings.* Augusta, Ga.: Harbor House.

Fodor, Nandor. 1964. *Between Two Worlds.* W. Nyack, New York: Parker Publishing.

———. 1966. *Encyclopedia of Psychic Science.* New York: University Books.

Fortune, Dion. 1981. *Psychic Self-Defence*. Northamptonshire, U.K.: Aquarian Press.

Frank, Gerold. 1966. *The Boston Strangler*. New York: New American Library.

Freud, Sigmund. 1923. "A Neurosis of Demoniacal Possession in the Seventeenth Century."

Fuller, John G. 1976. *The Ghost of Flight 401*. New York: Berkley Publishing.

———. 1986. *The Ghost of 29 Megacycles*. New York: NAL.

Gilmore, Mikal. 1994. *Shot in the Heart*. New York: Doubleday.

Glass, Justine. 1969. *They Foresaw the Future*. New York: G. P. Putnam's Sons.

Glatt, John. 2002. *Cradle of Death*. New York: St. Martin's Paperbacks.

Gomez, Alan. 2009. "Military Focuses on 'Internal Insurgents' in Suicides." *USA Today*, March 25, 1.

Goodman, Felicitas. 1981. *The Exorcism of Anneliese Michel*. New York: Doubleday.

———. 1988. *How About Demons?* Bloomington: Indiana University Press.

Graysmith, Robert. 1987. *Zodiac*. New York: Berkley Books.

Guiley, Rosemary E. 2000. *The Encyclopedia of Ghost and Spirits*. New York: Facts on File.

Guirdham, Arthur. 1982. *The Psychic Dimensions of Mental Health*. Wellingborough, U.K.: Turnstone Press.

Guttmacher, Manfred. 1960. *The Mind of the Murderer*. New York: Grove Press.

Hall, Calvin. 1953. *The Meaning of Dreams*. New York: Harper & Brothers.

Hare, Robert D. 1993. *Without Conscience*. New York: Pocket Books.

Hartmann, Ernest. 1984. *The Nightmare*. New York: Basic Books.

Hawksworth, Henry. 1977. *The Five of Me*. Chicago: Henry Regnery Co.

Hayden, Torey L. 1991. *Ghost Girl*. New York: Avon Books.

Head, Tom. 2004. *Possessions and Exorcisms*. Farmington Hills, Mich.: Greenhaven Press.

Henry, Teuira. 1928. *Ancient Tahiti*. Honolulu: Bishop Museum, Bulletin 48.

Howard, Virginia. 1971. *The Messenger*. Tiger, Ga: Universal Faith in the Father Church and Missionary Society.

Hunt, Dave, and T. A. McMahon. 1988. *The New Spirituality*. Eugene, Ore.: Harvest House.

Hurwood, B. J. 1971. *Ghosts, Ghouls and Other Horrors*. New York: Scholastic Books.

Hyslop, James. 1918. *Life After Death*. New York: E. P. Dutton. Internet Archive website.

Inglis, Brian. 1977/1992. *Natural and Supernatural*. Dorset, U.K. and Lindfield, N.S.W.: Prism-Unity.

Jelinek, Pauline. 2008. "Military Suicide Rate at Record Level." *Atlanta Journal Constitution,* May 30, A3.

Jelinek, Pauline, and Kimberly Hefling. 2009. "Army Suicides at Record High, Passing Civilians." *Associated Press.* Jan 29.

Jones, Aphrodite. 1999. *The Embrace*. New York: Pocket Books.

Keyes, Daniel. 1981. *The Minds of Billy Milligan*. New York: Random House.

Kirwin, Barbara R. 1997. *The Mad, the Bad and the Innocent*. New York: HarperPaperbacks.

Klausner, Lawrence D. 1981. *Son of Sam*. New York: McGraw-Hill Book Co.

Kueshana, Eklal. 1970. *The Ultimate Frontier*. Chicago: Stelle Group.

Kuhn, Lesley. 1963. "Exorcising a Demon in the Bronx." *Fate,* April, 26–30.

Lancaster, Evelyn. 1958. *Strangers in My Body*. New York: Signet.

Langley, Noel. 1967. *Edgar Cayce on Reincarnation*. New York: Hawthorn Books.

Lavergne, Gary. 1997. *A Sniper in the Tower*. Denton: University of North Texas Press.

Levenkron, Steven. 1991. *Obsessive Compulsive Disorders*. New York: Warner Books.

Lhermitte, J. 1963. *Diabolical Possession, True and False*. London: Burns and Oates.

Lindsey, Robert. 1988. *A Gathering of Saints*. New York: Dell Publishing.

Lissner, Ivar. 1962. *The Silent Past*. New York: G. P. Putnam's Sons.

Lunde, Donald T. 1976. *Murder and Madness*. New York: W. W. Norton.

Lysiak, Matthew. 2013. *Newtown*. New York: Gallery Books.

Mackenzie, Andrew. 1972. *A Gallery of Ghosts*. New York: Taplinger.

Markman, Ronald, and Dominick Bosco.1989. *Alone with the Devil*. New York: Doubleday.

Martin, Malachi. 1976. *Hostage to the Devil*. New York: Reader's Digest Press.

Martinez, Susan. 2009. *The Hidden Prophet*. Amazon POD, ISBN 97814495055162015.

———. 2015. *Delusions in Science and Spirituality*. Rochester, Vt.: Bear and Company.

Maurey, Eugene. 1988. *Exorcism*. West Chester, Penn.: Whitford Press.

Mayer, Robert. 1989. *Through Divided Minds*. New York: Doubleday.

McGinniss, Joe. 1983. *Fatal Vision*. New York: Signet Book.

Michaud, Stephen G. 1998. *The Evil That Men Do*. New York: St. Martin's Press.

Michel, Lou, and Dan Herbeck. 2001. *American Terrorist*. New York: ReganBooks.

Miles, Jim. 2000. *Weird Georgia*. Nashville, Tenn.: Cumberland House.

Mones, Paul. 1991. *When a Child Kills*. New York: Pocket Books.

Monroe, Robert A. 1971. *Journeys Out of the Body*. New York: Doubleday.

Montandon, Pat. 1975. *The Intruders*. New York: Coward, McCann & Geoghegan.

Moody, Raymond. 1975/1988. *Life After Life*. New York: Bantam Books.

———. 1993. *Reunions*. New York: Villard Books.

Morehouse, David. 1998. *Psychic Warrior*. New York: St. Martin's Press.

Morrison, Helen. 2004. *My Life Among the Serial Killers*. New York: William Morrow.

Morse, Melvin. 1991. *Closer to the Light*. New York: Ivy Books.

Naegeli-Osjord, Hans. 1988. *Possession and Exorcism*. Oregon, Wis.: New Frontiers Center.

Naifeh, Steven, and Gregory White Smith. 1995. *A Stranger in the Family*. New York: Onyx Book.

Newbrough, John. 1874. *Spiritalis*. New York: Self-published.

Newton, Michael. 1998. *Rope*. New York: Pocket Books.

Noll, Richard. 1990. *Bizarre Diseases of the Mind*. New York: Berkley Books.

Noorbergen, Rene. 1976. *The Soul Hustlers*. Grand Rapids, Mich.: Zondervan.

Oahspe: A New Bible in the Words of Jehovih and His Angel Embassadors. A Sacred History of the Dominions of the Higher and Lower Heavens on the Earth for the Past Twenty-four Thousand Years. 1960. Raymond Palmer Edition. (Orig. pub. 1882.) New York & London: Oahspe Publishing.

O'Brien, Darcy. 1985. *Two of a Kind, The Hillside Stranglers*. New York: New American Library.

———. 1989. *Murder in Little Egypt*. New York: New American Library.

Oesterreich, T. K. 1935. *Obsession and Possession by Spirits Both Good and Evil*. Chicago: DeLaurence.

Olcott, Henry Steele. 1972. *People from the Other World*. Rutland, Vt.: Charles E. Tuttle.

Olsen, Jack I. 1975. *The Man with the Candy*. New York: Simon & Schuster.

———. 1983. *Son*. New York: Dell.

———. 1993. *The Misbegotten Son*. New York: Delacorte Press.

——. 2002. *The Creation of a Serial Killer.* New York: St. Martin's Press.

Owens, Darrin. 2006. *Reader of Hearts.* Novato, Calif.: New World Library.

Peck, M. Scott. 1983. *People of the Lie.* New York: Simon & Schuster.

——. 2005. *Glimpses of the Devil.* New York: Free Press.

Picknett, Lynn, and Clive Prince. 2001. *The Stargate Conspiracy.* New York: Berkley.

Pienciak, Robert T. 1996. *Mama's Boy.* New York: Onyx Book.

Powell, A. E. 2007. *The Etheric Double.* San Diego, Calif.: The Book Tree. First edition published in 1925 by the Theosophical Society London.

Ramsland, Katherine. 2001. *Ghost: Investigating the Other Side.* New York: St. Martin's Press.

Randall, Kate. 2008. "Returning US Veterans' Lives Shattered." WSWS: News & Analysis: North America, July 15.

Rapoport, Judith L. 1989. *The Boy Who Couldn't Stop Washing.* New York: New American Library.

Rawlings, Maurice. 1978. *Beyond Death's Door.* New York: Bantam Books.

Ressler, Robert. 1992. *Whoever Fights Monsters.* New York: St. Martin's Paperbacks.

——. 1997. *I Have Lived in the Monster.* New York: St. Martin's Press.

Ring, Kenneth. 1992. *The Omega Project.* New York: Wm. Morrow.

Rivers, W. H. R. 1914/1968. *The History of Melanesian Society.* Cambridge, U.K.: Cambridge University Press.

Rogo, D. Scott. 1979. *The Poltergeist Experience.* New York: Penguin.

Roll, William G. 2004. *The Poltergeist.* New York: Signet.

Rose, Ronald. 1957. "Crisis Telepathy in Australia." *Tomorrow* 5, n. 2.

Rule, Ann. 1986. *The Stranger Beside Me.* New York: New American Library.

——. 1988a. *The I-5 Killer.* Waterville, Maine: Thorndike Press.

——. 1988b. *Lust Killer.* New York: Signet.

——. 2004. *Green River, Running Red.* New York: Pocket Star Books.

Russell, George. 1918. *The Candle of Vision.* New York: Macmillan.

Ryzl, Milan, and Lubor Kysucan. 2007. *Ancient Oracles.* Victoria, Canada: Trafford Publishing.

Sagan, Samuel. 1997. *Entity Possession.* Rochester, Vt.: Destiny Books.

Sarchie, Ralph, and Lisa Collier. 2001. *Beware the Night.* New York: St. Martin's Press.

Sargent, Epes. 1876. *Does Matter Do It All?* Boston.

Schechter, Harold. 1989. *Deviant.* New York: Pocket Books.

Schoenewolf, Gerald. 1991. *Jennifer and Her Selves.* New York: Donald I. Fine.

Schreiber, F. R. 1973. *Sybil.* New York: Warner Books.

———. 1984. *The Shoemaker.* New York: Signet.

Schwarz, Ted. 1981. *The Hillside Strangler.* New York: Signet Books.

Scott, Beth, and Michael Norman. 1985. *Haunted Heartland.* New York: Barnes & Noble Books.

Shah, Tahir. 2006. *The Caliph's House.* New York: Bantam Books.

Shapiro, Rami. 1994. *Open Secrets.* Miami, Fla.: Lighthouse Books.

Sharkey, Joe. 1990. *Death Sentence.* New York: Signet Book.

Shelton, Harriet. 1957. *Abraham Lincoln Returns.* New York: Evans Publishing.

Smith, Carole. 1998. *The Magic Castle.* New York: St. Martin's.

Smith, Hester Travers. 1919. *Voices from the Void.* New York: Dutton.

Smith, Michelle, and Lawrence Pazder. 1980. *Michelle Remembers.* New York: Congdon & Lattes.

Smith, Susy. 1968. *Prominent American Ghosts.* New York: World Publishing.

———. 1970a. *Ghosts Around the House.* New York: World Publishing.

———. 1970b. *Widespread Psychic Wonders.* New York: Ace Publishing.

Spence, Lewis. 1942. *Will Europe Follow Atlantis?* London: Rider and Company.

Spencer, Judith. 1989. *Suffer the Child.* New York: Pocket Books.

Spraggett, Allen. 1967. *The Unexplained.* New York: New American Library.

Stillman, Deanne. 2001. *Twentynine Palms.* New York: William Morrow.

Stillman, William. 2006. *Autism and the God Connection.* Naperville, Ill.: Sourcebooks.

Styron, William. 1990. *Darkness Visible, A Memoir of Madness.* New York: Random House.

Suggs, Robert. 1962. *The Hidden Worlds of Polynesia.* New York: Harcourt, Brace & World.

Thigpen, Corbett H., and Hervey M. Cleckley. 1957. *The Three Faces of Eve.* New York: Popular Library.

Thompson, Mark. 2015. "Unlocking the Secrets of PTSD." *Time,* April 6, 41–43.

Titus, Justin. 1971. *Eternal Progression.* Lakemont, Ga.: CSA Press.

———. 1976. *Alpha & Omega.* Amherst, Wis.: Palmer Publications, 1976.

Twigg, Ena, and Ruth Hagy Brod. 1973. *Ena Twigg: Medium.* New York: Manor Books.

Twitchell, James. *Carnival Culture.* New York: Columbia University Press, 1992.

Tymn, M. 2008. "Interview." *Searchlight,* March, 8.

Ullman, Montague, ed. 1999. *The Variety of Dream Experience*. New York: State University of New York Press.

Underwood, Peter. 1986. *Queen Victoria's Other World*. London: Harrap.

Van de Castle. 1994. *Our Dreaming Mind*. New York: Ballantine Books.

Van Praagh, James. 2008. *Ghosts Among Us*. New York: Harper One.

Vidal, Gore. 1995. *Palimpsest*. New York: Penguin.

Vronsky, Peter. 2004. *Serial Killers*. New York: Berkley Books.

Waite, Robert G. 1977. *The Psychopathic God*. New York: Signet.

Walsh, John. 1998. *No Mercy*. New York: Pocket Books.

Warnke, Mike, Dave Balsiger, and Les Jones. 1972. *The Satan-Seller*. Plainfield, N.J.: Logos.

Webster, James. 2009. *The Case Against Reincarnation*. Surrey, U.K.: Grosvenor House Publishing.

Weisman, Alan. 1977. *We Immortals*. New York: Pocket Books.

Wenzl, Roy et al. 2007. *Bind, Torture, Kill*. New York: HarperCollins.

West, Cameron. 1999. *First Person Plural*. New York: Hyperion.

White, John. 2014. "Reincarnation and Survival." Dec., unpublished paper.

Whitton, Joel, and Joe Fisher. 1986. *Life Between Life*. New York: Dolphin Book.

Wickland, Karl. 1924/1974. *Thirty Years Among the Dead*. Tarzana, Calif.: Newcastle Publishing.

Williamson, R. W. 1933. *Religious and Cosmic Beliefs of Central Polynesia*. 2 vols. London: Cambridge University Press.

Wilson, Colin. 1973. *Strange Powers*. New York: Vintage.

Wolfe, Linda. 1986. *The Professor and the Prostitute*. New York: Ballantine.

Zung, Thomas, ed. 2001. *Buckminster Fuller: An Anthology*. New York: St. Martin's.

INDEX

Page numbers in *italics* refer to illustrations.